C000318673

THE ANTS FOUND HER FIRST

The small, nude woman sprawled on her back a few feet from the edge of Scenic Loop, a now-empty two-lane country road. Double lines cut into her flesh and circled her throat like a necklace, causing a swollen, purple discoloration. Bruises tinted her face, as well as her right breast and thigh. She had landed with her head turned to one side, her chin touching her shoulder, and a trickle of blood had dried on each side of her mouth. Her left arm lay across her chest and her slim legs were bent grotesquely at the knees, splayed out in frog fashion. Next to her body, was a small neat roll of the clothing she had been wearing when she died.

In the darkness of the hot San Antonio night, she remained unnoticed ... except by the column of fire ants crawling methodically up her right hand.

REAL HORROR STORIES!
PINNACLE TRUE CRIME

SAVAGE VENGEANCE   (0-7860-0251-4, $5.99)
By Gary C. King and Don Lasseter
On a sunny day in December, 1974, Charles Campbell attacked
Renae Ahlers Wicklund, brutally raping her in her own home in
front of her 16-month-old daughter. After Campbell was released
from prison after only 8 years, he sought revenge. When Campbell
was through, he left behind the most gruesome crime scene local
investigators had ever encountered.

NO REMORSE   (0-7860-0231-X, $5.99)
By Bob Stewart
Kenneth Allen McDuff was a career criminal by the time he was
a teenager. Then, in Fort Worth, Texas in 1966, he upped the ante.
Arrested for three brutal murders, McDuff was sentenced to death.
In 1972, his sentence was commuted to life imprisonment. He
was paroled after only 23 years behind bars. In 1991 McDuff
struck again, carving a bloody rampage of torture and murder
across Texas.

BROKEN SILENCE   (0-7860-0343-X, $5.99)
The Truth About Lee Harvey Oswald, LBJ,
and the Assassination of JFK
By Ray "Tex" Brown with Don Lasseter
In 1963, two men approached Texas bounty hunter Ray "Tex"
Brown. They needed someone to teach them how to shoot at a
moving target—and they needed it fast. One of the men was Jack
Ruby. The other was Lee Harvey Oswald. . . . Weeks later, after
the assassination of JFK, Ray Brown was offered $5,000 to leave
Ft. Worth and keep silent the rest of his life. The deal was ar-
ranged by none other than America's new president: Lyndon
Baines Johnson.

*Available wherever paperbacks are sold, or order direct from the
Publisher. Send cover price plus 50¢ per copy for mailing and
handling to Penguin USA, P.O. Box 999, c/o Dept. 17109,
Bergenfield, NJ 07621. Residents of New York and Tennessee
must include sales tax. DO NOT SEND CASH.*

A CLUE FROM THE GRAVE

Irene Pence

Pinnacle Books
Kensington Publishing Corp.

http://www.pinnaclebooks.com

Some names have been changed to protect the privacy of individuals connected to this story.

PINNACLE BOOKS are published by

Kensington Publishing Corp.
850 Third Avenue
New York, NY 10022

Pinnacle and the P logo Reg. U.S. Pat. & TM Off.

First Printing: June, 1997
10 9 8 7 6 5 4 3 2 1

Printed in the United States of America

DEDICATION

To my sisters

Gloria Rorick Bennett
Peggy Rorick Oltmanns

*For the encouragement, the confidences,
and the laughter.*

ACKNOWLEDGMENTS

I am most grateful for information and photographs from the victim's family, Nadine Adams and Darlene Adams Sanford. Many thanks to the following for their generous help: OSI's Dr. Charles P. McDowell, Special Agent Barney Stegall, and Special Agent Herb Shipman; Investigator Tom Bevans; Bexar County Sheriff's Department investigators Sgt. Dalton Baker, Sgt. Sal Marin; and Lt. Al Ramon, and Dr. Robert C. Bux, medical examiner and the victim's co-workers, Olga Spindle and Sarah Bowers. Also, thanks to Bill Lipscomb for providing me with information only he could know.

A sincere ''thank you'' to my agent, Janet Manus, for her faith in a non-published author. To my writing consultant, Pam Renner, who helped me grow.

Heaps of gratitude on my readers and support group: Julie Benson, Jim Loose, Heiko Mueller, and Alpha Ward-Burns. A special thank you to Jane Graves, who donated her Fourth of July weekend line-editing my manuscript, and to Dan Hurwitz, who sat with me for hours after my old computer blew up, and helped me salvage and transfer the manuscript to the new.

Special thanks to my wonderful family: my husband, Brad Pence, who read the manuscript and gently made suggestions; my son, Mark Pence, a San Antonian who helped with local color; my daughter, Lisa Pence, for her critiques; and my daughter, Laura Pence Johansen, my attorney and adviser.

My sincere gratitude to my editors at Pinnacle Books: Editor in Chief Paul Dinas, Consulting Editor Karen Haas, and Editorial Assistant Katherine Gayle.

AN EXPLANATORY NOTE

This story has been carefully researched from more than 3,000 pages of court records, statements, and files of the United States Air Force, its Office of Special Investigation, the Bexar County Sheriff's Department, and the Guidry Group, private investigators.

Dialogue has been extracted from court documents and tapes, and in numerous cases is the actual words of the people involved. Some dialogue has been reconstructed based on the author's interviews. Where conflict in version exists, the author has chosen to elect the version most consistent with the facts of the case as presented in court records.

Some scenes have been dramatically recreated to portray episodes that occurred.

The author has chosen to change names of some individuals in the story to afford them privacy. Any similarity between the fictitious names used and those of living persons is entirely coincidental.

Chapter One

The sultry night loomed midnight black as he navigated the two-lane country road in search of the perfect place. He had been at the wheel for an hour. At one time, he became lost and wandered through a small town where a policeman tailed him, almost sitting on his bumper. He thought his heart would pound out of his chest when he glimpsed the cop in his mirror. But after several agonizing moments, the policeman passed him and once again he was alone.

Finally, disoriented, scared, and in a state of panic, he spotted an area not invaded by either houses or streetlights, and pulled off the road. Dressed inconspicuously in a black T-shirt and blue jeans, he jumped out and struggled to open the catch of the truck's tailgate. He yanked vigorously on the handle and finally metal scraped metal, the catch released, and the tailgate fell with a thundering crash. He wondered if anyone had heard it. Nah, who would hear anything way out here?

He inhaled deeply, expecting new strength, but his nerves caused his breath to expel in short, panting gasps. With the truck lights turned off, he stretched inside the camper shell to grope for the cord of the duffel bag and grunted as he dragged it toward him. The bag felt like dead weight. She couldn't have weighed more than 110 pounds, but tugging on that bag was like pulling a boulder to him.

His imagination ran wild in the intimidating blackness, and he questioned how securely she had been tucked into the bag. A limp hand dangling out would unnerve him for sure. With clumsy and rushed actions, he fumbled with the knot. Shutting his eyes before the bag completely opened, he blindly grabbed the duffel with both hands, heaving it out of the pickup. It hit the ground with a thud. He held onto the underside and vigorously shook the canvas fabric to eject its contents. Only after he turned from the body did he open his eyes. Now he could distinguish dim outlines of a fence and trees in the sparse moonlight, so he was sure he didn't want to turn around and glance at what he had just planted.

He ditched the bag in the back of the truck, and as he slammed the tailgate shut it pinched his thumb. He spit out a muffled curse, and felt blood dampen his fingers. Trying to shake feeling back into his hand, he dashed to the driver's side and jumped in. Gravel sprayed and tires dug a trench as he fled.

The small, nude woman sprawled on her back a few feet from the road. Double lines cut into her flesh and circled her throat like a necklace, causing a swollen, purple discoloration. Bruises tinted her face, as well as her right breast and thigh. She had landed with her head turned to one side, her chin gently touching her shoulder. She looked oddly demure. But there was nothing demure in her position—left arm flung carelessly across her chest, and her slim legs grotesquely bent at the knees, flayed out in frog fashion. She remained unnoticed, except by the column of fire ants crawling methodically up her right hand.

* * *

Monday, June 9, 1986, promised to be another sweltering day, but located 150 miles north of the Mexican border, summer always arrived early and heated the humidity to steam in San Antonio, Texas.

James Slides steered his Ford Pinto onto Scenic Loop, a two-lane country road where yellow and purple wildflowers grew, and cicadas, nestling in old oaks and pines, added their ceaseless din to the pastoral scene. At 6:15 a.m., the sun had already burnt away the morning haze.

Five days a week, Slides drove this route to his job at Kelly Air Force Base, and his familiarity with the road made anything unusual stand out. What he saw lying ahead off the west shoulder was definitely not normal. He drew closer, and his palms felt moist as they gripped the steering wheel. Even from this distance he knew he was approaching a body. The bacon and eggs he had gulped down half an hour ago suddenly churned.

He didn't want to look, let alone stop, but he slowly brought his car to a halt at the side of the road where rough, scratchy-looking grass shot up between patches of gravel. He squinted at the pallid, twisted form and shook his head.

Opening his car door, he crept timidly toward the body, hearing the crunch of his own shoes on the gravel. Now closer, he could see a trickle of dried blood on each side of her mouth, and she was shrouded with bites—ants still crawled all over her. He looked around hurriedly and saw a white clapboard fence at the entrance to a ranch about a hundred yards from where he stood. He scrambled back into his car and headed for the house and a telephone.

Slides alerted the Bexar County Sheriff's Department and told Officer Robert Morales what he had stumbled upon. Then he went back to stand guard over the woman who had light blond hair, gray lips, and hands that had hardened into fists.

Slides breathed a sigh of relief when he saw Officer Morales' squad car pull up at 6:58. The officer quickly wrote down Slides' reenactment of finding the body.

"Did you touch anything?"

"God, no!" Slides looked repulsed by the idea.

Morales grabbed a roll of yellow crime tape from his car and strung it over a wide area surrounding the body, then called the office dispatcher. "Get me Sgt. Dalton Baker in Homicide. Tell him to get out here real quick."

The sheriff's office sprang into action. In less than twenty minutes, five additional squad cars had screeched to the scene. A corps of blue shirts, pointed cowboy boots, and white Stetsons roamed the area.

Like insects drawn to a carcass, the once-deserted area became alive with people. The sporadic traffic on Scenic Loop clustered as it moved past the body. Curious onlookers, trying to get a glimpse of the victim, were blocked by the deputies' cars parked adjacent to the body. Patrolman Morales waved his nightstick, signaling the drivers to move on.

The sheriff's men fanned out to search for evidence, but kept returning to study the woman. It was a grotesque scene— men in their uniforms, loaded guns, and heavy boots, and the defenseless victim lying amid gravel and rocks, contorted, naked, and vulnerable.

John C. Hubbard, evidence technician, lugging both his Polaroid and a 35-millimeter camera, shot 34 colored photographs of the woman, some from as close as six inches.

Hubbard's photographs would create a significant record of the crime scene as it now appeared, because after the body was removed and autopsied, memories would dim as to the juxtaposition of the evidence. Then he diagrammed the terrain—measuring the distance of the body from the road, from the large oak tree, and from a barbed wire and wood fence.

His sketches would add detailed dimension for the photographs and hopefully jog memories later.

Sergeant Baker jotted down notes for his report. "Have you noticed how clean she smells? It's like someone had just bathed her with a bar of Ivory."

Hubbard and Morales nodded in agreement.

"Look here," the sergeant said. "Someone's rolled up her clothes." He snatched them from under her right foot. "Notice how neat they are. Why do you supposed someone would go to all the trouble to make them so precise? It's a pair of Levi's and a T-shirt." He examined the tag.

"'Made in Turkey'. Anyone find anything else? Murder weapon? Footprints?"

The officers shook their heads. By now the officers' boots had obliterated the tire tracks left by the quickly escaping truck.

"Take a look at the bottom of her feet. Completely clean. She had to be killed somewhere else and brought here." Baker continued taking notes. "Okay, unidentified white female. Let's say about five-foot-one or two, late teens to early twenties."

By 9 a.m., Investigator Gene Biggs of the medical examiner's office arrived. He frowned and muttered, "It's all the worse when they're so damn young." He declared her DOS—dead at the scene—and pulled on rubber gloves to begin probing her body. "Can't find any gunshot or stab wounds. There's blood in her mouth and ears." Carefully, he turned her over. Rigor mortis had set in and her body moved like a statue, legs paralyzed in their peculiar position.

Biggs resumed his narration. "She's been here for a while, I'd say four or five hours. See how purple her back is from blood draining there? There's more blood around the vagina and anus. Probably a sex crime," he said under his breath. "Look at the inch gap in the strangulation mark at the back of her neck. Bet the murderer stood behind when he choked her. Also, there are small amounts of blood in several places on her head." He stood up and brushed off his denims. "Okay, that'll do for now. Let's get her to the morgue. We'll need a full autopsy.''

Sheriff Jimmy Ray Frazier pulled up, red and blue lights flashing. Unlike the deputies, the investigators and the sheriff didn't wear uniforms, but their clothes were the same Western style. The buttons on Frazier's white shirt gaped over his belly, and his cowboy jeans were cut long, completely covering the back of his high-heeled boots. His brown leather belt held a holster with a deliberately visible .38-caliber revolver.

The sheriff strutted over to the body, his shiny five-point badge on his chest duplicating the big lone star welded to his belt buckle. Hooking his thumbs in his belt loops, he hiked up his pants. ''Another damn murder,'' he said in a deep voice. ''What are we getting now, about one a week? Let's hope to hell we solve this one.''

''This is all we've found,'' Sergeant Baker said, holding up the jeans and shirt. ''There's not a single clue.''

The sheriff stared a moment longer at the woman, then rubbed his chin. ''Hey, I think I know her. If I remember correctly, her name is Lita Jean Schrader.'' He told no one his source of information, and the deputies, anxious to find a quick solution, didn't ask. ''Let's pull in her ex-husband. We've got some questions to ask.''

An hour later, Sheriff Frazier stormed through his office door, took off his hat and tossed it on the rack 10 feet across the room. He was proud that he had a 90 percent success rate at hitting the hook. Still hot from his romp in the country, he wiped perspiration from his forehead and sat down at his desk. His brown hair remained indented where his hat had stuck to his head.

Glancing at his watch, he saw that in 30 minutes the ex-husband, Philip Schrader, would arrive. He had instructed his secretary to call and politely invite Mr. Schrader to his office.

"If the gentleman objects after you let him know why we want him here," he told her, "we'll get tough and personally escort him."

There had been no objections. Philip Schrader seemed genuinely shaken when he heard from the sheriff's secretary and anxiously agreed to come. Frazier prided himself on spotting an actor, but when he heard about Schrader's apparent grief, he wasn't so sure.

He studied the Polaroids Hubbard had taken and their quality was only adequate. The 35-millimeter shots would be more precise, but they wouldn't be ready until tomorrow.

He punched in the number for the investigation administrator, M. R. Rose, and barked into the phone, "Rose, take Sergeant Baker with you and get over to Heimer Road. That's where the woman lived. Nose around and see what you can find. Could be the crime scene. Might be signs of a struggle. Call me back as soon as you find out something. Anything."

In less than an hour, tall, thin Philip Schrader entered the sheriff's office, compulsively rattling the change in his pocket.

Frazier stood and shook hands, but still didn't know whether to offer Schrader condolences or treat him like a murderer. "I've got some photos I want you to see and I need to warn you they're not pretty."

"I would think not," Schrader said, reaching for the pictures. Color drained from his face and he grimaced over the photos. He stared in silence at the ant-bitten body and the grotesquely swollen neck. He slowly nodded. "This could be her. Same blonde hair. Same small body." Then he said quietly, "Yes, I think it's Lila."

With the identity of the victim established, Sheriff Frazier felt a sense of satisfaction with how the case was progressing. Then his secretary buzzed him from her outer office with an urgent phone call from Sergeant Baker.

"All right, put him through," he thundered. "Okay, Dalton,

what did you find?'' The sheriff's eyes widened. He frowned and stared at Schrader, who looked bewildered.

Frazier hung up the phone. ''That was about your ex-wife. She's alive and well. And quite mystified why we sent two men over to check on her.''

The sheriff glanced at his watch—2 p.m. The murdered woman had been discovered eight hours ago, and now her identification had just evaporated.

Chapter Two

Dr. Robert C. Bux, a Bexar County medical examiner, pulled the cart closer to him. The pale white form resting on it had just been delivered to the county morgue on Martin Street, and soon he would begin her autopsy.

In the meantime, the sheriff had asked radio stations to air the woman's discovery and description every 30 minutes, and requested television channels to display the same information hourly. But not one response was received from the entire city of San Antonio.

Directly across the street from the morgue, and surrounded by a spattering of palm trees, stood the yellow-white brick Brady Green structure, part of the huge University of Texas Health Science Center. Summer brought no vacation relief to San Antonio's busy medical university; the sprawling campus ran full-steam 12 months a year and stretched all the way from the core unit in north San Antonio to this near-downtown branch

at Brady Green. Today the clinic was experiencing a particularly
hectic Monday morning. At 8:30 a.m., a secretary in the research
office, Vivian Gabrillo, answered the phone. It was Bill Lipscomb wanting to speak with his wife, Kathy.

"Kathy hasn't come in yet. Can I have her call you?"

"She's not there? This is crazy. I can't imagine what's happened. I was supposed to take the kids back to her last night
after their weekend visit with me and she wasn't home."

"That's not at all like Kathy."

"Well, tell her to call me at work as soon as she gets in.
Thanks."

Vivian felt apprehensive as she jotted down the message and
put it on top of the growing tower of memos for Kathleen
Lipscomb, a senior research nurse in the Department of Obstetrics and Gynecology. Vivian knew Kathy as a conscientious
worker, as well as a loving mother who would never have
neglected her children.

An hour later, Sarah Bowers, an attractive woman with ash-
blonde, shoulder-length hair, walked into Kathy's office to talk
with her. The accumulation of telephone notes surprised her
as Kathy had said she'd be in the office first thing this morning.
Sarah, a physician's assistant and a close friend of Kathy's,
was on call at the hospital Sunday and knew Kathy had been
there Saturday because she had seen patient charts with Kathy's
notations on them. She wondered if Kathy had made a last-
minute trip to Washington D.C., where she frequently badgered
doctors at the Surgeon General's Office for grants to underwrite
her pet research projects: venereal disease, premature births,
and at-risk pregnancies.

A sense of foreboding crept over Sarah, prompting her to
call Kathy. She let the phone ring 10 times, but no one answered.
When Kathy still hadn't arrived 30 minutes later, Sarah called
again, and once more received no response. She hung up and

alerted their boss, Dr. David Pearle, who headed obstetrics and gynecology at the university. He'd know if Kathleen was in Washington.

"That's incredible," he said. "I can't imagine that nobody's heard from her. I know she's in town because I saw her Saturday. She seemed fine then. Tell you what, take Olga Spindle and get over to Kathy's. Maybe she's real sick, hurt, or something. Find out what's going on."

Olga and Sarah took Sarah's car.

"Dr. Pearle sounded worried," Sarah said.

"So am I," Olga replied. Olga, another close friend of Kathy's, was also a nurse. Her normally extroverted, vibrant personality seemed subdued during the drive.

Fifteen minutes later, the women pulled up to Kathleen's pastel brick and wood apartment complex. They hurriedly parked and dashed over to Kathy's ground-floor apartment where they found two notes stuck to her door. One was written in a child's large, uneven print: "Mommy, we love you." The second, from her estranged husband, Bill, read: "We were here at 6:45 and we will try again later."

They rang the doorbell, then knocked on the door and tapped on windows. Finally, they called her name. But the place was as quiet as a tomb. The women sat on the wall of the apartment's sequestered patio to think.

"We need to tell Pearle" Olga said. "Let's use the manager's phone."

Dr. Pearle had left word with Vivian that he should be interrupted for any word on Kathy.

"Get a key from the manager and check the apartment," he told them. "Make sure everything's okay."

They explained the situation to the manager, who was reluctant to hand over a key to Kathleen's apartment. But after listening to the women, she consented to accompany them to investigate.

The manager unlocked the door and stepped aside so the women could enter.

They all could see that the living room appeared completely in order. A fashionable cream-colored sofa and matching chair sat by a coffee table. Two end tables held matching lamps. A bookcase filled with books, family photos, and porcelain birds also held a television set.

Sarah couldn't shake her nervous jitters. She walked through the room, glancing at Kathy's colorful oil paintings, and they brought to mind Kathleen's sister, Darlene Sanford, who had painted them.

The three women hesitantly approached the next room, stepped past the dining room table and chairs, and continued to the kitchen. The dishwasher door lay open with the rack pulled out, and an oily wok sat on the countertop. Other than that, the place appeared spotless.

Olga strolled over to the coffeemaker. ''You know what a big coffee drinker Kathy is. Look, not a cup in sight, and the coffeemaker hasn't been used recently. She must have eaten dinner here last night, then darted out. It doesn't look like she's been back since.''

Kathleen had moved into the apartment the previous weekend, and five packing boxes sat on the outdoor balcony. It appeared she had worked rapidly in the past week to create an organized home for her family. The children's room, situated across the hall and toward the back of the apartment, held a neatly made double bed. Some drawers where clothes were stored remained open, perhaps hurriedly pulled out. But for a room used by two small children, nothing seemed out of the ordinary.

They had put off investigating Kathy's bedroom, but now it was the only room left. Sarah looked over at Olga, who was visibly shaking, and knew they both dreaded entering that room. The women took a deep breath and walked through the open door of the master bedroom. The tension lessened when they saw its condition. The drawers of the green antique chest and matching dresser were closed, the queen-sized bed was made, the clothes picked up, and all accessories put away.

Sarah shrugged, then realized the only place left to check was Kathy's bathroom. Again they were filled with anxiety as they headed toward the bath and peered in. But it too was empty. Sarah knelt down and touched the tile floor of the shower. "The shower's dry, and so are the towels. You're right, Olga. Kathy probably didn't spend the night here." Sarah sighed audibly.

They thanked the manager and walked back to the parking lot feeling empty-handed and puzzled. Olga said, "You know, if anything happened to her family in Houston, Kathy would call us before going there."

"I still want to phone her mother," Sarah said.

Sarah hurried back to Brady Green and rushed into her office to punch in Nadine Adams' number. Nadine lived in New Caney, a small town north of Houston, but worked in Houston as the assistant office manager for the U.S. Secret Service. She had spent over 20 years working for civil service.

"We're very worried," Sarah told Kathleen's mother. "It's not like Kathy. Bill can't find her, either. He just called again. I guess he had the children over the weekend. He wants to know if he should bring the kids to the office."

"I haven't talked to Kathy since Friday," Nadine said, with worry edging her voice. "I don't like the sound of this one bit. I'll call Bill right now."

Technical Sergeant Bill Lipscomb was teaching a class, so Nadine left a message for him to call her. Bill had entered military life at 18, directly out of New Caney High School. Now he worked as a training instructor at Lackland Air Force Base, where he turned airmen into mean and tough drill sergeants. He had been a drill sergeant himself for five years, and still carried the swagger. His broad shoulders and narrow hips made his body look like a ''V,'' and his handsome Nordic features—piercing blue eyes and dark blonde hair—crowned the total picture, making him seem much taller than his five feet, eight inches.

On January 22, 1978, when Lipscomb wore the four stripes of a staff sergeant, he married Kathleen. They had two children, a 7-year-old daughter, Mary Ann, born nine months and five days after their wedding, and a 4-year-old son, Billie.

Lipscomb called Nadine between classes and almost stuttered in his haste to ask her if she knew anything of Kathy's whereabouts.

''That's why I'm calling you,'' she said.

''I have no idea. I had the kids all weekend and was supposed to take them back to Kathy's apartment around 6:45. I went over there and she wasn't home. I went back about an hour later and she still wasn't there. The kids and I left notes and I kept calling her until eleven. I can't figure out what happened. I'm worried, too. I told her not to move to that area, because it just isn't safe. There are a lot of strip joints and bars. But she said it's close to her work and told me to mind my own business.''

''What did you do with the kids?''

''I took them back to my place and we went swimming. Then I put them to bed and started calling Kathy again this morning.''

''No, I mean what have you done with them now?''

''I dropped them off at Los Angeles Heights Day Care. Same one Kathy uses.''

''Have you called the police?''

''Yeah, a couple hours ago, but they said she had to be missing for twenty-four hours for them to take a missing persons report. This is the worst day, Nadine. My grandmother Lipscomb died this morning. I've been running around base trying to get the paperwork to go back to Virginia for her funeral.''

"I'm sorry about your grandmother, Bill. I'll call San Antonio's missing persons from here. Give me a call just as soon as you hear anything."

"I will. This is really scary."

Lipscomb had been particularly close to his paternal grandparents, Jeffrey Lipscomb. They had lived on a farm next door to his parents in West Point, Virginia, until Bill was 10, and he felt like he had lost a parent.

Nadine dashed off to see the Secret Service manager, Special Agent Jim Steele. The two had worked together for four years, and during that time Nadine had confided in him about her family, especially the trauma of Kathleen's divorce. As she explained her phone call from Sarah, Steele's handsome face creased with concern and he shook his head in disbelief.

"Let me help you file a missing persons report," he suggested. "We'll need to call the San Antonio Police Department. You'll have to give the specific information on Kathleen, but I can open the channels."

At the same time Nadine was filing her report, a Bexar County homicide investigator, Sal Marin, was notifying the same agency about the unidentified white female they had found that morning. Five minutes later, Missing Persons alerted Marin that a Mrs. Adams had just reported her daughter missing. The daughter lived in San Antonio.

Sergeant Marin, a kindly, round-faced man, had served 10 years as a deputy with the sheriff's department. He wasted no time contacting Nadine. She gave him Kathleen's address and her date of birth—September 1, 1956. That date puzzled Marin. Kathleen would be 30 in less than three months. Could it be possible that the woman they found looked only two-thirds of her actual age? Nadine went on to describe Kathleen's skin as flawless with no scars or birthmarks, no identifying marks whatsoever, save two pierced ears. Marin could hear Nadine's trembling voice. Having five children of his own, he had no problem empathizing with her. He hung up the phone and studied both reports. The many similarities of the reports were just too obvious to ignore.

Chapter Three

Agent Jim Steele went to see if Nadine Adams had learned anything about her daughter. But when he walked into her office and saw her slumped over her desk sobbing, he knew.

"Nadine? My God, what did you find out?"

"I just got a call a few minutes ago from the Bexar County Sheriff. They found a small blonde woman this morning. They think she's younger than Kathleen. Maybe as much as 10 years. But everything else adds up. We're waiting for positive identification."

"This is no place to wait. Let me drive you home."

Ushered by the agent, Nadine left her office in a mental haze. She remained silent, her eyes staring straight ahead as grief crept over her. When they arrived at her house, Steele stayed to become part of her support team.

Nadine's next-door neighbor and long-time friend, J.O. Williams, was a Houston policeman who had served the force for 22 years and was well-known as an officer who wore his heart on his sleeve. Earlier, Nadine had called him at work, and as soon as he wound up his shift, he and his wife, Pat, dashed over to be with their widowed neighbor. The Williams' were like family even before their daughter, Debbie, had married Nadine's son, Chuck, six months earlier. There was something comforting about Pat. She could sit for hours, quietly reassuring a friend. The four sat and waited, hoping for a call to tell them this wasn't really happening.

Nadine had also called her younger daughter, Cynthia Darlene Sanford. Darlene, currently on maternity leave, worked as a secretary for the Federal Bankruptcy Court. She had given birth to her second daughter prematurely in May 1986. She would later say that her mother called every five minutes that day to update her on news of Kathleen.

Although Darlene was three years younger than her sister, they were as close as twins, and had shared a double wedding ceremony they had planned since childhood.

Kathleen's natural propensity to take care of people made choosing a nursing career an easy decision. She had been born beautiful, but Darlene was born with a cleft palate. Darlene's childhood, spent enduring countless rounds of plastic surgery, was cushioned by Kathleen's help. Kathleen hovered over her like a mother hen, running to her with pain pills, toys, books, or whatever she wanted. No sister could ask for more.

Vivian Gabrillo couldn't erase Kathy from her mind all day and still thought about her when she drove home from work around 5 p.m. She searched her car radio for news and heard the tail end of a report about a woman found in northwest Bexar County.

She raced home to get more facts from television news and heard an announcer relating a story about a small blonde woman, early 20s, found strangled on Scenic Loop Road.

Vivian, struck with the terrifying realization that the newscaster most probably was describing Kathy, dialed the San Antonio Medical Examiner, who directed her to the sheriff's department. It was a chilling experience.

"I'm afraid the murdered woman you found is my friend." When she shared Kathy's description with the deputy, he insisted that she come immediately to their office.

Vivian called Olga and Sarah. Both women had heard the same news upon arriving home and were devastated. They, too, held Vivian's conviction. Olga was tied down with two small babies, but Sarah was only minutes away from being able to give a statement to the sheriff.

While waiting for Vivian to arrive, Fred Moreno and Sal Marin busily sorted through the gruesome pictures taken earlier that day, looking for the most palatable head shots. Finally, they settled on two photos. Despite the blood that stained the victim's face, the woman looked more asleep than dead. The pictures were the best they could do. Nevertheless, the shots were ghastly.

At almost 7 p.m., 44-year-old Vivian walked into the sheriff's office. Her husband accompanied her and she tightly held onto his arm.

The deputies offered her a chair and something to drink.

She shook her head and anxiously reached for the pictures. Holding them under a light near one of the desks, she moaned, "Oh yes, this is Kathy. This is my supervisor, Kathleen Lipscomb. I just knew it was going to be her. I work . . . worked with this woman every day." Her voice trailed off and tears filled her eyes.

"Then, ma'am, I need you to accompany me to the county morgue," Lt. Moreno said.

Vivian stared at the investigator as if to will the words back into his mouth. "The morgue?"

"Yes, we need positive identification. Sorry to ask you to do this, ma'am, but it's real important."

Marin and Lt. Moreno drove Vivian and her husband to the building across the street from where she had worked all day. The officers were sympathetic, well aware that these were circumstances no one wanted in their worst nightmares.

When they walked inside, Vivian said, "I can't believe she's been right across the street from us. We've looked everywhere for her."

Vivian tried to breathe calmly as they led her past the double doors of the refrigerated room and into a small viewing room no larger than a walk-in closet. Sal pulled a white-covered cart closer to them and reached for the sheet. Vivian clutched her husband's arm so intensely she knew he had to feel her fingernails through his shirt. Her eyes stared wide as Moreno pulled back the sheet, exposing Kathy's purple, swollen face.

Vivian gasped and began shaking. "Yes, it's Kathy," she cried. "Oh my God, Kathy!"

After Vivian returned to the waiting room, it took several minutes before she regained her composure. Marin waited until she stopped crying before he said apologetically, "Ma'am, it's real necessary that we go back to the sheriff's office so you can give us a written statement. I hate askin'. But this is the first step in finding Kathleen's murderer."

Vivian looked at him for a moment, then appeared to find new resolve. "Of course I'll help. I can't imagine who would want Kathleen dead. Everyone loved her so."

At the sheriff's office, it took Vivian almost an hour to give a step-by-step account of what had happened from the moment she discovered Kathy was missing until she identified her in the morgue.

"So this woman was your supervisor?" Moreno asked.

"Yes, my direct supervisor. She was a program coordinator at the university."

"Her mother told us that she and her husband were separated. Did you know anything about that?"

"I knew Kathy was getting divorced. In fact, her husband called several times today looking for her. He sounded very concerned."

"Have you any idea why she wanted a divorce?"

Vivian shifted in her chair. "I think her husband spent a lot of time at work. He was real intent on getting promoted to master sergeant."

"Was there another man, Vivian?" His voice was calm, but insistent.

Vivian glanced at the floor, then raised her eyes to meet the investigator's. "She had a supervisor, Dr. David Pearle. He heads Obstetrics and Gynecology at the medical school. They've been seeing each other."

Marin glanced at Moreno. "See if Captain Sanchez can get Pearle on the phone. We need him down here. You call the victim's almost ex-husband and have him come in for questioning. And I'll call the victim's mother." He stood up to get Nadine's phone number to do the task he hated most.

As the investigators made their calls, Sarah Bowers came in to give her statement. It was obvious she had been crying, and she was accompanied by her husband, a young medical student.

Dalton Baker listened to Sarah describe how she and Olga had investigated Kathleen's apartment earlier in the day when she hadn't come to work. The sergeant made a note to send a crew there tomorrow morning to conduct a thorough investigation.

"What can you tell me about her divorce?"

Sarah didn't hesitate to explain what she knew. She spoke quietly when she said how close she felt to Kathy. "Kathy often told me about the marital problems that she and Bill had. I don't know of any time he actually got violent with her. Kathy did tell me Bill threatened that if she told anyone about some illegal activity he was involved in that the other people who were also involved would get her. The illegal activity was cheating on promotion examinations.''

"Illegal activity?" Baker exclaimed. Sarah had definitely captured his attention. "What people would get her?"

"She never said. I just assumed they were friends of Bill's. I'm sorry I have no names to give you."

Baker frowned. "I would sure like to know who she was talking about. Let me know if you hear anything.

"I've got just a couple more questions. Kathleen was found with no underwear. Do you know if she'd wear any if she wasn't at work?"

Sarah shrugged. "She usually didn't wear a bra."

"What about panties?"

Sarah looked uncomfortable. "I don't know if she wore panties or not."

"I know she was your friend, but tell me what kind of person you thought she was."

"Kathy was a very good person. She didn't hang out at bars. Really wasn't a drinker. Quite often we'd go out together for Chinese food."

"Mrs. Bowers, do you have any opinion of who could have killed Kathleen?"

Sarah looked directly at Sergeant Baker. "I have no idea."

Darkness settled in the New Caney dusk, but no one in the Adams' household bothered to turn on the lights. Conversation droned on, and the mood was quietly somber. The ringing of the phone jangled everyone's nerves.

"I'll get it," Steele said.

On the other end, Sergeant Marin identified himself. "We're ninety-nine percent sure it's Kathleen Lipscomb." It was conventional police procedure—always give the next of kin a tiny piece of hope that maybe this wasn't their loved one.

"We'll grab the next plane and be there as soon as we can," Steele told him. He turned to tell the others, but from the looks on their faces, they already knew.

"They're ninety-nine percent certain," he said.

Nadine began to tremble and grabbed her head to keep it from exploding. But she didn't cry. "Call Darlene," she said. "This will kill her, but she needs to know right away."

J.O. picked up the phone and spoke softly to Darlene's husband, then told Nadine, "Gary and Darlene will meet us at Hobby Airport."

J.O., Pat, and Steele insisted on flying to San Antonio with Nadine and she was too paralyzed to resist.

"Let's get going," Steele said. "The last Southwest flight to San Antonio leaves at nine."

Despite Steele's driving well over the limit, the trip to Hobby took 40 minutes. They arrived shortly after nine and Agent Steele had his Secret Service ID ready to brandish. He ran to the gate, panting and flashing his badge. "Hold that plane, we've got an emergency here!"

The ticketing agent looked startled by his outburst, but had to apologize. "I'm sorry, sir. The plane is airborne. There's no way."

Darlene and Gary Sanford quickly followed them to the gate. Darlene's face was wet and she kept dabbing at her red eyes.

"No dice," J.O. told them. "The plane's already left. We'll have to drive." He reached out to hug Darlene. When he released her, Darlene ran to embrace her mother. Darlene, brunette and five-foot-seven, had to bend down to grasp her petite mother. Nadine was as composed as a rock, but later she would say that she had been in shock and her mind operated on automatic—just trying to determine her next step.

"Mom, I want to go with you. You need me right now. I

can't stand for you to be put through something like this by yourself. You need to be with someone who loves you.''

"I know, Darlene, but you go on home. Your baby needs you, and there will be things I'll want you to do for me in Houston.''

Darlene hesitated. ''If that's what you want. But Gary will go. He'll be your right-hand man, Mom.'' Nadine gratefully embraced her tall son-in-law.

Darlene looked so heartbroken that Pat rushed to hold her. ''You all go on to San Antonio. I'll stay here with Darlene.''

Nadine nodded her approval and the men led her to the car for the 180-mile odyssey to San Antonio.

Their road was paved with every courtesy law enforcement could render. Agent Steele alerted the Secret Service to summon the first police escort. After that, each patrolman called ahead to the next destination. As they reached each city, a patrol car met them at the outskirts with lights flashing and escorted them all the way through that town and to the edge of the next, where they were intercepted by a different policeman.

At 10:35 p.m., Bill Lipscomb came to the sheriff's office, appearing drained and disheveled. His face was wet with perspiration, and his eyes held a glassy stare.

''I came as soon as I got your call. I didn't know about Kathy. I can't believe she's dead.''

"We want to ask a few questions,'' Sergeant Baker began, leading him to an office where Sal Marin waited. Baker's eyes scanned Lipscomb's arms, hands, and face. There were no bruises. No fingernails had sunk into his flesh, no sign at all that he had manhandled anyone.

''Would you mind making a statement for the department?'' Sal asked. ''Just tell us what you know, when you last saw your wife, what you were doing, that type of thing. Okay?''

''Sure. Anything I can do to help.''

Sergeant Baker read him his Miranda rights and a stenographer came in to take his statement.

"I am giving my statement to Sergeant Dalton N. Baker, who has identified himself to me as an investigator for the Bexar County Sheriff's Department. I have been advised of my rights and I fully understand these rights. I wish to waive my right to an attorney and give the following statement:

"I would like to say that my wife, Kathy Lipscomb, and I have been separated since around the 23rd of May, 1986. Kathy and I went to court on the 28th of May and I have been living at my apartment and Kathy has been living at hers.

"The last time I saw Kathy was Friday evening around 6:30 p.m., when I went to her house to pick up my two children. I visited with Kathy for a few minutes and then my children and I went to my apartment.

"I was supposed to take the children back to Kathy around 6:45 p.m. Sunday. I took the children home at that time because I was trying to go by what my preliminary divorce guideline told me to do. When I got to Kathy's, she was not home. I left a note telling her that I had been there and then I took the children back to my house.

"I tried to call her several times Sunday night, but couldn't get an answer. I tried to call her at work Monday, but she wasn't there. I tried calling her so many times, I really can't remember.

"Kathy is a good woman, and I don't know who could have done this to her. I didn't know she had been killed until Lieutenant Moreno told me about it tonight. I don't know anything about Kathy's death and I have told all I know about the incident. I have made my statement to Sergeant Baker and I have not been promised anything

nor have any threats been made against me by Sergeant
Baker or any other peace officer representing the state.''

Lipscomb read over his statement after it had been typed,
then leaned over Baker's desk to sign it. As he did, loud voices
came from the office next door. ''Who's over there?'' he asked.

''Dr. David Pearle. Do you know him?''

''Yeah, that's who Kathy worked for. What's he doing
here?''

''I understand they've been having an affair.''

''An affair?'' Lipscomb snapped, raising his voice. ''What
kind of bullshit are you trying to hand me?''

''That's what I heard. Kathy's co-worker identified her in
the morgue and apparently went right out and called Pearle.
He planned on coming down before we called him. Seems real
shook up. Brought his wife with him.''

Lipscomb stood up and kicked his chair out of the way. His
brow knitted together and his eyes squinted angrily. He stomped
out of Baker's office, glancing at the closed door of the office
next to them. ''Sonofabitch,'' he yelled at the door, then hurried
out of the building.

Baker stared at Lipscomb's back as he raced out the door.
Something about the man bothered the investigator. Lipscomb
was cooperative, and he obviously didn't have a mark on him.
He seemed genuinely concerned about Kathleen's death. Baker
thought a moment longer, then realized what had flagged his
attention. Lipscomb showed a lot of emotion. He even cried—
but there had been no tears.

Marin and Baker went next door to join Capt. Gene Sanchez
and Dr. and Mrs. Pearle, who were seated in front of Sanchez's
desk.

Dr. David Pearle, dressed in flawlessly tailored clothes,
seemed devastated by the murder. As Marin described him nine
years later: ''He was shaking and scared as hell—a nervous
wreck who was falling apart.''

"I came as soon as Vivian called me. Well, actually after I explained the situation to my wife. I knew this thing with Kathy would be better coming from me. My wife's been wonderful." He put his arm around the stiff shoulders of the unsmiling woman.

"I just can't believe Kathy's dead—and murdered in such a brutal way. I saw her Saturday," he offered, looking self-consciously at his wife.

"We'd like for you to answer a few questions, if you would, Doctor." Sanchez read him his rights and a sheet of ice formed over the man.

"Where did you last see the victim on Saturday?" Sanchez asked.

There was silence as David Pearle appeared to struggle for words. "I really think I need to talk with my attorney."

Sanchez pushed the phone toward the doctor, who reached for his small black leather address book inside his jacket. He searched for a number, quickly punched it in, and seemed relieved to hear his attorney's voice.

"Jeb, I need you to meet me at the sheriff's office—right now!"

"We'll let you know when he gets here," Sanchez said as he, Baker, and Marin got up and left the doctor and his wife alone in the office.

A half hour later, Jeb Francis arrived at the sheriff's office and Marin directed him to the small room where his client waited. An older man with his right arm in a cast, he received sympathetic stares. Francis immediately got down to his client's business.

He looked at Captain Sanchez. "With what is my client charged?"

"Absolutely nothing. We just brought him in for questioning."

"Then you have no reason to keep him?"

"We're hoping he can help us. We know he's one of the last people to see the deceased alive."

Francis glanced at Pearle. "I don't believe a statement would be in my client's best interest. Come on, David, let's go."

Dr. Pearle was allowed to leave with his attorney.

Marin waited until the doctor left and turned to Sanchez. "Pearle sure seemed obvious about not wanting to talk. What do you make of that?"

Sanchez didn't hesitate. "Could be we have just found the murderer."

Chapter Four

The journey to San Antonio became a frenetic, almost three-hour voyage guided by flashing red and blue lights.

Nadine's head ached with thoughts of what monster could have murdered her daughter. "I wonder about Bill. He fought Kathleen so much over this divorce. But recently he did change his mind and allowed her to have custody of the children. That's when things became peaceful and they were able to settle their differences. Thank goodness."

"What about Dr. Pearle?" Gary asked. "Do you think he got cold feet and thought Kathleen was pushing him into marriage?"

Jim told him, "This wouldn't be the first time I've seen a guy lose enthusiasm once his girlfriend became free to marry."

"Pearle had separated," Nadine said.

"Yeah, but he hadn't completely cut his ties," J.O. told them. "He might have had second thoughts about splitting everything he owned with an ex-wife. In a community-property state like Texas, she'd have cleaned his clock. Besides, he'd have too much to lose. He had a high-level position at the university. I think he's too high-profile to do something like this.''

"You know the one who'd have the most to lose is Mrs. Pearle,'' Nadine said. ''If she got wind of the reason for this pending divorce, she could have killed Kathleen to save her marriage and her lifestyle.''

"Now that's a possibility,'' Agent Steele said.

"Maybe it's none of them. It could have been a total stranger. I can't imagine that solving this will be easy.''

At 1 a.m., Nadine and her entourage arrived at the sheriff's office, housed in the massive four-story courthouse, a San Antonio landmark since 1889. The red, rough brick building sat in the middle of a one-time town square, less than a half mile from the Alamo.

The sheriff's department had rows of tightly packed gray steel desks lining each wall, and even at this hour, several uniformed deputies hunched over their computer screens. The deputies had tagged this place the ''bull pen.'' There were two investigation rooms for scrutinizing the more serious crimes, and a segregated office for the sheriff; otherwise, everyone felt penned up with no privacy.

Sergeant Dalton Baker, dressed more like a cowboy coming off a roundup than an investigator, shook hands with Nadine and her friends. A tall man with a stocky build, his full mustache enhanced his handsome features. Baker had been at the crime scene before 7 a.m. the previous morning, and still had not been home. Frequently working 36 to 48 hours at a stretch, he would turn off the lights in his office and take cat naps at his desk when he couldn't stay awake another minute. This was no job for a family man, he often said, and his two ex-wives probably agreed.

He ushered his visitors into one of the investigation rooms and introduced Sal Marin, the other detective on the case, who was also dressed like a cowboy.

"Mrs. Adams, I'm sorry to ask you here under these circumstances," Baker said. "We'll try to make this as quick as possible." He waived his hand toward the chairs set aside for visitors.

"I'd appreciate that," Nadine replied, and introduced the three people with her.

The sergeant pulled his chair next to Nadine. "Do you happen to have any pictures of your daughter?"

"I brought a couple," she said. "This one is older—it was from Kathleen's high school graduation. Here's a more recent one, taken about a year ago."

Sergeant Baker studied the photographs for a few moments, saying nothing. Nadine waited, scarcely breathing. Baker turned and looked sympathetically at her, then tapped the second picture with his right index finger. "I'm terribly sorry, Mrs. Adams. This one matches the body."

Nadine covered her face with shaking hands. They had said they were 99 percent sure, and now she realized her one percent option had expired. It was especially hard because all day she had mentally replayed the scenario of what she knew—that a young woman had been ignominiously dumped, completely nude, in a desolate area. To now learn that the young woman was her daughter became insufferable. Gary quickly stood up and rushed to her, throwing his arms around her shoulders. She reached for his support as tears rolled down her face, but nothing could cushion the sting of Baker's words.

Sergeant Baker waited a few moments for the shock to dissipate, and then continued. "Mrs. Adams, when was the last time you saw your daughter?"

Nadine tried to find composure, but words were lost to her. She took another deep breath. "Last weekend," she managed. "My youngest son, David, and I helped her move into her apartment."

"And when did you last talk with her?"

"Let's see. It was Friday. She had to work at the hospital

over the weekend. She told me her husband would have their children.''

"We've talked with a Dr. Pearle. Do you know him?''

"Yes, I know him. I mean, I know *of* him. For the last six months, Kathleen was always so happy when she talked about David Pearle. She loved him. Was he able to help you?''

Baker stood up and tucked his thumbs in the waistband of his pants. He looked calm, but his placid outward demeanor was defused by nails bitten to the quick. "No, he wasn't a big help. Apparently he and your daughter had been involved for quite some time. He came in after one of his employees told him what happened to Kathleen. And he brought his wife with him. Evidently he told her about the affair before he got here.''

Nadine's mouth opened in shock. "His wife? I thought they were separated. What on earth was she doing with him?''

"Well, Mrs. Adams, first of all, he's not separated. That may be what he told your daughter, but as far as we can tell, he's definitely married.''

"What did she say?''

"What would your reaction be if your husband told you that a woman he'd been having an affair with had just been murdered and he had to go to the sheriff's office for questioning? She didn't say much, but apparently she's sticking by him.''

"I can't believe it. Kathleen *told* me he was separated. They were planning to be married . . .'' Her words trailed off and she looked bewildered.

Gary asked Nadine, "Did Kathleen ever mention anyone she was afraid of?''

"Not really, Gary. I have no idea who would kill her. She and Bill bickered throughout this entire divorce, but I just can't imagine his doing anything like this.''

"Mrs. Adams, I'd be happy to answer any questions you had for me,'' Baker told her.

"What about Bill? Have you talked with him?''

"Yes. But I'm afraid he wasn't much help either. He came

in and we showed him some Polaroids, but he said he didn't know anything about the murder.'' Baker moved a toothpick from one side of his mouth to the other. "He's got an alibi—he's been with his kids all weekend.''

"Did you talk to the kids?''

"No, he didn't bring them in.'' Baker leaned back in his chair and propped his feet on his desk. "Bill seemed to be pretty interested in why Dr. Pearle was in the next room, and when we told him about Kathleen's affair, he got plenty riled up.''

Nadine shook her head. "That's strange. I thought he knew about Dr. Pearle. Well, another thing, a co-worker of Kathy's, Sarah Bowers, called me today after she went to Kathleen's apartment looking for her. She doesn't remember seeing her car in the parking lot. Have you found it?''

"No, haven't looked. What did she drive?''

"A white 1986 Nissan Sentra, two-door.''

"Okay,'' Baker said, writing down the information. "We'll check this out and let you know when we find it.''

Nadine remained silent for a moment and then stared intently at Baker. "Sergeant, I would like to know as much about what happened to my daughter as you can tell me.'' Although confident at first when she said those words, Nadine started to cry. "Maybe that will help me deal with this better.''

Sergeant Baker glanced over at Detective Marin, who had been silent up to now. A 37-year-old deputy who had been married for twenty years knew the importance of family. It had been the experience of the sheriff's department that the good families of victims always cooperated and deserved to know about their loved ones.

Marin nodded his approval.

"Your daughter was strangled,'' Baker told her. "I'm afraid she was slapped around a little. Not beaten up, just slapped about the face.'' He detailed how Kathleen had been found. "Whoever put her there didn't toss her out of a car or throw her on the ground. Looks to us like he lifted her out of the trunk of a car and gently laid her down because she didn't have any scratches on her body and there wasn't any grass in her hair. Our guess is that whoever did this knew your daughter and cared about her.''

Nadine had trouble understanding how someone who cared for Kathleen could have murdered her.

"Probably a lover's quarrel," Baker continued. "Anyway, he didn't mess her up too bad, just slapped her around, then strangled her."

Gary and Nadine winced at the officer's description.

Nadine watched Baker as he spoke and realized how matter-of-fact he seemed. To him this murder was probably no different from the last, nor would it be any different from the next, but to her it was crushing.

She stood up and wiped her eyes, then glanced down at her suit and tried to smooth out its wrinkles. "I would like to see my daughter now."

Baker frowned. "I wish you wouldn't. Kathy's co-worker made physical identification, and now that you've given me these photographs, I'm positive the body we have is your daughter. Don't put yourself through that. It would just make things harder on you."

Nadine looked frustrated.

J.O. stood up. "Nadine, if you want a final word that this is Kathleen, I'll go see her. I'd rather do that than to have you."

"Oh, thank you, J.O.," she said, patting his arm. She felt as if she had aged five years in the last few hours. Then she turned to Gary, "Would you please take me outside for a few minutes? I need some fresh air."

Gary escorted her outside, then stood hugging her tightly in grief-filled silence.

They walked back inside just as J.O. returned from seeing

Kathleen. No verbal confirmation was necessary. His red-rimmed eyes confirmed that, indisputably, Kathleen had died.

Nadine prided herself on being a strong woman, but the conversation with Sergeant Baker had had the same effect as hollowing out a sturdy oak. They had been discussing her first born. Now emotionally and physically exhausted, Nadine and the men dragged themselves to a La Quinta Hotel, a few blocks from the sheriff's office.

Nadine barely closed her eyes all night, but it was only the beginning of many sleepless nights. Kathleen's face shimmered in her mind, and Nadine remembered how Kathleen had suffered more than her siblings from being an Air Force brat. Because her father had been in the Air Force during all of Kathleen's elementary school years, Kathleen had drifted in and out of schools as her father's relocation orders arrived. Finally, Kathleen had stopped trying to make friends, realizing the townspeople knew she was a sergeant's child and would treat her as only temporary, knowing she would be moving on. As a result, she appeared timid and quiet with people she didn't know. Once a person became her friend, however, Kathy was a friend for life.

Kathleen had been both a member of the National Honor Society and chosen for *Who's Who in American High Schools*. Her brightest moment had been her election as "Most Likely to Succeed" by her classmates. She had graduated sixth in her class, lettered in track and volleyball, and proved to be an accomplished writer for the New Caney High School newspaper, the *Eagle's Talon*.

Kathleen had gone on to college, the first in her family. She attended Stephen F. Austin University in Nacogdoches, Texas, for two years before transferring to West Texas State University for another year. Even after she had married Bill Lipscomb and given birth to two children, she still found time to enroll in nursing classes at the University of Texas in San Antonio, graduating with a degree in nursing in May 1984.

The San Antonio Light hit the streets with headlines screaming, "NUDE BODY OF WOMAN FOUND," and as a subheadline, "Medical Examiner Says 29-Year-Old Strangled." The *Humble Echo* also ran the article: "OFFICIALS IDENTIFY NUDE WOMAN'S BODY." Both newspapers disregarded the family's sensitivity by vividly describing Kathleen in her nude state—"face up, brutally strangled with an electrical cord or telephone wire, and covered with fire ants."

Around 11 a.m., the group from San Antonio met for breakfast in the hotel coffee shop in the same clothes they had worn the night before. During the somber breakfast, Nadine outlined the day's activities. First, they had to go to Kathleen's apartment to get the clothes for her funeral.

Entering Kathleen's apartment proved not to be as easy as Nadine had anticipated. The apartment's management shied away from accepting responsibility for missing items that had once belonged to Kathleen, thus forcing Nadine to convene with the attorney representing the complex and sign forms releasing them from liability.

Finally inside, they were met by a half dozen investigators from the sheriff's department in the process of conducting a search. The investigators crawled over Kathleen's apartment, stripped her bed and took the pink sheets and pillowcases for hair, fiber, and semen samples. They also took hair samples from the bathtub, sink, and commode. The specimen would be sent to the FBI Crime Lab in Washington, D.C. After photographs were shot of each room, the detectives sprinkled black, baby powder-soft graphite over everything in search of fingerprints, making the once-immaculate apartment look dirty.

J.O. and Jim stayed with the investigators while Nadine and Gary went to Kathleen's bedroom. Nadine had to steady herself when she opened Kathy's closet and saw all the familiar clothes. She reached for a blue silk suit, recalling how it complemented Kathy's blue eyes. Then she stopped, realizing those eyes would be closed. She rehung the outfit, and chose the coral linen suit she had made. Even though Nadine had an important, time-consuming career, she still sometimes sewed for her daughters, as she had since they were little. Hopefully the coral would make Kathy's skin look more alive. She folded it over her arm, and bent down to look for matching shoes before she realized Kathy wouldn't be needing shoes.

Nadine hurried out of the bedroom and joined her friends to leave the apartment. While the forensic investigators were busy gathering samples, Nadine saw Kathleen's date book by her phone and slipped it in her purse. Once outside, Nadine checked Kathleen's mailbox and found an envelope with the return address of Kathy's attorney. She ripped it open to find Kathy's divorce papers, already signed by Lipscomb and his attorney. All they lacked to be legal and final was Kathy's signature.

Kathleen's grief-stricken friends in San Antonio wanted a service for her there, even though the main funeral would be the day after in Kingwood, Texas, 25 miles north of Houston. Gary accompanied Nadine to the funeral home to finalize arrangements, and as they stood in the entry, Bill Lipscomb came rushing in.

"Can you believe this?" he said with tears in his red eyes. His rough, unshaven face looked drained. "Who could have done this to our Kathy? My kids don't have a mom anymore. Now, I've really lost her."

Nadine and Gary stared at the shaking form in front of them. They had not seen Lipscomb since before Kathleen's murder, and they couldn't believe this was the same macho, I've-got-all-the-answers Bill. His eyes were swollen, and he kept dabbing at his runny nose with a wet handkerchief.

Gary, a computer expert, usually gritted his teeth and put up with his boastful brother-in-law, who normally made condescending remarks about Gary's lack of athletic ability. Now Bill looked so pathetic that Gary felt sorry for him. As Lipscomb continued to pour out his grief, Gary became convinced. Bill was innocent.

Thursday morning, the gloomy day after the San Antonio service, the funeral home placed Kathleen's tortured body into a silver Suburban that the funeral home had converted into a hearse and transferred it to Our Comforter Lutheran Church in Kingwood.

Around one, an hour before the service, the family went to see Kathleen. Not one of them had seen her since she had been killed.

They nervously clustered at the far end of the church. Darlene's older brother, Chuck, an army sergeant, had flown in on emergency leave from Germany. David, her younger brother and the only child living at home, had taken the week off from his classes at North Harris County Junior College.

Darlene glanced around and was reminded of her father's funeral in this same church. Charles had died of cancer in 1977, five years after he had retired from the Air Force. Darlene had been barely seventeen and she had thought burying him had been the hardest thing she had ever done. Today was far worse.

Kathy's blonde hair was visible from across the room. Perky daisies, Kathleen's favorite flower, graced her casket and the room smelled of all the flowers sent by her friends and co-workers.

Darlene started toward her sister's casket, passing by the bouquets of roses and lilies, until she reached her sister. Then her mouth gaped open and her stomach heaved as she stood by Kathleen, whose face was so swollen it could have been another person. Her neck and chin, fat and grotesque, melted into each other, and her beautiful hands were hidden under white gloves. Darlene felt weak and clung to the casket.

"Oh, Kathleen!" Nadine screamed, suddenly appearing beside Darlene. "What have they done to you?" Sobbing, Nadine leaned down into the casket. Her tears fell on the lifeless figure.

Darlene put her arms around her mother's shoulders and gently pulled her back, then looked at Chuck. Darlene had always been able to communicate with her 25-year-old brother with just her eyes. Darlene realized that this body was not the Kathleen the family wanted to remember. Nor would Kathleen have wished them to see her like this. Chuck reached up and closed the casket. Then they all held each other and cried.

Later, Darlene stood at the church entrance, greeting friends filing in for the funeral. She had not seen Lipscomb since Kathleen had died, and was impatiently waiting for him to bring the children. Gary's words after he returned from San Antonio still echoed in her head: "Bill didn't do this, Darlene. You should see how broken up the guy is. This murder has just crushed him."

Lipscomb walked in holding hands with little Mary Ann and Billie. His somber-looking parents, who that morning had flown in from Virginia, followed behind. Darlene rushed up and hugged the children, expecting them to be devastated. Instead, the children simply smiled and said, "Hi, Aunt Darlene." She thought their young age had insulated their grief. Lipscomb embraced her, and she began crying on his shoulder.

"Who could have done this?" she asked.

"I don't know, Darlene, I don't know," he said softly. "But I'd sure like to get my hands on him."

"Sergeant Baker called last night," she told him, "and now I'm really scared. Kathleen's neighbor, Gina Riegel, reported that yesterday, right before the funeral in San Antonio, some man called her and said in a low voice, 'You're the next one to die.' Can you imagine?"

Lipscomb looked startled. Gina Riegel, a close friend of Kathy's, also had an Air Force husband, children, and a nursing career. "Do they have any idea who called?"

Darlene shook her head. "I'm afraid. I really am. First Kathleen, and now a threat against her good friend. I'm thinking, what about me? I was so close to Kathleen."

Lipscomb gave Darlene another hug and went to sit with her family. During the funeral, Darlene's eyes searched the congregation, wondering if the person who called Gina could be sitting among them.

At the close of the ceremony, the family was escorted down the aisle, and Dr. Pearle stood up and hugged Nadine. He began crying and said, "I loved your daughter very, very much. She was so special to me. I want you to know that."

"Yes, I know," Nadine said, her posture stiff and her face unsmiling. The doctor stood staring at her meekly, his misery so apparent that she felt forced to reply. "She loved you too, and talked about you often."

Pearle nervously fingered his tie. He lingered a moment as though he had something else to say, but finally he quietly nodded and stepped aside to let Nadine pass.

The next day, Kathy would be put to rest in Haughton, the small Louisiana hometown of the Adams, where her father was buried. So after today's service, the family visited with their friends in the back of the church.

Nadine and Darlene sat together on a pew when Lipscomb appeared and crouched down to whisper, "Nadine, I hate to talk to you about this right now, but I need to get into Kathleen's apartment."

"I can't let you in there. They won't even let *me* in."

"How'd you get in for the burial clothes?"

"I had to go to an attorney and sign a document stating what I needed before they would let me in. What do you want? I gave you the children's clothes."

"I need to get her Lutheran Brotherhood insurance policy. I have the others. I would wait to talk to you about this, but I have to leave town tomorrow."

Nadine sat twisting her hands until the tissue she held crumbled and white fragments fell on her black dress. She began to cry.

Darlene, listening to their conversation, could not believe her ears. She wondered if Bill had any idea how greedy it made him sound to ask about Kathleen's insurance.

"See what you're doing to my mother? She can't talk about it now. How can you be asking for my sister's insurance when we haven't even buried her yet?"

Lipscomb looked up at Darlene. "I don't understand why you or your mother are making a big deal over this. I was the one who paid the premiums."

Darlene couldn't imagine that the one person Kathleen hated was asking for her policy. "You're divorced, remember? She wanted Mary Ann and Billie to have the insurance." Darlene stood up to go to Kathleen, thinking Bill wouldn't follow, but he did.

Lipscomb put his arm around her as they stood in front of the casket. "I know this is tough for you and I apologize for that. But life goes on."

"Life doesn't go on for Kathleen," Darlene said, turning abruptly to face him. "It stopped for her three nights ago."

Inexplicably, Lipscomb's expression changed. He grabbed Kathleen's coffin and began rocking it—shaking it so hard the handles rattled. "When are they going to open this thing?"

Darlene reached out to steady the wooden box, and thought the entire moment seemed like a bad dream. "They aren't," she said firmly. "Chuck closed it before the service and when he did, the latch broke. We don't want it opened because she looked so bad."

Disgusted with Lipscomb's actions, Darlene hurried back to her mother and took her arm. "It's time to go," she said and headed for the door.

The next day Kathleen's body arrived in Haughton, Louisiana, outside of Shreveport. The family's grief had been stretched and elongated until it had occupied the entire week. Kathleen had been killed on Sunday, found on Monday, and it was early Tuesday before Nadine gave Sergeant Baker the photographs for identification. The San Antonio funeral was Wednesday, another funeral had been held on Thursday, and the burial was today on Friday. The entire process had been like a sledgehammer, driving the grief deeper into the family.

After the burial, everyone walked away from Kathleen's coffin as it cantilevered over the open grave. Nadine overheard Bill's father, Nelson Lipscomb say, "Let's get the hell out of here. This place gives me the creeps."

Nadine turned to Bill. "We'd love to have Mary Ann and Billie come stay with us." She stroked Mary Ann's silken blonde hair. "They're the most precious memories we have of Kathleen. Can they stay for a while?" She now held Billie's small hand.

"No, they can't," Bill said sharply. "We're leaving from here to go to Virginia. You know my grandmother just died. I wasn't able to go to her funeral because of Kathleen's, and I want to be with my grandfather. I need to grieve with *my* family." He jerked the children away from Nadine and left.

Chapter Five

Technical Sergeant William Thomas Lipscomb, a good-looking, muscular athlete, joined the Air Force on October 2, 1974. Each year since that date, his annual evaluations glowed beyond any of his contemporaries. They were written by his supervisors all the way up to the highest ranking officer presiding over his section. The evaluations made up one of two significant keys to his rapidly-acquired promotions. His performance reports were rare because of their consistent perfection. On a scale of zero to nine, Lipscomb scored a *nine* in all sixteen categories ranging from "performance of duty" to "bearing and behavior."

On Lipscomb's 1983 review, M.Sgt. William Harris Jr. wrote: "Staff Sergeant Lipscomb's devotion to duty, knowledge, cooperative attitude, and absolute unselfish loyalty are his greatest strengths."

In May 1984, an opening existed for a military training instructor, and the coveted position would catapult Lipscomb from being a drill sergeant to teaching others to shoulder that responsibility. His most formidable competition was Staff Sgt. Roger Anthony Barrelo, who had six years of Air Force experience under his belt.

Both airmen had undergone extensive written and oral testing in addition to personal evaluations by their superiors for the position, but by far, Sergeant Lipscomb was considered the front-runner. Wanting to be the only one chosen, Lipscomb was dismayed when M.Sgt. Leon Owens revealed that the recruitment committee had decided to choose both Lipscomb and Barrelo.

After Lipscomb's appointment, his 1984 report contained remarks from Maj. Kerry Green: "Technical Sergeant Lipscomb is absolutely the finest young Non-commissioned Officer (NCO) I know. Promote at the earliest opportunity," and Col. James Wilhelm said, "Absolutely superior is the watchword for this young NCO. Few NCO's accomplish in a career what Technical Sergeant Lipscomb has done in one reporting period. He is performing at the Master Sergeant level better than many who wear the grade. Promote." In the same year, Capt. Michael H. McKenna characterized Lipscomb as, "An outstanding role model for the entire Air Force." Maj. Gen. Carl R. Smith wrote: "Technical Sergeant Lipscomb's impeccable appearance and unusual ability made him a natural choice to serve as one of my flag bearers. Promote."

The praise continued the following June when Col. Hubert C. Place exalted Lipscomb as, "A razor-sharp NCO. Because of his crisp professional presence and polished speaking ability, he was the keynote speaker at a recent Aerospace Medical Division's NCO Preparatory Course. Promote immediately." And promote they did, at the rate of every other year.

Lipscomb's success as a training instructor ranked above all others. After he experienced the highest student success rate on base, the Air Force recognized him as the Air Training Command Master Instructor of 1985.

Lipscomb handled personnel problems with the adroitness

of a psychologist, but for him, his pride rested in his men's impeccable loyalty.

The other key to Bill's promotions was The Weighted Airman Performance System test (WAPS). The next rank was master sergeant. Bill desperately wanted that promotion, for at 30, he would be one of the youngest master sergeants in the entire United States Air Force. The exam would be given in six months, and by then Bill felt he would have memorized everything he needed to know to pass.

Lipscomb and Tony Barrelo had become good friends after working together, and that friendship carried over into their leisure hours. Lipscomb frequently worked out in the gym to maintain his phenomenal upper body strength, and Barrelo worked alongside him. One day in late fall, while in the gym lifting weights, they discussed the upcoming WAPS test. Lipscomb wondered if he should suggest a plan he had toyed with for almost a year, a plan that would assure success on all future promotions.

Every job Lipscomb undertook in the Air Force received an excellent rating, but in promotion testing, he lacked perfection. With one exception, he had passed the promotion test on the first try, but he usually missed about 15 questions out of 100. When he tested for staff sergeant, he had embarrassingly failed the test first round, but passed it on his second try. He wanted to make sure that he would never fail a test again. Now he decided to take a shot at discussing his plan with Barrelo.

"That test is taken by thousands of guys every year," Lipscomb began. "You'd think we'd be able to get our hands on those questions. It would cut our studying time in half and guarantee getting the next rank."

"Come on, Bill, you know it's illegal even to discuss it," Barrelo said. "Besides, people don't want to tell you what's on the test. You might get a better grade than they do. That lessens their chance for promotion. Nah." He shook his head, "Guys won't do that."

"They'd talk if there was an incentive."

"Like what?"

"Say we put together a test we all could share, one complete with current questions and answers. Everyone in on it would get a little gravy. Wouldn't you like to be assured of getting your next promotion to tech sergeant?"

"Who wouldn't?" Barrelo said, "But how you gonna find out what they'll ask?"

"We'd talk to people who just took the test, and ask them to highlight their PFE [Promotion Fitness Exam] manual when they see a question they were asked. Then we'd highlight a master study guide on questions they tell us about. We could make this a long-range project and highlight it with different colors for each year."

"You think people would remember the whole test?"

"If they know they had to give us their highlighted manuals immediately after taking the test, they'd put out a major effort to remember. Let's get a dozen or more people involved. That would increase our chances of covering the entire test. I could be the clearing point who everybody reports to."

"You wouldn't be afraid to take that kind of chance?"

"I'd have the control because I'd be the only one with the manual. I'd know exactly who'd get to look at it."

"If you'd be willing to do that, it might just work," Barrelo nodded slowly. His misgivings gave way to strategizing. "But we couldn't use a whole bunch of people on this base. Someone's bound to talk."

"You want different bases?" Lipscomb asked. "I've got a good friend going up for master sergeant at Maxwell Air Force Base. He'll help us. Another friend I served with here was transferred to Elmendorf outside of Anchorage. He'll cooperate."

"Yeah, that reminds me," Barrelo said with a big grin, "I've got a cousin at Hickam in Hawaii, and a good friend in Germany at Ramstein. This just might work,'' he said, and high-fived Lipscomb.

The two men headed off to the showers and Lipscomb suggested, ''Come over to my house. We need to start studying.'' They both laughed.

Barrelo followed Lipscomb home and soon they covered the dining room table with maps and lists of Air Force bases around the world.

An hour later, Kathleen came in wearing her medical scrub suit and carrying two bags of groceries, followed by Mary Ann and Billie, whom she had just collected from day care. She stepped into the dining room and asked, ''What are you two doing?''

''We're studying for WAPS,'' Lipscomb told her with a mischievous grin.

''With maps and telephone numbers?''

''It's our new innovative approach,'' Barrelo laughed. ''Kinda the work-smart-instead-of-hard school. Hey, Bill, tell her you'll buy her a new dress with your master sergeant's raise,'' he said, eyeing Kathy's scrubs.

Kathy wrinkled her nose and appeared puzzled. ''I'm getting my nursing degree this month. That will give us plenty more income.''

''In those clothes you look like a nurse already,'' Barrelo said.

Kathy smiled. ''I guess I do. I'm a nurses' aide in pediatric ICU at the hospital, and the job helps pay for my college expenses.''

''Don't believe her, Tony. Kathy is already talking about buying a bigger house when she gets her degree. We always seem to need more money.'' Bill, the third oldest of six children in a big Catholic family, grew up knowing the problems of a family trying to stretch its income. Being a middle child, he learned to be competitive early in life. When he had turned eleven, he had started working a paper route, and through the monetary rewards of work he had experienced the joy of financial and social independence. That experience included a twenty-year-old woman on his route who had found him particularly attractive, and had coaxed him inside her home for more than newspaper delivery. Long ago he had forgotten her name, but he still remembered her strip-tease and dance to lure him into his first sexual encounter. At the same time, she had introduced him to alcohol and cigarettes, but those two vices didn't stay with him when athletics in school changed his goals into body building.

At eleven, Lipscomb had mistaken his new activities for maturity, but his parents had found his behavior inexcusable. Determined to hold onto his new lifestyle, he had responded by running away from home. He still remembered his father's outrage when he had met him at the police station, and the sad, angry face of his mother looking back at him from the front seat on the ride home. He had convinced them that he only wanted to find his grandparents, who he had missed terribly since the family had moved over a year ago. Each summer thereafter, his parents had sent him to live with his grandparents, much to the envy of his brothers and sisters.

Kathy and Bill had attended New Caney High School together. Kathy knew of Bill because he was a wrestling and varsity football star who drove a snappy yellow Corvette convertible and he knew about her because she was one of the most popular girls in school, but they never had dated each other.

In the fall after graduation, Lipscomb had driven through the east Texas town of Nacogdoches one weekend to visit a friend who had just lost his leg in a motorcycle accident. On the way, he had stopped by Stephen F. Austin University to look up Kathy. He had poured out his heart about his friend and Kathy had been sympathetic because she had just lost her father. This marked the beginning of their romance, but Lipscomb had his heart set on entering the Air Force.

He had left in October for Barksdale Air Force Base in Louisiana while Kathy had continued her studies. They had dated only briefly before the Air Force sent him to Okinawa. After that, they had relied on letters to further their romance. When Lipscomb had proposed and Kathy had accepted, he had unromantically mailed her an engagement ring, and they had planned to marry two weeks after he returned home.

As their wedding date had drawn closer, Kathy did not confide to any one that she had serious doubts about marrying Lipscomb. Ever since she and Darlene were little, they had fantasized about a double wedding. Darlene's fiancé, Gary Sanford, was the only person she had ever dated, and Kathleen hadn't had the heart to disappoint her sister. So she had married Bill.

Kathy left the WAPS studying session to change her clothes, and Barrelo turned to Lipscomb.

"That wife of yours is sure some looker."

Lipscomb looked at him soberly. "Just remember, she's my wife. Now get your mind off Kathy and start making some phone calls. We've got a world organization to put together."

Chapter Six

Eduardo Pettavino, hospital administrator of U.T.'s Health Science Center, called the sheriff's department the week following Kathleen's murder. He talked with Sergeant Dalton Baker.

"I really need to tell you about one of our nurses," he began with a certain reluctance in his voice. "We've been throwing this around ever since Kathy Lipscomb died. It's possible that one of our male nurses, Vince Robideaux, might have had something to do with it."

"What makes you think that?," Baker asked.

"First of all, Robideaux worked with Kathy and he also lived in the same apartment complex. So he had an opportunity to be around her at home in addition to seeing her at work."

"That's only a coincidence." Baker began to feel this call would end up wasting his time.

"Maybe. But I have some serious doubts about Robideaux. He was a different sort. Kept to himself and didn't say a whole lot. But the main thing bothering us is that we can't find him anywhere. Last weekend when Kathy was murdered happened to be the end of a pay period. He didn't come by on Monday to pick up his check. No one has seen him since. And now he's made himself scarce since the murder investigation began. It's waving a red flag around here.''

''And you've questioned everyone he worked with?''

''Everyone on his shift. No one has seen or heard from him. At least we'd expect him to call and tell us where to mail his check. We know he's from the Galveston area, but we don't have the authority to go after anybody there. Rumor has it that he's either gay or bisexual, but don't quote me on that.''

''Okay, I agree this could be something,'' Baker said, warming to the possibility. ''We'll get out crew over to his apartment.'' He jotted a note to himself, ''Get search warrant. Bag fingerprints and hair samples. Check for any sign of a struggle.''

Even before Baker got around to investigating that lead, he received another phone call the same afternoon. This time it was one of Kathleen's neighbors, Hector Salquero. His apartment sat directly across the parking lot from hers, allowing him full view of any visitor she might have.

''I saw Mrs. Lipscomb leaving with someone on the day she was killed.'' Salquero spoke hurriedly. ''I've been thinking about it, and know it's my civic duty to call you. Goodness knows I wouldn't have thought to stop her. But now I can't get it off my mind. I'm really upset.''

''What did you see?'' Baker asked.

''I just happened to glance out my window and saw Mrs. Lipscomb leave with a dikey-looking woman. The woman wore a blue blouse with white polka dots. She had dark, short, kinda reddish hair. I don't remember exactly what time, but it was early afternoon.''

Amazed to be handed another lead so quickly, Baker hurriedly scribbled Salquero's address and promised to send a deputy out that afternoon to take his statement. An early forensic report had determined that they had found red hair on Kathleen's orange T-shirt.

* * *

Gary Sanford called Baker as soon as the family returned from Louisiana, eager to be updated on the case.

"We located Kathleen's car," Baker told him. "It was in a Luby's parking lot about a mile from her apartment. The manager called us Tuesday after seeing it there since Sunday night. It wasn't locked and there were no keys in it."

"Do you have any suspects?" Gary asked.

"As a matter of fact, we have four." He ticked off the possibilities: Lipscomb, Pearle, the male nurse, and the redhead. "So there might be more to this than we think. We ran a check on Lipscomb and the doctor, and found both men to be clean, really clean. There were no 911 calls. No reports of spousal abuse. We do want to question Lipscomb further when he returns from Virginia. Any idea when he'll get back to San Antonio?"

"He didn't tell us," Gary said, pleased that the sheriff's office knew Lipscomb's whereabouts. "He said he'd give us a call when he comes home."

"Okay, let me know."

The sergeant sounded intent on ending the conversation, but Gary hesitated. "I have one more question." He cleared his throat. "When Nadine and I were in San Antonio to identify the body, we asked if Kathleen had been raped or anything. At that time you told us no. I'm reluctant to discuss this and it's kind of embarrassing, but we've been hit with a rumor that she was . . . well, Kathleen's friends have heard that she might have been sodomized. This is awkward for me to talk about, but we really need to know. This whole thing is hard enough, so if she wasn't sodomized, knowing that would make us feel better." He sounded relieved to get the words out of his mouth.

"Gary, we're sure Kathleen had relations with someone on Saturday," Baker said matter-of-factly. "We know from our crime lab that the vaginal swab showed twenty-hour-old sperm.

Dr. Pearle has admitted being with her then, but as far as we know, she wasn't raped. I'm not positive about the sodomy part, and won't be until the autopsy report comes back. I promise we'll let you know one way or the other.''

On June 18th, Rance Grafton, managing partner of the law firm that represented Kathleen in her divorce, called Nadine and told her to go to San Antonio immediately to be established as the administratrix of Kathleen's estate.

''What's the hurry?'' Nadine asked as a wave of apprehension swept through her.

''We just heard that Bill's trying to get Kathleen's insurance. If you don't do this right now, that divorce could be annulled and Bill will stand to collect the money that otherwise would go to Mary Ann and Billie.''

Within two hours, Nadine, Darlene, and Chuck were in the car headed for San Antonio. When they reached Grafton's office, he had all the forms ready to authorize Nadine as the administratrix, and told them to go immediately to the three insurance companies and file a copy of the appointment with each one.

They stopped at the University of Texas' Insurance Department where Aetna Insurance guaranteed Kathleen's life for $228,000, then at Lutheran Brotherhood Insurance which held a policy for over $64,000, and finally, the state comptroller's office to alert them not to pay Bill Lipscomb the more than $22,000 on a Teacher's Insurance Policy. Since Kathleen worked in a teaching hospital, she held eligibility for their coverage. Each time the three swept into an office, they found that Lipscomb had been there only a scant 30 minutes before. Each claims departments echoed the other's comments: Bill had been terribly rude and irritated when told the proceeds couldn't be released without his prior appointment as the administrator.

As they left the last claims department, Darlene said, "Mom, what do you make of Kathleen having so much insurance? Did you know about all that?"

"I knew she had two insurance policies through her work, but I had no idea they were for that much. She had a small policy with Lutheran Brotherhood. We took out a $5,000 policy for each of you when you were little, but nothing like $60,000."

"That's over $300,000," Darlene quickly added. "Kathleen only made $23,000 when she died. Why would she have so much insurance?"

"I'm just amazed," she told Darlene. But as they discussed the insurance, Nadine seemed preoccupied. "While we're in San Antonio, we might as well go by the sheriff's office. We can get the release forms for Kathleen's car."

Ten minutes later, Darlene asked Baker, "Did you know that Kathleen had over $300,000 in life insurance?"

"No. I hadn't heard that figure."

"My mom's been made administratrix of her estate, so Bill can't get the insurance. In case she doesn't get to control the estate, you wouldn't let Bill collect, would you? Since he's a suspect?"

"That's really out of our hands, Darlene. If we don't have a probable cause to arrest him, then we can't keep him from getting the proceeds if he's the beneficiary."

"Can't you give him a lie detector test, or something? You can't force him?" Dismay laced Darlene's words.

"No, all we can do is ask. He has hired an attorney so we have to go through him to talk with Bill, and the lawyer's no help. His attorney put on the gag rule, which means we'd have to take Lipscomb to court in order to have a conversation. In court, the judge can say, 'Go ahead and interview him,' and Lipscomb can take the fifth."

"I can't believe a suspect can tie your hands like this."

"Heck, all our ability to question suspects ended in 1982 with the Miranda case."

"So if he doesn't cooperate, he could get the insurance," Darlene said, and fought for patience. Then she decided to try a different approach. "You talked about probable cause. How about over $300,000 in life insurance money. Isn't *that* probable cause?"

"That's hard to say, Darlene. Since they were married, Bill would be the logical one to receive the money."

"You mean you'd actually let the murderer have the life insurance on someone he's killed?"

"Darlene, you heard the sergeant," Nadine said. "They don't know that Bill killed Kathleen, and if they can't indict him, they have to assume he's innocent."

"That's right," Baker said, smiling at Nadine. "I'm glad you understand, Mrs. Adams."

Nadine tucked the release forms into her briefcase, and appeared ready to leave. They drove to the County Point where they picked up Kathleen's impounded car, finding it covered with fingerprint dust.

As they started to head back to Houston, Nadine asked to visit Kathleen's apartment, "One last time."

The manager, Sandra Donaldson, remembered them. She accompanied them inside Kathleen's apartment and then locked the door behind them.

"I never thought Bill could be as big a jerk as Kathy let on," Sandra said. "But I met him the other day, and he really is a nut case, isn't he?"

"He was here?" Nadine asked.

"Yes. He said he had some property in the apartment, needed some insurance policy or something."

"Did you let him in?"

"Goodness no! I could get in all kinds of trouble if I had. I only let you in today because I knew you had the proper—"

There was a loud knock on the door. They all stared at each other.

"Who could that be?" whispered Darlene.

"No one knows we're here except my office employees," Sandra said.

Darlene tiptoed to the door and looked through the peephole. She turned around and mouthed, "It's Bill!"

"I locked the door," Sandra said quietly. "Don't answer it. He doesn't know we're here."

"I guess it's about time Bill caught up with us," Nadine said. "We've been within thirty minutes of him all day."

Lipscomb repeatedly slammed his fist against the door. "Nadine? Nadine? I know you're in there because I saw your car. Open this door. Do you hear me? Nadine? Let me in!"

"Mom, what are we going to do?" whispered Darlene.

Chuck went to the door and peered through the peephole. Finally, after some time, he signaled that Lipscomb was leaving.

"Whew, that was close," Darlene said. "Bill scares me."

"Ha!" Chuck grunted, puffing out his chest. "I bet he wouldn't be beating on that door if he knew *I* was in here."

Darlene knew her brother was probably right. Bill had been afraid of only two people—her father and Chuck, who had a reputation for acting on his temper.

The telephone rang and Sandra answered it, then said, "Tell him we'll be back soon. Have him wait there. Thanks."

She turned and said, "Well, looks like he's decided to wait for you. There's only one way out and it's through the reception room, where he is. If he tries to start anything, I'll call the police.

"Okay, Mom," Chuck urged, "Let's go get him."

Lipscomb was leaning against a pool table, tossing a cue ball back and forth between his hands.

"Nadine, why didn't you answer the door when I knocked?"

"I don't know, Bill. I guess I didn't want to."

Lipscomb began tossing the ball gently into the air. "I know you filed the papers for Kathleen's estate. Why are you doing this to me?''

"I'm looking out for Mary Ann and Billie. I'm doing what Kathleen would want me to.''

"Are you going to let me in to get that policy I was talking about?''

"No. I can't get anything right now. Rance's waiting to get the recorded documents we filed back from the courts, and until then I can't touch a thing.''

Lipscomb slammed the cue ball onto the pool table. "I am not going to be divorced. Do you hear me? I will fight you on this if you force me. I will *not* be divorced!''

"We'll talk about this later, Bill. I've got a long ride back to Houston and I'm tired. Do *you* hear *me?*''

Lipscomb's face reddened. "Nadine! We can be friends, or we can fight. It's totally up to you. I repeat, I will not be divorced!''

Chapter Seven

On July 15, the Bexar County Sheriff allowed Bill Lipscomb to receive Kathleen's life insurance. The news caught the family off guard and left them reeling.

When Darlene Sanford called Sergeant Baker for an explanation, he told her that they were forced to do so because the insurance company was under a time limit to pay *some* beneficiary, and sufficient evidence to arrest Lipscomb just hadn't surfaced.

"Did you talk with all those people whose names we gave you?" Darlene asked.

"I'm sure we did," he said. "There wasn't anything there."

"What about Ricky Rios? You know, that sergeant and all those other guys Bill worked with?"

"They couldn't really tell us anything."

Darlene was appalled. Even though the sheriff still considered Bill a suspect, since they had failed to prove anything, Bill would be free to collect more than $314,000.

* * *

Nadine felt that she had somehow failed Kathleen and desperately wanted to prevent the insurance payment to Lipscomb. Under Rance Grafton's directions, she contacted the judge in San Antonio who had presided over her daughter's divorce. The judge agreed to let Nadine, as administratrix, sign the final divorce papers for Kathleen postmortem.

However, through Lipscomb's network at the sheriff's department he heard about her plans, and his calls took on an ominous, threatening tone. In early August he told her, "If you fight me on this, I'll drag Kathleen's name through the mud. I'll take all of you to court and have Kathleen's aunts and friends testify about her. Your whole family will have to get up and say she was guilty of adultery, and if you don't, you can be indicted for perjury, because I can prove you knew about her affair."

Lipscomb's words weighed heavily upon Nadine. She called Grafton and told him of Lipscomb's threats.

"I think he could have something there," Rance said in a resigned tone. "He might win in a civil trial because it may look like you covered up facts to get the insurance."

"It would be outrageous if he got a penny out of this."

"I know, but he hasn't been arrested, and he and Kathleen are not considered divorced. Legally, he is the beneficiary."

"You mean to tell me that there is nothing we can do about this?"

"Nothing that doesn't come with the risk of losing a court case and ending up with all the attorney fees to pay. Knowing Bill's personality, he'd be so bent on revenge that he'd keep your grandchildren from you."

Confrontation had always troubled Nadine. She asked herself if more than $300,000 was worth her peace of mind and the cohesiveness of her family. Her only ties to Kathleen now were her grandchildren. She decided to cave in to peace and family.

The next time Lipscomb called, Nadine told him of her decision, and he suggested that his children fly to Houston for a visit.

On July 19, 1986, Darlene gathered up her two daughters and drove over to Nadine's house after Lipscomb arrived. Kim ran outside to play with her cousins, and Darlene carried Julie in an infant seat. Bill sat watching television in the den. He was wearing a royal blue Ralph Lauren polo shirt and tan chino slacks. His bare feet were tucked into Gucci loafers.

"You sure look sharp, Bill. What gives?" She took a chair near Lipscomb and put Julie on the floor beside her.

"I can look sharp now," he said, flicking a thread from his slacks. "Ever since we were married, Kathleen complained when I bought clothes. Remember how great I used to look in high school? I can't believe I came in second for 'Most Handsome'." He started to laugh.

"All I remember," Darlene said flatly, "is your buying a formal dress uniform when Kathleen needed glasses. So she went without glasses."

The smile faded from his face. "Darlene, let's not start that, okay? I came down here so you could see the kids. I won't stay here and be measured up to Kathleen."

His chiding tone made her angry, and Darlene couldn't help but notice how Lipscomb's temper seemed to flare more easily lately. She chose her words carefully. "I thought you'd be happy knowing you'll get all the insurance."

"Well, I can't believe I had to fight your mother over it when I had a wife who ran around on me. There's no doubt in my mind that Pearle did this. Kathleen was probably pushing him into marriage, or threatening to tell his wife."

A cold silence permeated the room before Lipscomb spoke again.

"Has anyone at the sheriff's office told you what happened to Kathleen?"

Answering in a whisper, Darlene said, "Sergeant Baker said she had been slapped and strangled." A sob almost closed her throat. "But I get sick just talking about it."

Lipscomb ignored her remarks and continued. "She wasn't just slapped and strangled." He turned to look at Darlene, staring at her face to gauge her reaction. "She had been beaten real bad." He moved his hand over his own body to indicate where Kathleen's bruises were located. "Her right breast, here on her left thigh, on her throat, and her face, too. They could have been the 'slap' marks you mentioned. And Darlene, she had been raped and sodomized. If anyone knew Kathleen's sexual preferences, I did, and she would never consent to sodomy."

Darlene was both embarrassed and irritated by his words. How did Bill know all this? She wondered because the sheriff's office hadn't told them. She struggled with the uncertainty that Bill had raised, and could only think of two logical explanations: Either Bill was getting his information from the contact they suspected inside the sheriff's office, or he had murdered Kathleen.

The next day Darlene spent 45 minutes on the phone with Sergeant Baker, relaying her conversation with Lipscomb. He said he would jump right on it and find out how Lipscomb knew. Excitedly, he told her this was their first big break.

A month later, it wasn't difficult to spot Lipscomb's flashy new van in a restaurant parking lot in Schulenberg, Texas, the halfway point between Houston and San Antonio, where Nadine Adams had arranged with Lipscomb to collect Mary Ann and Billie for one last visit before the children's school started.

"What do you think of my new wheels?" he asked. "I bought it when I received Kathleen's Teacher Retirement Insurance. It's got a television, a VCR, headphones . . . name it, it's there. I really had it customized.''

Darlene and Nadine stared silently, unable to believe he would flaunt such a thing in front of them.

Lipscomb patted his shirt pocket. ''I have Kathleen's autopsy here. Anyone want to read it?''

Nadine shook her head. Darlene knew that that report was not how her mother wanted to remember Kathleen.

Undaunted, Lipscomb continued. ''This is really interesting. I think you'd be surprised with what you'd learn from it.''

Darlene stood in the parking lot listening to Lipscomb speak with such self-assured authority. She wondered what secret he wanted them to know. Finally too curious, she said, ''I'll read it.''

Nadine flashed her daughter a glare of disapproval.

Lipscomb handed Darlene the autopsy report and told her to take her time. She could read it in Nadine's car while he showed everyone else the latest in custom vans.

Darlene shut the car door and hesitantly unfolded the papers, remembering her sister telling her how she had watched an autopsy as part of her nurse's training, and remarking that she would never want that for her own body. ''They slice you up, and put your brain in one bucket and your heart in another. It's terrible. They just hollow you out.''

Seeing the weight of her sister's brain described so graphically dismayed Darlene. According to the report, Kathleen had eaten Chinese food shortly before her death and the image of the wok on Kathleen's countertop came instantly to mind. She rushed through the cold clinical terms until she got to the last two pages.

A drawing of Kathy's bruises showed them to be exactly where Lipscomb had said they were. Kathleen's neck had two marks where a cord had been wrapped. The section on rigor mortis described her position. All folded up, Darlene thought, like she had been put in something confining. Maybe a small vehicle—like Kathy's Sentra! Bill had told them shortly after her death that Kathy had been placed in her own car and that was why he didn't want it. Color drained from her face as she realized he'd known all along. Suddenly she became anxious to return the report and tell her mother what she had discovered.

Lipscomb took the autopsy, folded it and shoved it back into his pocket. "What'd you think?" he asked, taunting her.

"It was gross." She swallowed hard, trying to manage a reply. "It's the worst thing I ever saw. I can't even discuss it now."

"Yeah, it was kinda gross," he allowed, "but did you see where her blood was perfect, no alcohol or drugs?"

"Why should that surprise you? Kathy never did drugs and rarely drank."

Lipscomb sat in the front seat of his new van, stroking the soft leather. "She was in perfect health. It was a real shame."

On the way home, Darlene made sure the children were sound asleep before she told her mother about the new information she had learned. "Mom, remember last month when Bill told me about all the places where Kathleen had been bruised?"

"Yes." She kept her eyes on the road.

"Well, I know you didn't want me reading that autopsy report, but I found out he was right. He knew exactly where each bruise was, and how else could he have known? That was before the report came out."

"The sheriff's department could have told him."

"Why didn't they tell *us*? Do you remember the reason he gave for not wanting her car?"

"Yes, he thought she had been put in it, but the deputies didn't think that was the case."

"Listen to this. The report said that Kathleen was found in a frog-like position. Picture that." Darlene struggled to pull up her long legs in the car seat and fold herself into what she imagined her sister must have looked like. "Where could she have been to stiffen like that? It might have been in her car. Bill just may be right!"

"He was wrong, Darlene." Her hands tightened on the steering wheel. "You saw all the fingerprint dust on her car. The deputies would have detected something if that were the case."

"I've got to see for myself. As soon as we get home, I'm going to thoroughly check out her car."

They arrived home an hour later. Determined, Darlene walked over to Kathleen's car and opened the trunk. Some loose pieces of cardboard covered the short pile of the gray carpeting. She carefully lifted them out, but underneath, she found that the carpet was clean. Her hands touched every square inch of the rough fiber, but nothing indicated Kathleen had been there. Replacing the cardboard, she felt along the sides of the trunk and down deep into the crevices. All she found was lint. She shut the trunk and moved to the front of the car. She opened the driver's door and searched the floor, taking out the mats and looking under the seats, until a flicker of something shiny caught her eye. Her heart raced. She had to put her head almost on the floor to fish out a set of keys. The sheriff's report had specifically said no keys had been found. She clutched them in her hand and slowly stood up, realizing that someone had probably hidden them there. What else had the investigators missed?

On the last day of their visit, the children begged Nadine and Darlene to take them to Astroworld, a huge amusement park across the freeway from the Astrodome. Only Darlene felt brave enough to ride Billie's favorite—the Looping Starship. Afterwards, neither could walk a straight line, and they held onto each other as they exited.

When they stepped onto the sidewalk, Billie pointed to the surrounding dirt and gravel, and said, "Aunt Darlene, was that where my mama was?'' His voice sounded frightened, but his expression remained wide-eyed.

''What?'' Darlene asked, startled.

''Right there on the gravel,'' he said still pointing. ''She was beat up, too.''

''No, Billie. She wasn't beaten,'' Darlene said as she tried to cushion the story. She bent to her knees and attempted to console him.

''Yes, she was. My daddy said so. But I miss my mama. I miss her so much.'' Billie started to cry.

Darlene looked around for a bench and motioned to Nadine to take Mary Ann and Kim away so she could be alone with Billie.

They sat down and Darlene wiped his tears. ''I miss her too, Billie, and I loved her so much. But you know what?''

''What?'' he said, sniffling.

''She wouldn't want to see you crying like this. She's looking down at you right now saying, 'Puppa, don't be sad. I will always be with you.' You liked her to call you Puppa, didn't you?''

''Yeah, but I don't know why she did,'' he managed a small, tentative smile.

''You were so anxious to be born you arrived a month early and were real tiny. Do you remember seeing those pictures of you in the hospital?''

''Uh huh,'' he nodded his head.

''When your mama brought you home, she said you were as small as a puppy. But she didn't want to call you 'Puppy.' She didn't think that sounded right. So, she called you 'Puppa.' Only those who love you know why we call you that . . . it can be our secret, okay?''

''Yeah. I can have a secret with my mama, right Aunt Darlene?''

''Yes, Billie, and always remember how much your mama loved you. She's in heaven now. She looks down on you, and knows when you're happy. You can talk to her if that will make you feel better.''

''My daddy said mama's a star. Is that right?''

''I bet your daddy's right.'' Darlene smiled, pleased with Bill's description. ''Let's see if we can find your mama's star.''

Billie stared up at the night sky. From all the glittering stars, he selected the brightest one. ''There she is, over there!'' he said, pointing into darkness.

He was quiet for a moment. Then he looked up at Darlene and hesitantly confided, ''I have a secret with my daddy, too. But he says I can't ever tell anyone.''

Chapter Eight

Darlene was surprised at Billie's comment. "Billie, I'm Aunt Darlene. You can tell me what the secret is if it has anything to do with your mother. She would want you to tell me."

Tears began to form again and Billie looked down at his hands. He shook his head. "Daddy would get real mad. He told me so."

"Maybe it's something we could use to help find who killed her. Don't you think your daddy would want us to find the person who hurt her?"

Billie buried his face in Darlene's arm. "Don't make me. Please don't make me tell. Daddy would give me a real hard spanking."

Darlene put her arms around him, rocking him gently as he cried. The child had been through so much. She couldn't bring herself to continue with questions that added to his misery.

The sheriff's office had already indicated its lack of interest in Kathleen's murder. Sergeant Baker had never called Darlene

Sanford regarding how Bill Lipscomb knew about the condition of Kathleen's body. The family had turned over all the evidence they had, including the date book that Nadine had found in Kathleen's apartment. They had also bombarded the sheriff's department with the many names of Kathleen's and Bill's friends. But the family had not received any information from the Sheriff about the investigation of these people.

Now Nadine's many calls to Baker remained unreturned, prompting her to put her unanswered questions, meshed with bitterness and resentment, into a letter.

Three days later, on October 7, 1986, she received his reply apologizing for the unanswered phone calls and admitting that all the information the family had given them proved to be true. But he stated that there had been nothing to substantiate any allegations made against Lipscomb and Dr. Pearle because both men had been cleared through lab analysis, although they would remain suspects until the case was solved. The lab had also found that the red hair samples had been dyed and had no roots which precluded them from accurately determining the sex. Baker assured Nadine that the hair samples removed from the male nurse's apartment were not Kathleen's, nor was his hair found to be on Kathleen's clothes at the crime scene. However, they were still looking for the male nurse. Baker ended by assuring Nadine that her correspondence would be kept confidential because they didn't want to interfere with the visitation rights of her grandchildren.

Nadine's letter to Sergeant Baker stressed that the family suspected someone in the sheriff's office of giving Bill information and she tried to impress upon the sergeant the importance of his keeping her information secret. A few days later, Lipscomb called Nadine to ask what she expected to gain from the letter she had just written the sheriff. She desperately wanted to ask how he knew, but he would only laugh, enjoying the mind game.

* * *

Lipscomb's job performance report on November 14, 1986, demonstrated that he was progressing at an even faster clip than before Kathleen's murder. Having sailed through his WAPS test by missing only two questions, his promotion to master sergeant would soon be a reality.

On Lipscomb's November evaluation, M. Sgt. Raymond A. Martin, the school's commandant exclaimed: "T.Sgt. Lipscomb is the total professional . . . and his selection to Master Sergeant is well deserved. Greater responsibility is warranted—impressive results will follow. Promote ahead of contemporaries." Even though he had just received a promotion, his supervisors called for more, as did Maj. Gen. Chris O. Divich, the Commander of the Military Training Headquarters: "Lipscomb demonstrated the traits of a senior NCO long before his recent selection to master sergeant. Assign him to tough jobs and promote . . . he's good!"

J.O. Williams frequently called Darlene for reports on the investigation, and he always sounded disgusted over such scant progress. One day he mentioned that he and his wife, Pat, had a week's vacation coming and were contemplating going to Galveston. He asked if that was where the male nurse came from.

Darlene realized J.O. was going on purpose. She told him he was right and reminded him the nurse's name was Vince Robideaux.

J.O., famous for his long-standing friendships with police around the state, had apparently decided that the unanswered question about the nurse was important enough to cash in on some of those contacts.

Two days later, J.O. phoned Darlene to say he'd found him.

She had to smile. How could J.O. make it seem so easy? ''What was he like?''

''He's kind of a thin guy with a mustache. Not too many Robideaux in town, and someone at the station here remembered a Robideaux whose son was a nurse. You know how that would stand out in a small Texas town. I went over and talked to the family. They had no trouble remembering when he suddenly showed up here last June and told them he had decided to move back home. The family also remembered Robideaux being shocked and saddened when he heard about Kathleen. The murder was in the papers here. Robideaux got a job right away in the emergency room of a Galveston hospital.''

''Why did he move so abruptly to Galveston?''

''I asked him that. He said he just felt like it. But his sister teased him about having a tiff with a boyfriend, and that made him decide to get out of San Antonio.''

''After talking with him, do you think he could have done it?'' Darlene asked.

With all of J.O.'s experience, he didn't hesitate. ''Not a chance.''

It wasn't until December 10, 1986 that the family found out Bill Lipscomb secretly had applied for a Humanitarian Transfer to Virginia, convincing Air Force Personnel that the loss of his wife made it imperative that he live near his family, where he could find emotional support and his children would benefit from their grandparents' care.

Once Lipscomb had transported the children from Texas, he called Nadine.

''I want you to know we've been relocated to Langley Air Force Base in Virginia,'' he said tersely.

At first Nadine thought it was a joke. ''That's impossible. Why didn't I hear about this earlier?'' Then Nadine remembered that at Thanksgiving Bill had told her he found single parenting exhausting and needed a break. The children had visited her without their father, and they had told her that it would be a long time before they saw her again. Obviously they had known about the move—one more secret they were forced to keep. Nadine thought about the secret Billie had with his father. Could this have been it?

"Hey, they only gave me two days to get up here."

"Bill, don't tell me that. My husband was in the Air Force for twenty years, and they never gave him only two days to transfer to another base. You *knew.*" Her voice held a bitter edge of skepticism. "Besides, you were doing so well as an instructor. What's your job there?"

"Actually, I got burned out on teaching. Now I'm the Vehicle Operations Supervisor. You know how mechanical I am. I've always been able to do virtually anything with a car or truck."

Lipscomb's words triggered a long-forgotten event. Kathleen had wanted to go shopping and he had told her she couldn't. After he had left the house, she had decided to go anyway, and had gone out to start her car. As soon as the engine had rolled over, all of the water had gushed from the radiator, making it impossible for her to leave. Kathleen had summoned a repairman, who showed Kathleen where someone had punched a hole from inside the radiator.

"Nadine, this is really what I want."

Nadine realized Lipscomb always got what he wanted. He had talked her out of all of Kathleen's furniture and belongings because he had leased a spacious home after the murder, "so the children would have a nice place to live." She especially hated giving him all of Kathleen's possessions because she remembered how bitterly he had fought Kathleen over everything, even to the point of arguing who would keep an old cedar chest. Now all those things were in Virginia.

"I only wish you would have told us," Nadine said. "You *had* to know."

"You're lucky I didn't just move without telling you at all."

There was the click of disconnection, and Nadine was left to consider how much more difficult it would be for the sheriff to investigate Lipscomb now that he had moved to Virginia.

The first Christmas without Kathleen was the saddest her family could remember. Having Kathleen's children could have helped fill the tragic void, but Lipscomb denied them that comfort.

After an uncountable number of phone calls to Virginia, Nadine finally convinced Lipscomb to send Mary Ann and Billie to Houston for two weeks during the summer. He put the youngsters on a plane, and they arrived on Monday, June 8, 1987, one year to the day that Kathleen had been murdered.

Mary Ann looked noticeably taller, and Billie had more freckles. They were happy children, and anxious to tell their Houston family every detail of their new life.

"My daddy's gonna buy me a horse," Mary Ann enthused.

"Where will you keep it?" Nadine asked.

"He bought us a big house on Chesapeake Bay, even bigger than the one in San Antonio. It's on two and a half acres." She bubbled with excitement. "Daddy's gonna build a stable and everything!"

"I'm happy for you, honey," Nadine sighed, and listened to the two discuss their future with childish jubilation. Nadine hoped their resiliency would last through the painful, motherless years ahead.

The next Sunday, Nadine took the children to Our Comforter Lutheran Church, where Kathleen's funeral had been. They sat listening to Darlene sing in the choir.

"Aunt Darlene's nice, isn't she Grandma?"

"Yes, she is, dear. Now remember, we don't talk in church."

Mary Ann was quiet for a few minutes, then she put her lips to Nadine's ear and whispered, "Grandma, my daddy lies."

"Lies?"

"Yeah, he lied about where he was the night my mama was killed."

Nadine forgot about not talking in church.

"Where was he?"

"I don't know, but he wasn't with us."

"Where were you?"

"In his bed, asleep."

"If you were asleep, how did you know he wasn't with you?"

Mary Ann leaned closer to her grandmother. "Because, silly, we woke up."

Billie, looking pale, glanced at Mary Ann. "We're not supposed to tell," he said to his sister in a shaken voice.

"It's okay," Mary Ann replied. "It's only Grandma."

Her answer mollified Billie. He thought for a moment, then cautiously entered the conversation. "Yeah, that night, Grandma, we woke up to go to the bathroom, and Daddy wasn't there."

Nadine became aware that people around her were clearing their throats and shuffling in their seats.

"Save this for after church," she told them. "Aunt Darlene will want to hear."

Darlene met her family in the narthex. "What was all that talking going on?"

"We may have solved the puzzle," Nadine said.

"The puzzle?"

"*The* puzzle." Her mother looked like she would explode. "Let's hurry up and get to the car."

Once inside, Darlene asked Mary Ann, "So what's all this about?"

"My daddy lies," she said, seeming to enjoy the excitement her statement generated, then filled Darlene in on the information she had shared with Nadine in church.

"Okay, you woke up and your daddy wasn't there. You didn't know where he had gone?" Nadine asked.

"He wasn't in the apartment. We looked all over for him."

Nadine knew a one-bedroom apartment wouldn't require an extensive search.

"His truck wasn't there either," Billie added.

"What time did you wake up?" Darlene asked.

"At one o'clock. It was dark outside," Mary Ann replied.

Darlene pointed to the digital clock on the dashboard and asked, "What time does that say?"

"Twelve-seventeen," she answered proudly.

"Good, Mary Ann, you *can* tell time. And you said his truck wasn't there?"

"Nope. It was gone," Billie said. "It had been parked in front of the apartment. But that was before we went to sleep."

"How do you know?"

Mary Ann explained. "Billie woke up first to go to the bathroom and then woke me up. Daddy wasn't in bed. So we both called, 'Daddy, Daddy,' and he didn't answer. So we looked all through the apartment. Then we thought we'd go down to the pool, because he might be there. We got out on the porch. That's when we saw that his truck was gone. We knew if his truck was gone, then he wasn't at the pool, because he could have walked there."

"So what did you do then?" Nadine asked.

"We went back inside and got up on the couch. We waited, but we fell asleep. We couldn't stay awake that long."

"Where were you when you woke up?" Darlene asked.

"In bed with Daddy. It was light outside."

"Where was the truck?"

"In the same place as when we first went to bed."

"Did you say anything about knowing he had left or ask him where he went?"

"We started to ask, but he put his finger to his lips and said, 'It's a secret.'" Guilt flashed across Billie's face.

"Mary Ann, would you tell this story to J.O. when we get home?"

"Sure," she said.

Nadine quickly drove home and Darlene ran to phone J.O. She relayed what Mary Ann had told her.

"I'll be right there," J.O. said enthusiastically. "Bexar County needs to hear this."

Mary Ann felt comfortable with J.O. She thought of him as an uncle since he and his wife had been around her since her birth.

Mary Ann repeated the story for J.O., but this time she appeared worried. "Is my daddy in trouble?" Her face turned ashen. "Aunt Darlene, are you going to tell my daddy?"

"No, I won't, honey. I promise."

"Daddy would be real mad. He'd spank me. He wouldn't want us telling anybody."

J.O. bent down until he was eye to eye with Mary Ann. He looked into her innocent blue eyes and would have loved to tell her the truth. "I have a friend who would like to hear your story. Would you tell her?" J.O.'s 16 years experience with the Houston Police Department's Juvenile Division had given him a special talent for communicating with young people. Often, he had talked juveniles out of running away from home, or convinced them to enter drug rehabilitation programs.

Timidly, Mary Ann asked, "Will your friend tell my daddy?"

"Absolutely not," he said placing his arm around Mary Ann's narrow shoulders. "You won't have to tell anyone else, and after you tell her we won't talk about it again. Okay?"

"It will be our secret, J.O.?" She looked up into his face for assurance.

J.O. felt deceptive as he looked into her trusting face. "Cross my heart," he said drawing an X over his chest.

Monday morning, J.O. took Mary Ann to the Juvenile Division to be interviewed and videotaped. He had called the Bexar County Sheriff's Department earlier and was pleased with their enthusiasm.

"This could be the break we've been looking for," Sergeant Baker had told him. "Tape her and send it to me right away. We'll see if we can't finally get him."

Sergeant Delores Cassidy, a specialist in interviewing juveniles, smiled as she walked into the waiting room and saw Mary Ann sitting next to J.O. "You must be the pretty little blonde he's always talking about."

"I guess so," Mary Ann said shyly.

"Would you like me to show you some things we have here that no one else has?"

"Yeah." Mary Ann eagerly jumped off her chair to follow Sergeant Cassidy.

Cassidy gave Mary Ann a tour and showed her a bulletin board displaying pictures of children she had located. "See, we help people here. That's my job. Do you like helping people?"

"Yes, except when it comes to drying dishes."

"I don't like doing dishes either. I can see we're going to get along just fine. Would you like to help me? Will you tell me what you told J.O.? We can stop whenever you like."

Mary Ann looked into Cassidy's eyes and asked, "You won't tell anyone else?"

"No," she said honestly. "But if it's all right with you, I'd like to take your picture while you're talking. Have you ever been on television before?"

"No, but I've always wanted to be."

Cassidy smiled at Mary Ann's eagerness. "Great. Now you can do two things at once. Are you ready?"

"I guess so," Mary Ann said and followed the sergeant into the video room.

The video lasted just over an hour, and once again, Mary Ann told the same story without a single hesitation or change. Cassidy took several minutes to write a formal report to accompany the interview, then took Mary Ann back to the waiting room and handed J.O. the report and the tape. He clutched the tape eagerly and thanked the sergeant. Then he and Mary Ann went to the post office to send overnight both the tape and the report to the Bexar County Sheriff's Department.

"The D.A. says it won't work," Sergeant Baker told Darlene the next day. "He said it was good, but not good enough for us to issue a warrant."

"Why not?" Darlene asked, stunned.

"He said she was coaxed."

"Coaxed? What do you mean, coaxed?"

"Just what I said. He thinks your mother probably told the little girl what to say. I'm not saying I buy that, but he's the one who has to approve these things."

"That's bullshit!" Darlene roared, unable to remember when she had been so angry.

"Yeah. I know."

"It's not fair! We did *not* coax her! Not one bit. Bill killed my sister and y'all are going to let him get away with it. What else do you want? A photo with his hands around her neck? He got the kids. He got all that insurance money. Those things alone should have raised a red flag. Especially when we told you that he bought the last policy seven months before she died. Now his daughter, his own flesh and blood, is telling you that he lied about where he was that night, and you won't listen."

"It's out of my control, Darlene. I can see that you're upset, and I understand why. I personally wanted to use that little girl's statement. But without the D.A.'s say-so, there's nothing I can do.''

Darlene tried to calm herself. She thought if she heard, ''There's nothing I can do,'' one more time from him, she'd scream. ''Tell me one thing, then I'll leave you alone.''

''Shoot.''

''Do you honestly believe this case will ever be solved? I want your honest answer. I deserve that much.''

Baker hesitated for a few moments, then said, ''No, I really don't think it will. I hate to tell you that, but something needs to happen first thing out of the box if we're going to get anywhere with it. When the evidence gets cold, and the memories aren't clear, it's just not probable that the case will be solved. But the statute of limitations for murder never runs out. It could be solved ten or twenty years from now if the right piece of evidence comes up.''

''After what we just gave you, I can't imagine what kind of evidence you're talking about. But I have a gut feeling that Bill killed my sister, and so help me, I'm going to prove it.''

At the end of the children's two-week visit, Nadine put them on a plane for Virginia, and not long afterward she learned that her relationship with them would soon change. Within a month Lipscomb tightened the screws to force her to kneel to yet another of his demands.

Lipscomb had used the insurance money to buy a large boat and a luxurious two-story Southern colonial home graced by four white pillars in front. It backed up to a lushly wooded creek. He added a wrap-around deck in back that cantilevered over a sparkling swimming pool. The home was stuffed with expensive furniture.

His pride in his new home and surroundings compelled him to send photos to Nadine. It was an unwise gesture, since it gave her proof of his high living, and she knew exactly what money supported that life-style. Obviously, his customized van had been only an overture to his many purchases.

With all he had, Lipscomb still was not satisfied. He wanted Kathleen's wedding ring—a two-carat pavé diamond band with a large diamond set in the center. Kathy had given the ring to Nadine a few weeks before her divorce. Kathleen had cherished her two diamond rings, but unbeknownst to her, Lipscomb had smuggled her dinner ring out of their house and sold it. The ring had first belonged to Bill's grandmother who had given it to Kathleen because the two women had a very special relationship. The ring was fashioned of gold nuggets with several diamonds sprinkled among the gold mounds. Fearing the same fate would befall her wedding ring, Kathy had given it to her mother.

"Please take it," she had told Nadine. "I don't want it on my finger to remind me of Bill. And if he had it, he'd only sell it." Nadine had placed the ring in a bank vault to save for Mary Ann, hoping the little girl might cherish it in the future. Nadine couldn't bear to release another item that had belonged to Kathleen.

Now Lipscomb was holding his children as ransom for the ring. "I'd sure like to let you talk to the kids," he told Nadine during one of her many calls, "but until you send me that ring, I just don't see how that's going to happen."

In October 1987, Nadine managed to speak with her granddaughter. When she called, Mary Ann answered without her father's knowledge. Nadine discovered why Lipscomb hadn't wanted the children to have any communication with her. During the relatively brief conversation, Mary Ann said, "And you know what else, Grandma? I have a new mommy."

"You what?" Nadine gasped, thinking surely she hadn't heard correctly.

"Yes, Daddy got married last week."

"Oh no," she said, feeling a knot tighten in her stomach. "We didn't know he was dating anyone."

"Uh huh, her name's Francine. She's got a boy and a girl. Joel is five and Peggy is seven. But sometimes her kids are kinda mean to us."

Nadine had trouble accepting what Mary Ann told her. Lipscomb had never given her the slightest indication of his intentions. Then she recalled his pestering her about the wedding ring, and thought she understood.

"Has he known her long?" Nadine asked.

"They met last Valentine's Day in a video store."

"Is she from Virginia?"

"I don't know," said Mary Ann. "But her mom and dad are, 'cause they come by to visit us often."

Nadine heard a click and realized that someone had picked up another line. She heard a man's muffled voice.

"I gotta go, Grandma," Mary Ann said anxiously.

She heard another click and her granddaughter was gone. Nadine sat down on her den sofa feeling dizzy and confused. How easy it had been for Lipscomb to replace Kathleen. That thought bothered her most of all. Later, she would come to learn the problems encountered with a stepmother raising her grandchildren.

A new marriage didn't slow Lipscomb's enormously successful career. His November 1987 reviews lauded his single-handed success in dispatching the transportation at the Tactical Air Command Headquarters. He broke records for time response for needed transportation, trimming the Air Force goal of 10 minutes to 6, and maintaining a vehicle readiness to an optimum never seen before. Senior M. Sgt. David Moses called him "one of the most outstanding noncommissioned officers in the United States Air Force." He applauded Lipscomb's "can-do attitude and will-do determination." Col. James Moen and Col. Richard Myers, as well as Gen. Henry Canterbury acclaimed his leadership ability and urged that he be promoted again.

As the new year, 1988, rolled in, Lipscomb continued to be masterful at his standoff, and the Bexar County Sheriff's Department had all but forgotten that a murder took place on June 8, 1986.

Nadine and Darlene had worked patiently with the sheriff the first year, but now they felt abandoned. This cast them in the role of keepers of the flame and made them feel personally responsible for solving Kathleen's murder. It overshadowed everything else in their lives. Darlene slept with a notepad on her nightstand. While she dozed, her subconscious brought forth memories of her conversations with Bill and Kathleen. During the night, Darlene would sit up and write down the words. It was the beginning of what became known as "Darlene's Diary."

Darlene had started working for the Houston law firm, Chamberlain, Hrdlicka, White, Johnson & Williams, as a legal secretary a month after her sister died. Between Darlene being surrounded by lawyers and Nadine managing the Secret Service Office, the two were recipients of abundant and sound advice, but still the murder remained unsolved as it approached its second anniversary.

Then one wet, wind-tossed March morning in 1988, something happened to change the situation.

Hurrying through the rain, Darlene rushed to her desk, completely oblivious to anyone around her.

"Well, good morning, sunshine," said a smiling Charlie Trotter, an attorney in her firm. He stood within 10 feet of her, talking with another attorney.

Darlene smiled self-consciously. "Hi, y'all. Sorry, my mind's somewhere else. I was on the phone with my mom this morning discussing what Sergeant Baker told me a while back."

"And what were the words of the tireless investigator?"

"Would you believe that Dalton Baker told me Kathleen's murder would never be solved? Can you imagine? A murderer, and you know who I'm talking about, is going to stay free—and rich with my sister's insurance money!"

"Darlene, that's only his viewpoint," he said. *"They* can't solve it. There's no reason for you to settle for that. Why don't you hire a private detective?"

Darlene gave him a skeptical look. "That's got to be expensive."

Trotter walked closer to her desk and looked directly into her eyes. "Depends on how important this is to you."

"You know it's the most important thing in the whole world to my mom and me." She paused. "Do you know of anyone?"

"I think so, and he's pretty good. Oh, what's his name?" he tried to recall. "He's a short little guy. A real wiry, energetic person. Probably doesn't sleep more than two hours a night." Then he finally came up with the name—Mike Guidry. "He has offices in Houston. You can probably find him in the phone book. At least talk to him. Get an idea of what he thinks of the case."

"I just might do that." Darlene wrote down Guidry's name. "I'll call my mom tonight and see what she thinks."

After work, Darlene picked up her two daughters from a neighbor who cared for them during the day. She was peeling potatoes for dinner when Gary came home. "Charlie Trotter gave me a great idea today," she said. "You know how the sheriff isn't doing anything about Kathleen's murder? He suggested in order to get off ground zero, I, or we, I mean, Mom and I . . ."

"What is it, Darlene?"

"He thinks we should hire a private detective to find her

killer." She tried to say her words quickly, hoping they'd be more palatable.

"I don't believe what I'm hearing."

"Gary, it's the only thing left to do."

"So, who says you have to do anything? I don't know how you can still believe that Bill killed the mother of his own children. It's just beyond me. I think you and Nadine feed on each other. And the cost, Darlene. Have you thought about that?"

"Yes. I'm going to suggest it to Mom tonight. She'll probably pay the major part, and my brothers could help."

"Your brothers?" Gary laughed. "Chuck hates Bill, but I don't think even *he* believes Bill would kill her. Think about the cost, Darlene. The kids are getting more expensive every year. There's only so much both of our paychecks will cover."

"Gary, it's all I think about. I loved my sister so much and knowing that her murderer is walking around just tears me up."

They were both silent for several minutes, then Gary said, "If this will bring closure to the worst thing that ever happened in your life, who am I to stop a duo as dynamic as you and your mother?"

That evening, Darlene approached her mother about hiring an investigator. Cautiously, she related her conversation with Trotter.

"I don't know, Darlene, my income is stretched pretty thin as it is."

"Gary and I will help," Darlene offered. "And I bet Chuck and David will kick in, too."

"I definitely like the idea of hiring a detective," Nadine said. "However, their bills can go on and on. Who knows what it would end up costing?"

"I'll call this Mike Guidry tomorrow and give him some

details of the case. Then we can see what he thinks it would run.''

When Darlene called the next day, she wasn't allowed to talk with Mike, but was passed to one of his detectives, Tom Bevans.

Bevans called back soon after conferring with his boss. ''Mike feels the investigation would run around $5,000, definitely not more than $7,500.''

Afterward, Darlene called her mother at work. ''What do you think?''

''I suppose we could live with that,'' she said after several moments of hesitation. ''I think we have to. There'll be no peace in this family until the question is answered once and for all—did Bill kill Kathleen?''

Chapter Nine

"Fiction has given us a picture of a private detective—a hulk of a guy sitting in his sleazy office ... In reality, the typical detective is someone like Mike Guidry. He's 5'-foot-6'' and 122 pounds soaking wet ... His well-appointed office ... has carpet on the floor and a security lock on the door."

—Jim Barlow, *Houston Chronicle*, May 3, 1987

Summer had arrived by the time an appointment was finally set for Darlene Sanford and her mother to meet the detectives. At noon on June 27, 1988, Mike Guidry and Tom Bevans joined them for lunch at Birraporetti's Restaurant near downtown Houston, across the street from Guidry's office in the Lyric Centre.

The four sat at a table discussing Kathleen's murder. Guidry's hyper energy made Nadine feel nervous and she thought she had never met anyone so intensely driven. Conversely, Bevans' easygoing, laid-back calm relaxed her.

Nadine didn't know that security and investigations had been Guidry's life ever since he took a part-time job in campus security while attending Lamar University in Beaumont. After graduation, he had become a Texas state trooper. But his week-end private under-cover work tracking corporate espionage net-ted him many times his salary as a trooper, so he left law enforcement to form his own company.

Tom Bevans, exactly twice Guidry's weight at 244 pounds, was a big, six-foot-two teddy bear of a man. A graduate of Texas A & M, he had been a member of the Corps. of Cadets—the university's gung-ho, tradition-steeped, military brother-hood. He still kept his raven-black hair trimmed militarily short. His boyish good looks and deprecating wit would have sent Nadine looking for a match if she had had a daughter the right age for the 25-year-old detective. Bevans came by his profession naturally from his father, who would eventually accumulate over 26 years as an FBI Agent.

If Guidry and Bevans had anything in common, it was their stare. They both had dark brown eyes that could pierce through a suspect. Eyes that darted around a room, as if casing it.

Reliving Kathleen's murder to write their notes forced Nadine and Darlene back into grief. Even though the story had spilled from their lips hundreds of times, they labored to be exact in their written account for the investigators.

Over lunch, the pair disclosed every detail of the last two years. Nadine became the authority on Kathleen and the Lips-comb family, while Darlene recounted the more technical aspects of her tribulations with the sheriff's department.

"We don't know for sure who killed Kathleen," Nadine began. "One minute we think it's Bill because of what he said and did in the past, and then we don't want to believe that Bill would do this to his own children." She shook her head. "Our family's so torn with all of the uncertainty that we just have to know for sure."

The detectives nodded and sat leafing through the notes on

the case. They wanted to hear more about basic information on Bill and his past behavior.

"Kathleen had tried to divorce Bill the previous year," Nadine began. "The paperwork had almost been finished when Bill called from the airport—only minutes before he took the children on a plane headed for Virginia. He threatened to take the children away for good if she didn't drop the divorce proceedings."

"So that's why she stopped the divorce?"

"Not right then. She thought he was bluffing. Then Bill actually took off for Virginia and handed the kids over to his mother. Kathleen couldn't even talk to them on the phone. She really panicked when she found out that Bill's father was to be transferred to Cairo, Egypt, with his company."

The men shook their heads.

"Bill fully intended to let the kids go to Egypt. Naturally, Kathleen told her attorney to put the divorce on hold."

Bevans whistled. "We're dealing with a real control freak here."

Guidry had been perusing the women's notes. "Can we get a copy of the tape of your granddaughter? I'd like to see how convincing she looks when she tells about her father."

Nadine promised to ask J.O. about getting a copy.

Guidry placed his elbows on the table and waited until he had both women's undivided attention. "You're really going to have to keep us up on the information. We'll need a list of Bill's and Kathleen's friends in San Antonio. We want to know what both of them liked to do, where they went, and who they saw. We need anything specific you can give us."

After lunch, the quartet strolled across the street to Guidry's office to continue their discussion. Guidry checked in with his secretary/receptionist/bookkeeper, Carol Johnson, a sweet motherly type who had watched over him since he launched his business five years earlier. In his first year of business, Guidry had been out of the country on assignment, and his partner at the time snatched the $65,000 they had amassed, borrowed an additional $65,000 on their joint line-of-credit, and vanished. In order to save his company, Guidry had to cut grass at night wearing a miner's hat to guide him through the numerous yards he had contracted to trim.

Guidry gathered his messages, and ushered his guests to a small, round table in a corner of his office that held a tape recorder. Unless someone objected, he always taped interviews in order to catch every word, innuendo, and verbal emphasis of the conversation.

"This case is right up our alley," he said enthusiastically. "You two have really stayed on top of this. That will make our job easier. Let me give you an example of what we can do for you. Last year we had a murder where the victim's body had to be exhumed so DNA tests could be performed. We had a good idea that this guy had been poisoned with arsenic because everyone he knew told us he looked jaundiced before he died. Arsenic causes that and also stays in the hair and nails even after embalming. So after the tests, we could prove that his girlfriend had every opportunity to drop some tablets into his morning coffee. We were able to trace it back to the druggist who supplied her. The victim's son got us involved." He turned to Bevans. "Remember the case?"

Bevans nodded. Although he wasn't the showman Guidry was, the hours he spent doing the detailed investigating that netted results made his clients respect him.

"Kathleen's murder will be easy in comparison," Guidry assured them. He ignited the women's hopes, convincing them that there would be a successful conclusion to their tragedy. For the first time in two years, the women looked hopeful. What Guidry didn't tell them was how the age of the case troubled him. Locating the people involved, especially under Air Force circumstances where personnel are routinely transferred, would be a monumental task. Even if found, the witnesses' memories might be diminished and evidence could go astray.

"Here's what I propose," Guidry said, "Why don't you let us go to San Antonio and check out the sheriff's files and see what he has? We can talk with the medical examiner and find out exactly what happened. Our rate is $600 a day per person, but I'll only charge for one person since this is a fishing expedition. What do you say?"

"That sounds like the logical first step," Darlene said, looking for her mother's reaction.

"Yes," Nadine agreed wholeheartedly. "We want you to get started as soon as possible."

Guidry asked, "Would tomorrow be soon enough?"

The next morning, Bevans pulled his shiny red 280 ZX out of his driveway at 4:30 and headed for Guidry's house. He found the color-blind Guidry looking for the correctly numbered tie to go with his dark gray suit. Guidry's ties and suits were numbered by color, taking the guesswork out of color coordination, a process especially helpful when he was between wives.

As they drove, they planned their strategy, knowing they had to tread lightly when invading the sheriff's turf to commandeer a case he couldn't solve. They had already read the numerous newspaper articles about the murder and still were troubled by the fact that Kathleen had been killed over two years ago. Such a time span was an eternity in investigative work, since the first two weeks are the most propitious time to solve a murder. Actually, the first 24 hours are best.

At the sheriff's office, Sergeant Baker greeted them politely, shook hands, then listened tolerantly to their request for his files.

"Since this is an ongoing investigation," Baker told them, "I can show you the file, but I can't let you make copies of our documents. If you'd like, you can use that desk over there and hand copy what you need.''

His suggestion sounded unnecessarily laborious to the detectives, but Baker was calling the shots. They waited a half hour while Baker hunted down the file, finally returning with a folder bound with duct tape.

Taking the file, the two PIs carried it to their assigned desk and began looking through the collection of papers. A mug shot of Bill Lipscomb slid out that had been taken at the sheriff's office the night he made his statement. Bevans drawing on his degree in psychology, thought Lipscomb had a psychotic look about him, and definitely felt that he could be capable of killing his wife.

They continued searching, but it was difficult to find many documents they considered important in the file. There were notes from phone calls, a few statements and the medical examiner's report. They didn't find anything that indicated to them that the sheriff's department had vigorously pursued the case. The initial statements given the night the body was identified had not been followed up with subsequent questions.

The investigators copied medical reports and the drawings from the crime scene. They took one break to go out for Mexican food, then returned to continue taking copious notes. Finally, the detectives asked to speak to the medical examiner.

Dr. Robert C. Bux, a Bexar County medical examiner was also a board-certified forensic pathologist. It was his job to determine the cause of death of anyone in the county had who died suddenly or unexpectedly. The handsome man in his early thirties offered to answer any questions the PIs had and to show them anything they wanted to see.

The doctor instantly remembered Kathleen's autopsy, even though he had performed hundreds since then. ''I remember her case especially because she was so young and obviously took such great care of herself. I later read that she was a research nurse with a very promising career, so this was a real tragedy." He pulled out two dozen colored slides of Kathleen, taken both before and during her autopsy, and dropped them into his projector cartridge. The ant bites were vivid and angry-looking on the slides, and the red and purple slices around her neck only intensified Guidry and Bevan's determination to find the killer.

"I've seen strangulations before that didn't look this bad," Guidry said. "What do you suppose the sonofabitch did?"

"Her strangulation could have been worse than most, because she suffered petechiae, which are hemorrhages that we found in the white part of her eyes. What happened is that her jugular veins became occluded, so blood couldn't flow out of her head, but the carotid arteries still pumped blood into her head, forcing increased pressure on these delicate capillaries that burst and hemorrhaged."

"Sounds painful," Guidry observed.

"Probably was. She would have sensed that her head was swelling. The carotid bone in her neck didn't break because—well, look here," he said, pointing at the two lines circling her neck. "The perpetrator placed the cord above the bone, so it didn't happen to break. Had he strangled her with his hands instead of a cord, that bone would have been crushed with the force he applied."

"What do you suppose caused those?" Bevans asked, pointing to darkened bruises on Kathleen's jaw and chest.

"It would take a pretty good blow from something blunt to get bruises like that. Also could have happened from being hurled against something. She was such a little thing. She wouldn't have had a chance against someone with a lot of strength. Look at these bruises on each side of her neck. Could have been the killer's knuckles against her throat as he held the cord, or it might have been Kathleen's hands, trying to stop him.

"She smelled so clean when she arrived at the morgue. But I doubt anyone had bathed her. She would have been hard to move and wash. Actually, her feet and hands were not dirty, and that led us to believe that they'd been bagged so they would stay clean. I think it took two people to put her on the ground in such an immaculate condition—no gravel, no dirt, no road hash.''

He moved to pictures of the orange T-shirt and blue jeans. ''They were rolled so neatly that the detectives here thought the murderer had to be someone involved with a precision-oriented occupation, such as the military or medicine.''

Dr. Bux picked up his copy of the autopsy. ''Here's something important,'' he said. ''Her stomach was full of Chinese food. She had just eaten, because it takes around two hours for food to digest, longer if the person gets excited. That told us she was probably killed around dinnertime—maybe six or seven.''

Dr. Bux went over Kathleen's autopsy in great detail as the investigators took notes to explain their findings to the family. He completed his slide presentation and returned the slides to the file. ''Yes, I certainly remember this case,'' he said again. ''It really was a shame.''

In the car driving back to Houston, they discussed the case.

''After looking through that file, I didn't see one person that Lipscomb knew who had been brought in for questioning,'' Bevan said.

''No shit, Sherlock,'' Guidry said, using his trademark response.

Tom said, ''The only statements in the file were from Vivian Gonzales and Sarah Bowers, who had volunteered them, and the one from Bill Lipscomb. Even though Dr. Pearle had accepted the sheriff's invitation to his office, there was not a word about the doctor. The scope of the investigation was pretty damn narrow. There sure are a lot of gaps.''

Mike started taking notes. ''We've got to talk to friends and co-workers of both Bill and Kathleen. I'd sure like to talk with that damn Dr. Pearle. He was supposed to be in love with her, but he did nothing to cooperate in finding her murderer.''

''I'd like to chat with Sergeant Baker at length to find out what the hell they actually did on the case,'' Bevans said. ''But I've got to come up with a better way of saying, 'Your case is full of shit. What about the interviews with possibly over sixty people you should have been doing if you had any hopes of solving this crime?' ''

''Tom, you're going to have to head this one because I'll be in and out of the country a lot. I've got to be in Korea the day after tomorrow.''

''Fine I'm used to it. Now, about the body—that's the damnedest position Kathleen was found in. After death, when rigor mortis sets in and the body hardens, there's no reflexive drawing up of the extremities. Those legs *couldn't* have automatically reverted to that frog-like position.''

Guidry nodded. ''She definitely was somewhere that formed her like that. How about this—we could get a picture from the crime scene and measure the distance across her knees to see what size the area had to be?''

''Knowing she was five-foot-two measuring a crime scene photo to scale wouldn't be hard,'' Bevans agreed.

''Then we could measure her bathtub, the trunk of her car, and Lipscomb's pickup if we can find it, to see if any of them were the right size to hold her in that pose until rigor set in.''

As they neared Houston, Guidry reached for the car phone. ''I've got to call Darlene and let her know how much we found.''

''What we found was that the sheriff's department did very little on this case.''

''That's the good news,'' Guidry assured him. ''There are a lot of people we can talk to that they didn't contact.''

Guidry sat up in the bucket seat when he heard Darlene's voice. ''Darlene, we had a fantastic trip! You're not going to believe everything we dug up. We've found so many damn holes in this case. We need to meet with you tomorrow in Houston to tell you all about it. I guarantee you, Darlene, we're going to nail that guy.''

Guidry met with the women and wasted no time supplying them with information on Kathleen's autopsy. The bruises they described were not as violent as Bill Lipscomb had indicated.

"I don't understand," Darlene said, looking puzzled. "Bill showed me the autopsy and the bruises looked much more severe than these."

"Weird," Bevans said. "Why would somebody change the autopsy to make it look worse than it was?"

"I have no idea," Nadine remarked. "Getting reasons out of Bill isn't easy."

"You'll be glad to know Kathleen had no defensive wounds." Guidry offered. "That tells us it happened so fast she didn't have time to react.

"Kathleen had been slapped in the face. Dr. Bux knew that because blood had pocketed in her mouth. The blood also revealed that some time after she had died, someone picked her up, and that caused her head to fall backward and the blood to form a 'Y' as it slid to the back of her throat."

Glancing at the women, Guidry said, "Do you want me to continue? I don't have to be this graphic if it bothers you."

"We're fine," Nadine said. "Please go on."

Guidry resumed, "The vaginal swab shows that she had intercourse some time on Saturday. There was no sperm found in the anal swab, but blood and contusions inside and around the anus indicated she had been penetrated."

Nadine closed her eyes.

Guidry moved on to the safer subject of clothing. "There were human and cat hairs on her clothes."

"Kathleen had a cat," Darlene offered.

"They found no sperm on the clothes or bed linens in Kathleen's apartment.

"When the evidence technician examined Kathleen's car, he found only her fingerprints."

"That's strange," Darlene said. "So there's no indication that someone else drove it? When I checked her car, I found her keys hidden underneath the front seat. Why would Kathy hide her own keys? She always locked her car when she got out and put her keys in her purse."

"There's lots of holes we have to plug," Guidry said, "but that's just a matter of time." Then he finished relating all that Dr. Bux had shared with them.

"The next step will be to form a plan of action. The only way we know how to solve a crime is hard, detail-oriented work—interviewing dozens of people, checking out numerous leads, and thinking up every possible scenario," he concluded.

The detectives returned to their office to jump-start a very closed investigation. They had to play catch-up with Kathleen's life up to the time of her murder. Referring to his notes, Bevans listed names of people he planned to interview, but he was forced to put the case on hold for a month.

Over a year earlier, Guidry had contracted to handle security for NBC during the Olympics in Seoul, South Korea. The next day, Guidry left for Asia and Bevans had to spend all his time running their office.

It wasn't until the second week of August, when he returned from Korea, that they were able to take up the case. As would be the detectives' custom, they invited Darlene to lunch to discuss their plans. On August 8, 1988, the men started explaining their approach.

Bevans said, "What really bothers us is that we have no time schedule for Lipscomb the night of the murder—just no idea of his whereabouts other than what he said. Lipscomb told both Sergeant Baker and Nadine that he was with his children and they went swimming in the apartment pool. But there's nobody to back his story. He told Baker that people walked by his apartment to do their laundry and saw him there, but two years later, finding anyone would be a miracle.

"Also, I watched the tape the Houston Police made of Mary Ann. I think there's more there. I'd love to question her, and since you said the kids are visiting now, I guess I could, but I'm afraid she'd tell Lipscomb about us investigating the case. What do you think?"

"Mary Ann's a sweetheart," Darlene told him. "She's easy to talk with, but it's like you say, she might feel she has to protect her father and tell him."

"Come by tomorrow morning and I'll have a list of questions for you to ask her. We'll give you a voice-activated tape recorder you can slip into your purse to record your conversation. Would you do that?"

"Of course," Darlene said, feeling torn. "I hate putting Mary Ann in that position again, but you know I'll do anything to help."

Darlene collected the list of Tom's 18 questions, and not wanting a gaggle of cousins to overhear the interview, asked Mary Ann to accompany her to Baytown, 18 miles south of Houston. Mary Ann, almost 10 now, smiled with delight to be the only one invited by her aunt and gladly accepted. Darlene drove to the Casa Ole' Restaurant. She began asking the questions before the waiter took their order.

"Mary Ann, I miss your mother so much. I need to ask you something about that day, okay?"

Mary Ann frowned. "Okay."

"You won't get in trouble, will you? I won't tell anyone about our conversation, and I don't want you to either."

"I won't tell," Mary Ann said softly.

"You said that you and your daddy drove through the parking lot at your mother's apartment on Sunday. Why did y'all do that? Did your daddy say?"

"I know why. Because we had to go home at 6:45."

"Did you get out and knock on your mother's door?"

"No."

"Why not?"

"We didn't knock because her car wasn't in the parking lot."

"Did your daddy get out, or let you or Billie out of the car?"

"I got out and put my note on the door that said 'I love you'." Each of Mary Ann's answers was softer than the one before. She whispered when she discussed her father.

"Did you go back to her apartment later?"

"Uh huh. Once about 6:45 and once after."

"Two times? What happened when you went back?"

"My daddy got out and pinned his note, giving the time we were there, next to mine on her door."

"Did your daddy write the note in his truck?"

Mary Ann shook her head.

"Did he already have the note with him?"

She shrugged and started to cry. "I don't know where he wrote the note. I can't remember all this."

"I'm sorry, baby, I don't mean to make you sad." *Oh, honey, stay with me on this,* Darlene thought as she watched tears form in Mary Ann's eyes. *If you only knew how badly we want to find out who put your mother through all of this.* "I just think if we talk about this long enough, we'll figure out who did this, because everybody liked your mother so much."

"Everybody likes me, too. They always say, 'Oh, you look just like your mother.'"

"You do look just like your mother," Darlene said, realizing how true those words were. "And that's good, because Kathleen was so pretty. And you're pretty too." Darlene smiled again at her niece. It was as if she were looking at a miniature Kathleen.

"Did you see anybody in the parking lot that night?"

"Nobody was there."

"None of your daddy's buddies were there, like Ricky or Tony?"

"Only Daddy."

"Did your daddy call your mother on Sunday?"

"Yeah, on Sunday morning. She got real mad at him, too."

"Your mother did? Why?"

"I think her face was turning red, she was so mad. I don't know why she was so mad, but she hung up on him."

"Your mother did?"

"Uh huh."

Darlene realized her probing was opening up more unanswered questions. "Did you have your suitcases with you when you drove to her apartment?"

"Uh huh. We packed everything in our suitcases to go home, but we left them in his truck."

"Why didn't you take them to the door?"

"Because we didn't see her car in the parking lot that time either." She looked more apprehensive as the questions continued.

"Oh, okay. Then what did you do?"

"We went back to Daddy's."

"Did you eat dinner there?"

"I remember what we ate."

"Okay, you went home, you made dinner, then you went to bed, right?"

"And then I got up to go to the bathroom. That's the time I told you about. When it was one o'clock. It was dark out and Daddy wasn't there. And his truck was gone." She reached over and dipped her tortilla chip in salsa and began nibbling on it.

"He didn't tell you where he went?"

Mary Ann shook her head. "I don't like talking about this."

"Well, I don't like talking about this either, Mary Ann. I keep thinking that if you remember driving through the parking lot, maybe you saw something or somebody."

"Nobody! Nobody was even in her apartment. I mean we even looked in the window and nobody was there either."

"Okay, when you got up Monday morning, did he dress you for school, for day care, where did he take you?"

"To Sergeant Martin's."

"On Monday morning? Even before you knew your mother was dead?"

"This is getting harder," she said, starting to cry again.

"Baby, don't cry. Just think." Darlene forced herself to forge ahead, to get it over with. "What did you do Monday morning?"

"We went back to see if the notes were still on the door." Her lower lip protruded.

Darlene reached out for Mary Ann's hand. "It's okay. I don't mean to make you cry. Did your daddy get out of the car?"

"No. We just drove by and saw the notes, and he said, 'Guess your mother's still not home.' "

"So that's when you went to Sergeant Martin's?"

Mary Ann nodded. "We stayed there all day. Then about eight o'clock the police called. They told daddy to go there later."

"Were you awake when your daddy came home?"

"No, we didn't see him 'til the next morning. He was crying when he walked in our bedroom. He said, 'Your mother died,' and we were like, 'How?' And he said . . ." Mary Ann's voice clogged with sobs.

Darlene put her arm around her. "It's okay, baby." She waited a few minutes before continuing. "Just a couple more questions, honey. Did you talk to him?"

"He just told us she died, then I forget what else he said. He went somewhere with Sergeant Martin."

"Did you go home that night?"

"We stayed that night with the Martins. We stayed with the Martins until we moved into our big house."

"Mary Ann, you didn't tell your daddy about the videotape J.O. helped make of you?"

"No. I really didn't want to do that tape. I didn't want to tell J.O. or the police what happened that night. Daddy'd get mad and whip me."

"We won't tell him. And we won't tell him that we talked today either, okay? It will be our secret." Darlene looked into Mary Ann's eyes and wondered how many more secrets she was forced to keep.

Mary Ann nodded, "Right. It'll be our secret."

"Just one last question. Earlier when we were driving here, you said that you bet the person who did this moved away."

"Yeah, my daddy said that whoever killed her maybe moved away to some place where they couldn't find him. And that if he hears they're looking for him there, he'll probably move again. What do you think?"

"I don't know, Mary Ann. I don't know." Darlene wondered if Bill had been speaking about himself, but Darlene didn't want to push it. For now she was filled with relief that the interview was over, but she had an empty feeling that there was still something Mary Ann hadn't told her.

Chapter Ten

Tom Bevans closed his door to muffle the sounds in the outer office and clicked on the tape recorder. Of the 18 questions he had prepared for Darlene to ask Mary Ann, he had one special question where he had underlined an important word: "Did they eat lunch and *dinner* at their dad's house?" Since the medical examiner had said Kathleen had been killed around dinnertime, it was extremely important to know Bill's whereabouts then.

Bevans listened intently as Darlene asked: "Did you eat dinner with your daddy?" and Mary Ann replied: "I remember what I ate." Then Darlene briefly summarized, "Okay, you fixed dinner at home and . . ."

Bevans sat back, astonished. How could Darlene have let Mary Ann's response drop without following it up? What would the child have said if Darlene had probed further? Mary Ann neither denied nor affirmed that she had eaten at home, or that she had eaten with her father. That time period was crucial. He guessed Mary Ann's frightened responses demonstrated she knew a great deal more than she said. Now he'd have to develop a new strategy to get that information.

The next day, Bevans left for San Antonio to investigate a lead from the sheriff's files. When they had first looked through the office records, they had found a reference to a Hector Salquero, dubbed the "Girl Watcher" by the deputies—the man who had said he had seen Kathleen on the day she was murdered. Bevans phoned Salquero and discovered he still lived in the same apartment near Kathleen's, and he seemed genuinely eager to answer Bevan's questions.

Salquero invited Tom into his small apartment, picking up a cat from the chair he offered. His slouching posture coupled with a permanent sneer led Bevans to suspect that the retired bachelor had nothing better to do than observe the comings and goings of his neighbors.

Salquero readily recalled talking with the deputies two years earlier. He asked, "Can you imagine I saw Kathleen on the last day of her life? If I had only known." He shook his head and looked depressed.

"But I understand you saw her with another woman."

"Yeah. That gal with her had short, dark reddish hair. Kinda cut butch-like, you know? I remember what she wore like it just happened yesterday." Then he whispered, "She had real small breasts—like I told the deputies, kinda dikey-looking."

Salquero had been the only one who had referred to red hair—the color of hair found on Kathleen's T-shirt. Bevans knew they needed to find that red-headed woman.

Bevans' next stop was to see Dr. Bux as they had yet to establish a firm time for Kathleen's murder. From Dr. Bux's office, Bevans phoned an insect specialist from his alma mater. The entomologist went into great detail about the nocturnal habits of the fire ant, a painful, stinging insect that can kill small animals. Fire ants swarm mainly at night, although frequently a pungent odor, such as a body, can entice the insects to come out earlier from their hiding places. Unfortunately this turned out to be only minimal help in determining the time frame.

"From the full stomach," Dr. Bux began, "we think Mrs. Lipscomb had been killed around dinnertime, and we know her body had been on the roadside long enough to have suffered the ant damage. There are a few unexplained hours here, however. She had to be kept some place until it got dark. Judging from her unusual stiff position, the murderer stuffed her somewhere long enough to mold her body that way, probably until midnight or 1 a.m., then moved her to Scenic Loop. That would tie in with the evidence we discussed about blood having drained toward the back of her mouth after she died, showing someone picked her up later to move her. Since she was still rigid when we first saw her, we know for sure that she was killed within the previous twenty-four hours, because rigor mortis disappears after that length of time and the body becomes limp again."

Bevans nodded and looked at a crime scene photo. Kathleen's position bothered him. What the hell did the murderer do to her to cause her legs to settle that way?

On September 15, 1988, an angry Bill Lipscomb called Nadine. He had received the same letter she had from Charlotte Kanzler in Rance Grafton's office about closing Kathleen's estate.

"This accounting on the estate is just not right," Lipscomb told her. "I never had the dryer or the freezer and couldn't care less, but I won't settle without that wedding ring. You know that, Nadine."

"Bill, how many times have we had this conversation? Kathleen gave me that ring and I intend to keep it."

"If that's how you feel, I'll take you to court," he bellowed.

"Then you'll be forced to give me the ring. I'll just say you stole it from me, and you can kiss your grandchildren goodbye."

Lipscomb's oft-repeated threat sparked a resolve in Nadine that she hadn't shown Bill before. "You just go ahead and sue," she snapped. "I would love to go to court and tell a judge just how I happen to have this ring. If a judge listens to how you took the first ring and sold it, and still wants me to hand over this ring, I will. But only if I'm ordered to."

That conversation prompted a meeting the next day among Nadine, Darlene, and Tom Bevans.

"I think one of you should call Bill and tell him you're going to proceed with the estate closing," Bevans suggested.

"I agree, Mom. Bill's just bluffing. If he's innocent of the murder, he'll go to San Antonio and tell his side of the story. He'd do that to get the ring back just so he can hurt you more. But if he's guilty, he won't show up at all."

Bevans suggested they call Bill when he got home from work, around six, and he would tape it. Darlene volunteered to speak to Bill.

Darlene was nervous to the point of shaking that evening when she went to Bevans' office. She hoped she wouldn't stutter on the phone and reveal her apprehension. The more determined she became that Bill had killed her sister, the more she grew to fear him.

Bevans connected the phone to a recorder, and Darlene dialed. When Bill answered she haltingly told him, "I was talking with my mom over lunch today, and we were trying to get this estate thing settled. What I don't understand, Bill, is what's going on with the estate closing?"

"Well, the only thing I'm going to do is just let it be. If the ring's that important to her, she can keep it. She says it's the *principle* of the thing,'' he said sarcastically.

"But that was Kathleen's ring. Mom wanted it as a keepsake. You have to realize that Kathleen was the star of the family. You know Mom. Kathleen was above all the rest of us.''

"Yeah, I know, that's how Nadine treated her.''

Bevans passed Darlene a note: "Swear at him, get him angry. He's too much in control.''

Darlene took a deep breath. "Bill, telling my mom you're taking Mary Ann and Billie away from her is just so much shit! After Kathleen, Mary Ann is easily her second favorite.''

Lipscomb's voice became edged with irritation, "I know.''

"She has been so nice to you. Grafton wanted her to go after you for the insurance money.''

"I don't believe that for a minute! Besides, I was thinking about suing Pearle. I could get him because of the affair. My attorney told me I could sue for alienation of affection, and collect Kathy's annual salary times the number of years she would have worked. But I didn't pursue it.''

Darlene knew he didn't try because he needed Sergeant Baker's word that Pearle had admitted having the affair. Baker would assist Lipscomb only if he agreed to come in first for a polygraph—a step Lipscomb refused to take.

Bevans kept passing notes with his suggestions. "Use words that you know will pull his chain.''

"You collected that insurance when Kathleen told Mom what a bastard you were to her.''

"What a bastard *I* was?'' Lipscomb's anger had finally surfaced. "For a year all I did was coexist with Kathleen. We had no relationship—''

"I know. You told me Kathleen wouldn't have sex unless you asked her permission first.'' Darlene had to fight to control her temper whenever Bill spoke negatively about her sister.

"Then I found out she was having an affair with Pearle. Don't you know how that hurts?''

"I found out about her and Pearle the weekend before she died. I was really upset. But, Bill, if you execute everybody who ever had an affair, half the world would be dead."

"Darlene, they found sperm in her," he almost yelled.

"So?"

"You know it's not mine. I had a vasectomy in 1980."

"She was also sodomized, and there wasn't sperm there," Darlene retorted. "That just might mean there were two people involved. So, see you're still not cleared." Darlene realized that was the closest she had ever come to confronting Bill about her sister's murder, and it chilled her.

"Well—"

"Bill, just don't take the kids away from Mom."

"That's up to her," he said with resignation. "Tell her to file the papers for the estate."

Darlene ended the conversation, hung up, and looked at Bevans. "What do you think?"

"He's a pretty sly guy—didn't tell us much. Remember you said he'd put up a fight if he were innocent? He caved in on the ring. But still he's plenty smart to have done this and gotten away with it for so long. With the sheriff's laid-back attitude, maybe dropping the body in Bexar County was the smartest, or the luckiest, thing he ever did."

On October 4, Tom Bevans accompanied Nadine Adams and Darlene Sanford to the estate closing at the Bexar County Courthouse. Bevans suspected the judge would not tolerate a detective's participation in the proceeding. Since Gary still felt Darlene was chasing butterflies, he had no interest in attending the closing, so Bevans posed as Darlene's husband. In case it turned out to be noteworthy, he stuck a tape recorder in his pocket.

The judge appeared incredulous when he learned that the Bexar County Sheriff had allowed Bill Lipscomb to receive the insurance proceeds when he remained a prime suspect in a case still under investigation. Also, the judge determined that Grafton had not properly filed the documents to close the estate.

The attorney appointed for the children, Richard Knutsen, listened to the facts and immediately asked to be withdrawn from the case. It was obvious that he didn't want to be responsible for the children's interest if Lipscomb were eventually found guilty.

The judge abruptly dispatched the proceeding by denying the closing, and in so doing, gave the family a morale boost. Now someone else understood the absurdity of Lipscomb's not being scrutinized more closely.

With only 10 minutes taken out of their day, Bevans recommended an early lunch so they could discuss their next move. Once they were seated, he said, "Now don't get mad at me, but I need to ask you a serious question. Are you both one hundred percent sure Kathleen was sexually straight?"

Darlene rolled her eyes. "Of course she was. What are you getting at?"

"There's a neighbor who said he saw Kathleen with a 'dikey-looking' woman. You have to admit that raises a question. I want you to think about any of Kathleen's friends who *look* lesbian. Remember, we're only talking about appearance."

Darlene thought for a moment, then said, "This is a stretch. I *know* this woman is absolutely heterosexual, but Angela Rios is a PE teacher and has that muscular build. She's the only one of Kathleen's acquaintances I can think of who could remotely look like someone the neighbor described. She teaches in San Antonio. And her husband is a good friend of Bill's."

That afternoon Bevans took Sergeant Sal Marin with him to call on the principal of Angela Rios' school. The principal willingly handed over a photo of Rios from the school files at the police's request.

On October 11, Bexar County called in Hector Salquero for the photographic line-up. He was unable to identify Rios or anyone else in the line-up as the woman he had seen with Kathleen.

The following week both Guidry and Bevans went to San Antonio. Bevans had made a point of meeting with Dr. Bux on each trip there.

At one of these meetings, Dr. Bux had mentioned that one of their long-time Bexar County deputies, Frank Castillon, had a son, Frank Jr., who headed the Homicide Division for the San Antonio Police Department. Upon Tom's request, Dr. Bux had introduced him to Frank Sr., who had gladly set up an appointment with the police department's homicide division.

Even though the city of San Antonio was choked with 200 murders a year compared to Bexar County's 25, the SAPD agreed to help Tom Bevans with the murder. The police felt that even though Kathleen's body had landed in the county, the murder most likely had occurred within the city limits. With that offer, the police department became the first in Bevans' accumulation of allies in his search.

Then the sheriff's department extended an olive branch and assigned a precise and thorough investigator, Al Ramon, to the case. The tall, dark-haired, Ramon had been a sergeant at the time of Kathleen's murder and initially had worked the case. Since then, he had been promoted to lieutenant.

At the time of the murder, Ramon had been one of the first investigators on the scene. The memory of the petite blonde who had been beaten, murdered, and dumped by a country road had never left his mind. Even though he had been transferred to robberies shortly after the murder, he frequently called homicide to check on the department's progress. That interest prompted the sheriff to ask him if he wanted to return to the investigation. Ramon jumped at the chance.

Lieutenant Ramon studied the reports and interviews, and reached the same conclusion as the others. "Everything points to Bill Lipscomb. But we need a search warrant to obtain body fluids and a hair specimen. Now that Bill Lipscomb lives in Virginia, we have no jurisdiction, so our hands are tied.''

Realizing that both the sheriff's department and the private investigators had met a brick wall in terms of their jurisdictional abilities, Ramon wrote a letter to the Office of Special Investigation (OSI), the Air Force's equivalent of the FBI. Its national jurisdiction as well as its military connections were the final hopes of solving this puzzle. The agency had the governmental ability to unlock doors that civilian police and private detectives couldn't.

The OSI agreed to a meeting on October 18, but for the agency to get involved, the case had to be Air Force related. So in concert with Mike Guidry and Tom Bevans, Ramon sought the agency's attention through the WAPS cheating scheme.

Guidry and Bevans traveled to the outskirts of San Antonio to Lackland Air Force Base, and visited the OSI. Their one-story, flat-roofed structure of World War II vintage recently had had stucco smeared over its original wood siding, giving it a Southwestern look.

They met with Herb Shipman, an OSI agent with 22 years of experience. The detectives outlined all of the information they had garnered on the scam. For its part, Shipman said the OSI would agree to compile a list of everyone who took the WAPS test between January and June of 1986. Then they consented to break down the results by squadron and have each commander meet with the sergeants to confront them on the scam. Guidry and Bevans would try to coax the commanders into asking questions about Kathleen's murder.

Agent Shipman was a little skeptical. ''This murder took place well over two years ago. There would be no crime scene. No forensic evidence to speak of. Witnesses have been scattered around, and if we can find them, their memories will be thin. As I look at what you brought me, I don't even see a logical place to begin. It's such a long shot.''

"We've talked to a lot of people already," Bevans assured him. "The family has a whole book they kept on this murder—dates, places, names of Bill's friends."

The detectives stressed the military tie-in. Mike explained that Kathleen had divulged details of the cheating scam to several of her close friends, and that she had explicitly planned to use that information to gain custody of her children.

"Bill would scare the hell out of her by saying she was making a lot of people mad, and they'd be out to get her," Guidry said. "He almost promised she'd end up on some slab in the morgue. We have written statements from those people. They're friends of Kathleen's, in addition to psychiatrists and psychologists at Lackland, and they want like hell to see this thing solved."

These details helped Shipman warm to the case. "You must be aware, though, that this can't be a crusade to 'get' Lipscomb. Our goal is to do the right thing, but we cannot cross the line." However skepticism crept back in when he read Lipscomb's glowing annual reviews that told them for the last 12 years, he had had a knack of collecting stripes and commendations at breakneck speed. He saw that Lipscomb's military accomplishments were lavishly recognized as the Air Force decorated him with the Merit Service Medal, the Commendation Medal, the Good Conduct Medal, and lauded his unit as the Outstanding Air Force Unit. In addition, they had pinned ribbons on his chest for his educational proficiency, dedication to duty, and leadership ability. Having been promoted faster than most any other Master Sergeant in the entire Air Force, it seemed indefensible that Lipscomb would have killed his wife.

"Look at it this way," Bevans said to the agent, "This guy is totally military, really into his career. He gets promoted like a rocket and he wants that upward spiral to continue. Then his little wife keeps saying 'I guarantee you the base commander will be interested to hear what you're doing.' It's his whole life. He's a stud, and he isn't about to be taken down by this girl who threatens to spill the beans about the WAPS. This is the only part of his life he doesn't control, and he's going to fix that.''

Agent Shipman listened carefully but he still had reservations. ''You have nothing actually tying him to the crime, right?''

Bevans and Guidry looked at each other. They knew there wasn't a shred of physical evidence, no fingerprints of Lipscomb's, no bloody clothes, and no one who had seen Bill near Kathleen that night. But even knowing the agent was absolutely correct, Guidry said in his most confident manner, ''We're closing in on him. It's only a matter of time.''

''Let me talk to OSI Headquarters on this,'' Shipman said. ''Kathleen was a military dependent at the time of her death, so there's a possibility her killer could be military. If we decide to get involved, we'll assign someone to the case and get back to you.''

Guidry and Bevans knew Shipman's guarded statement meant that he had to get authority from the top. They didn't mind waiting. OSI involvement would be the best news they could ever hear.

The next day Guidry called Darlene. ''I've been in touch with Pearle's lawyer and he refuses to let Pearle talk to us. Under *no* circumstances will he meet with us. He's the last person we know who was with Kathleen before she died, so she might have confided information to him that we could use. If we're going to get anything out of him, we need your help.''

Darlene willingly agreed.

''You know Pearle is a specialist for at-risk pregnancies. You've never spoken to him and I doubt he'll remember you from the funeral, so all you have to do is make an appointment under an assumed name and tell his nurse that you're pregnant and having lots of problems. Tom and I will be waiting, and once Pearle starts to examine you, we'll rush in and corner him. He won't be able to refuse talking to us then.''

Darlene pictured the detectives storming the room while she laid sprawled, almost naked, on the examining table. She couldn't help laughing, but she also made it clear that under no circumstances would she do that. She'd be happy to make an appointment and talk with Pearle, but not under the ruse of being pregnant.

''We need your help, Darlene. Whatever you think you can do. There's a much better chance Pearle will talk to you than with us.''

''Okay. I'll call him, then I'll be back in touch.''

Darlene phoned Dr. Pearle's office and gave her name to his secretary. The doctor called back within the hour.

''Is this really Darlene?'' Pearle gushed. ''Oh I should know because you sound so much like Kathy. In fact, I could close my eyes and think I was talking with Kathleen. How wonderful!''

Darlene was flustered by his response and not completely sure what she should say. She invented a story about having to be in San Antonio the following week and since her sister spoke so highly of him and loved him so much, she would like to meet him. Pearle proved more than amenable and they agreed on the following Friday, October 28, at 3 p.m.

On the preceding Thursday, Tom Bevans and Mike Guidry drove to San Antonio in Mike's new Mercedes. Darlene flew up on Friday. Having remembered well how beautiful her sister had been, she took more than normal care with her makeup and wore a stunning red suit. The investigators met her at the plane and drove to the U.T. Health Science Center Hospital for her appointment. They gave their solemn promise that they would not let her out of their sight. Their concern for her safety reminded Darlene that Pearle had first been a suspect.

Dr. Pearle rushed out of his office, smartly dressed in a cashmere sports coat with an Italian tie. He extended his hand to Darlene, and as she approached him, he surprised her by giving her a tight embrace. His sudden intimacy unnerved her. She didn't want to be alone with Pearle under any circumstances, and became suspicious when he suggested going somewhere more private where they could talk.

He grabbed her hand and walked her down long corridors, took elevators to lower floors, then traversed more passageways. She kept looking back to see if her protectors were following, but to her horror, Mike and Tom hadn't been able to keep up. Finally, David Pearle escorted her outside to a deserted patio. Still holding her hand, he ushered her toward an umbrella table and pulled out a chair for her. They sat down and Pearle stared at her.

Darlene's urge to leave grew stronger, but the PIs had given her a list of important questions to ask which she had memorized.

"When was the last time you saw Kathleen?" she asked timidly.

"Long, long ago."

"Did you take her to your apartment?"

"I didn't have an apartment. You know, Darlene, when I hold your hand, I can close my eyes and I hear Kathleen. Being with you is just like being with her." He started patting her arm.

Darlene's stomach lurched and she wanted to reclaim her hand, but she left it clutched in his hoping to hear some answers. Under these circumstances she couldn't believe she had agreed to the questions she had to ask.

"Did you and Kathy have sex the last time you were together?"

David put his head on his arm that rested on the table, striking a pose that suggested the question was too painful. He brought his head up shaking "no," that he wouldn't answer.

Darlene asked, "Did Kathleen bathe after sex?" She received the same silent response. He didn't seem irritated with her, nor did he try to leave. He only looked sad. The investigators had told her to ask: "Did you have sex in her apartment? Was Kathy wearing a bra? What about panties?" The questions about underwear were important because none had been found with Kathleen on Scenic Loop. But expecting the same silence, Darlene saw no reason to ask them.

She sat staring at him, wondering how to get a reply out of the man. Finally, she asked if he would speak with the investigators.

After a few moments, he replied, "I don't know your family, Darlene. I don't know what kind of agenda they have. I talked with the sheriff's department and gave them hair samples from my head and mustache. My lawyer told me not to speak to anyone else. No, I will *not* talk to the detectives. Perhaps my attorney will."

There was no denying the adamancy in his tone and Darlene felt frustrated knowing she had been so ineffective. Leaving him sitting at the table, she ran back into the building, trying to locate the path Pearle had taken. She took one wrong corridor after another. Finally she found the main entrance and rushed outside. There on the front steps sat her two heroes, looking very sheepish.

Chapter Eleven

"What a creep!" Darlene gasped. "I feel like I need to take a bath to get his handprints off me."

"He's a quick sonofabitch," Mike Guidry said. "He ditched us by the time we reached the first bank of elevators."

"What the hell happened?" Tom Bevans asked, once they were inside the car.

Darlene tried to detail everything she could remember that Pearle had said and done.

"I had no idea he'd come on to you like that," Guidry said. "He was too quick and smooth at getting you alone. Makes me think his affair with Kathleen wasn't his first. Chances are he only wanted to lead her on, because he never did leave his wife. And as fast as his wife forgave him, she must be used to overlooking his escapades."

"What a jerk," Bevans agreed. "He was just after your body. Sorry, Darlene, we couldn't have predicted that."

"It was dreadful," Darlene moaned. "I can't believe he's the man Kathleen wanted to marry. She must have been so sad in her marriage that she fell for the first person who was nice to her. Bill seldom spent time with her, and I know he rarely bought her gifts for special occasions. Pearle must have seen that loneliness and knew the right strings to pull. Poor Kathleen. She was so anxious to find love.''

''I have a completely different attitude about the doctor now,'' Bevans said. ''He's the type who's interested in lots of women. Kathleen wouldn't have been that important to him. If she had decided not to leave her husband, or for any reason dropped Pearle, he wouldn't have killed her. Doesn't seem the type to stick his neck out and take that big a risk.''

''I think you're right,'' Guidry said. ''Pearle didn't have anything to gain by murdering her. If Kathy broke it off, he'd just go after the next woman he saw.''

''Hell, he could have even gone home to his wife,'' Bevans quipped. ''But he had a lot to lose if he had killed her. Mainly, his career and all that status that attracts women in the first place.''

''I guess we're making progress,'' Guidry mused. ''We've cut our original list of four suspects in half. But we still have Lipscomb and the mysterious red-headed woman.''

Bevans and Guidry had scheduled a series of interviews with Kathleen's co-workers, so they headed back to the sheriff's office for the questioning. The detectives hoped to learn if Kathleen had confided anything to these people.

Sergeant Baker and the deputies were cooperating with them fully, and the sheriff allowed their use of an investigation room. It still bothered Bevans that Lipscomb appeared to be getting information from the sheriff's office. Whenever Bevans and Guidry entered the office, they glanced around wondering who could be the leak.

The first person they talked to was Olga Spindle, Kathleen's co-worker and good friend. The detectives wanted her viewpoint because it would be their first outside of the family's.

Arriving at the sheriff's office wearing her white uniform, her vivaciousness was contagious. The detectives found her to be an easy interview. It would not be necessary to pressure Olga into a statement. Barely five feet tall, she was verbal and animated, and carried her emotions outwardly. Her life was an open book, especially her friendship with Kathleen, and the investigators were welcome to glance at the pages.

"Bill has gotten away with this for over two years," she began immediately. "You should have seen him at the funeral, playing the grief-stricken husband. Telling us how much he cared for Kathy. He's a real actor, that one. He mustn't have any conscience to carry it off the way he did. He said he didn't know why she wanted the divorce. But we all knew Kathy was married to a monster." Olga's memories of Kathleen and Bill seemed as clear as if she had talked to them recently.

"Did you and your husband see them socially?" Guidry asked.

"Never. Bill was jealous that Kathy had completed college and had a nursing degree. He didn't want to be around her friends. In fact, he always put down her profession as well as her education."

Bevans jotted "jealousy" down on his notepad.

Olga didn't need to be asked questions, and continued, "Frequently Kathy and Dr. Pearle went to conferences in Washington D.C., and Kathy asked Bill go to along. His folks lived nearby and could take care of their children. But he always said no. He wanted nothing to do with her colleagues in the medical world."

Olga gave innumerable pertinent details about her friend. The detectives could only ask questions when Olga stopped long enough to take a breath.

"Kathy was absolutely wonderful—I'll never forget her. One day when we were at work, a call came in from some nurse friends of mine in OB. They wanted me to adopt a little girl who had just been born. I had adopted a baby boy only nine months earlier and I said definitely not.

"But Kathy overheard my conversation and she wouldn't let me say no. I remember her saying that children were a gift from God, and I couldn't say no to something like that. There were lots of tears that day and phone calls to my family, but because of Kathy, I adopted that baby girl. Thank God I did, she's been a perfect child.

"But Kathy wasn't just a wonderful friend and mother, she was also becoming well-known in her profession."

"In what way?" Guidry asked.

"Well, for example, she published articles in *Current Therapeutic Research* and *The American Journal of Obstetrics and Gynecology.*" Olga began ticking them off with her fingers. "I'm not talking about subjects like a nurse telling how she balanced her job, husband, and children. I mean, these were research studies like: 'Single-dose Prophylaxis in Vaginal Hysterectomy.' She was so bright."

Bevans nodded, realizing Pearle had it all with Kathleen— someone intelligent he could discuss medicine with and someone beautiful he could enjoy in bed.

"I also remember Kathy telling me how much she and Bill argued, and I worried for her." Olga's expression darkened as she was thrust back in her memories. "She told me about his cheating scam and how Bill had all those contacts to get the answers to that test. She warned him that if he didn't give her custody of the children she would turn him in, even though she knew it would mean a court martial. I kept cautioning her. I'd say, 'Kathy, I'm so scared he'll hurt you,' but she tried to brush off my concerns."

"Wasn't she afraid that if she told a lot of people about the tests, someone else would turn him in and she'd lose her leverage?" Guidry asked.

"I don't think so," Olga shook her head. "Those who knew

him were afraid to, and anyone else just didn't want to get involved.

"But one night after she died, Bill called me at home and told me that Kathy got what she deserved because she was having an affair. He implied that she was probably killed by Mrs. Pearle, who must have found out about the affair. He also told his children the same thing. When you're that young, you believe everything a parent says. I bet they believe him to this day."

Tom was aware that Mrs. Pearle had been suggested as a possible suspect, but he had never taken it seriously.

"I understand that Dr. Pearle sent you and Sarah Bowers over to Kathleen's apartment."

"Oh, that was so eerie," she said, her brown eyes widening. "When Sarah and I walked through the apartment, we were so scared. Of course, we only found that Kathy hadn't been there since the night before, but that was a frightening thing to do. We went right back and told Dr. Pearle. He was shaken, too.

"I went to both of her funerals. Seeing her in San Antonio was so hard. She must have suffered terribly. Her face and neck were swollen three times normal size, like it probably took her a long time to die. And in San Antonio, Bill took those children up to the casket and let them look at their mother in that condition. Can you imagine that? It was horrible. Just horrible." Emotions had built up in her, and now she couldn't stop the tears spilling down her cheeks.

Mike Guidry reached out for her hand. "We're gonna get him," he thundered. His determination even caused Bevans to give him a surprised glance. "Whatever it takes, we're going to do it, even if it means shaking apart the entire Bexar County Sheriff's Department. You're right, Olga. He *is* a monster. What he did was so horrible that I personally will see to it that Bill Lipscomb is indicted. You've got my word on that!"

"Oh, I hope so. I really do. The day Kathy came in and said

Bill had agreed to a divorce and told her she would get custody of the children, I knew there had been a terrible change.''

"Yeah, an interesting change. How long before she died did that happen?" Bevans asked.

"Only a couple weeks."

"That's important," he said writing it down. "It shows he planned the murder at least two weeks before."

"Longer than that," Guidry reminded him. "Bill had increased Kathy's life insurance several months before she died."

"No doubt all of this was planned for a long time." Olga nodded in agreement. "We knew something was wrong. Giving custody to Kathy was so out of character for Bill. And then the first weekend after she moved to her apartment, she disappeared. He planned this. He really did."

As Guidry questioned Olga, Bevans glanced at her short, compact body and her bobbed, auburn hair. An investigator had to suspect everyone, and her description seemed to match the one Hector Salquero had given.

"Olga, do you happen to have a photograph of yourself?" Bevans asked.

Olga didn't seem surprised at his question, since she was so intent on helping the detectives. "I have one in my purse, but Sarah Bowers is also in it. Will that do?"

"That will be fine," Bevans said, taking the picture. "I'll get this back to you in a couple of weeks."

Olga could have talked for hours, but it had not taken long for the men to catch the gist of her feelings: Kathleen was the sweetest person you'd ever want to know, and there was no doubt in Olga's mind that Lipscomb had murdered her.

As soon as Olga left, Bevans called Salquero and asked him to come to the sheriff's office.

Guidry dialed Gina Riegel's number from the sheriff's office. "Gina? Mike Guidry here. I talked with your husband earlier and he said you'd probably be home now. Did he tell you we're investigating Kathleen Lipscomb's murder?''

"Yes, and I'm so glad to hear that." Gina's voice was warm and friendly. "I had heard the family retained investigators."

"I've been looking at the report you gave the sheriff a couple of years ago. Tell me about the call you received right before Kathleen's funeral when you were told you'd be the next one to die."

"Oh, that was some experience. I've never been so scared."

"Did you recognize the voice?"

"No. I can't say I did because the man was whispering. In fact, it seemed like he was trying to disguise his voice. It sounded very strained."

"I understand you knew both Kathy and Bill."

"I'd met them four years ago when we moved near them, and we found out we had a lot in common. I'm a nurse and my husband's in the Air Force. Earlier that spring when I learned they were getting divorced, Kathy told me about her 'friend.'

"But after that, Bill came around often to talk about it. He didn't want a divorce and seemed very upset. He kept asking if she had a boyfriend. At one point, he told me he hoped Kathy's filing for a divorce wasn't because she was seeing someone else, because if that was the case, he didn't know if he could keep his friends from hurting her. Can you imagine him saying anything like that?"

"Did she give you any names?" Guidry jotted down her comments, thinking how many intimidating avenues Lipscomb had taken.

"No. She really wasn't specific. I just assumed she meant all those men Bill taught with. But his remark upset me so much that I immediately called my husband at work and told him."

"You must have thought back to that conversation after you learned she had been murdered," Guidry said.

"Even before that. I became suspicious when Bill and the kids came over on that Monday night—I think it was June 9th, around 7 p.m. He asked if we had seen or heard from Kathy. Bill looked awful—he had deep circles under his eyes and acted dazed. After Bill left, my husband and I discussed his appearance because he looked like he had gone through something traumatic."

Guidry wrote faster.

"Then a couple days later when my husband and I were leaving for her funeral, I received that phone call. It really unnerved me. I immediately called the sheriff and reported it."

"When you reported this, did you tell them about Bill coming over the night after the murder and how he looked?"

"Yes. When I called them, an officer came out to my house to take my statement. Later, they called to ask questions about Kathy's death, but I never heard from them again."

Guidry shook his head and continued to jot down notes. He wrote "helpful" by Gina's name.

While Guidry talked with Gina, Bevans left to check out the evidence locker and see what the sheriff had on the case. Dr. Bux had shown him photos of Kathleen's T-shirt and jeans, but the deputies had indicated there wasn't much there. The detectives already had seen the forensic reports, so they knew exactly what had been examined.

The deputy in charge of evidence led Bevans to a small dark room, the size of a large closet. The lighting was so inadequate that Bevans had to go back to the front office to borrow a lamp. The sergeant gave him a brown plastic bag with "K. Lipscomb" printed on a tag. Bevans pulled out the clothes. First he unrolled the jeans, then unfolded the T-shirt. He stopped and stared at it in shock, not believing his eyes.

Dozens of strands of hair still covered the shirt. How could the evidence people miss all this? He carefully spread the shirt out on a desktop. Taking a pair of tweezers from a manicure set in his briefcase, he spent the next hour picking hair from the shirt and placing it in a plastic bag to send to the FBI Crime Lab in Washington D.C. He meticulously rolled up the clothes and glanced inside the brown bag to see what else was there.

He found a booklet that was wrinkled and folded at the bottom of the bag. It was a Hallmark date book Kathleen had kept as a calendar. Thumbing through, he noticed she had written in the dates when Lipscomb took the WAPS exam and when he received information on it from other sergeants. Now Bevans possessed written data and the actual names of people who were contributing to the scam. He copied the information down, then replaced the booklet in the bag, astonished that this information hadn't been gathered earlier.

As he prepared the package to be sent to Washington, he asked the Bexar County serologist, Sergeant Jaynie Skow, if they still had the sperm sample they had removed from Kathleen. They did and he requested that another test be made of it. Sergeant Skow promised to send it to the lab in Atlanta.

Mike joined Tom.

"A few minutes ago, I learned something interesting from another nurse I called who was a friend of Kathy's, Jamie Richardson. Kathy had apparently confided a lot to her. Pearle was definitely the reason for Kathy's divorce. Supposedly Pearle promised to divorce his wife so he and Kathy could get married. He even talked about getting another academic position out of state. Jamie said Kathy was scared to death of what Bill would do if he found out about the affair."

"Yeah, so much for promises from Dr. Pearle," Bevans said.

"What are you up to?" Mike asked, noticing Kathy's scattered belongings.

"Look at all this stuff." Bevans showed Guidry the hair specimens he had collected and the names he had taken from Kathleen's date book.

Guidry nodded enthusiastically. "Okay, this is heating up. We're getting all these witnesses lined up, and the ones we've talked with are telling us it's Lipscomb. You're finding more evidence. We are really closing in on this guy.''

Bevans lowered his head to stare in Guidry's eyes. ''I wish I could be as optimistic, but we have nothing physical connecting this to Lipscomb. We have no idea what he did with his kids the night of the murder. We have no witnesses. No crime scene. Just a bunch of people telling us he's a bad guy. Face it, buddy, we don't have shit.''

On October 31, 1988, Dr. Pearle's attorney, Jeb Francis, called Darlene Sanford. He wanted Tom Bevan's address and phone number.

Darlene felt hopeful. Although she still considered the doctor repulsive, she thought maybe finally he wanted to help the detectives. With the possibility that he knew information no one else did, Darlene felt optimistic that what he had to say would almost make her stressful visit with him worthwhile.

Chapter Twelve

Hector Salquero was waiting for Tom Bevans at the front desk in the sheriff's office.

"Well I'll be darned," Salquero said when Bevans showed him the picture Olga had given him. "There's that gal I told you about. See that short reddish hair? And there's Kathleen with her. How'd you manage to get a picture of both of them?"

"That's not Kathleen. That's a woman named Sarah Bowers. They were friends of Mrs. Lipscomb's. Don't you think it's possible you saw them on Monday and not Sunday? They were at her apartment on Monday looking for her."

"Oh, I saw them on Sunday all right, because I read about her murder the very next day in the newspaper."

Bevans shook his head. "Although Kathleen had been murdered on Sunday, she wasn't found until Monday, so the article didn't appear until Tuesday."

"Oh," Salquero said dejectedly. "I see what you mean. Then I had to have seen them on Monday. Well now, gosh, how could I make a mistake like that?'' Salquero looked up, obviously embarrassed by his blunder. ''I just wanted to help.''

''And we appreciate that,'' Bevans said, guiding him toward the door.

Bevans went back to his suspect list to delete ''a red-haired woman.'' Now, only one name remained.

When the detectives returned to Houston, Guidry's secretary told him there was a visitor in his office.

A handsome, 30-something man dressed in a LaCoste shirt, casual slacks, and tennis shoes was sitting at the corner table leafing through a file folder he had apparently brought with him. The man stood up, smiled, and came forward with his right hand extended.

''Hi, I'm Special Agent Rich Fife. OSI sent me over to lend a hand with the Kathleen Lipscomb case.''

''Great!'' Guidry said, unable to hide his elation. ''We've been looking for you.'' He reached out to shake his hand.

Bevans was every bit as delighted. ''Now we'll really get rolling with this case.''

Fife's thick, well-groomed sandy hair matched his knit shirt, and his high, rounded cheekbones and short nose lent him an all-American appearance.

''I was going over some information you provided the OSI, and you'll have to fill me in on what you've done since. I can't believe the age of this case. What kind of luck are you having?''

''We're finding some people to interview, but they are mainly Kathleen's friends,'' Bevans said. ''You'd be a great help getting us Air Force personnel that we need to talk with.''

Bevans pulled out a list of people Darlene had provided, and those he had copied from Kathleen's date book. The list contained fellow drill instructors of Lipscomb's and his supervisor at Lackland.

They discussed the case for over an hour. At one point Agent

Fife complimented their ability to get the OSI involved. "I don't know what kind of song and dance you did for OSI, but our head murder investigator is going to run this thing. He's a criminal psychologist, Dr. Charles McDowell, and highly respected. I'll be the 'case agent' in San Antonio. Special Agent Barney Stegall will head the effort at Langley where Lipscomb's stationed."

Bevans and Guidry asked Fife to help them get access to interview Lipscomb's San Antonio co-workers. Fife enthusiastically agreed to do everything asked of him. Both detectives had instantly liked the agent, and years later, Tom would remember that when Rich Fife came to them, it had been their lucky day.

Darlene jotted down figures as she talked with her mother on the phone. "Okay, we paid Mike $600 for that first visit to San Antonio, then a week later he billed us for $1,000. It's been running about $4,000 a month and now we're up to $12,000. Mike said the max would be $7,500."

"I had no idea it had climbed that much," Nadine said. "This is just awful."

"What are we going to do, Mom?"

"We signed a contract, and unfortunately no maximum was written in. We've got to come up with the money somehow. But I don't have anything near that in savings and I doubt if I sold all my stock, I'd net that much." After a moment's hesitation, Nadine said, "There's only one thing we can do. I'll have to sell the house."

"Mom, you can't do that. It would just kill the family. The house was one of the last things Dad did for us. He wanted to see that we all had a nice place to live."

"It will break my heart, Darlene, but I can't think of anything else. If we quit now, we'll have wasted all the money we've already spent."

Darlene felt concerned about her mother. Ever since Kathy's death, Nadine had shown a resigned acceptance about any adversity. Darlene vowed not to let the growing cost continue forever. But now, with Tom and Mike getting the OSI involved, surely this investigation was coming to a close.

Rich Fife worked rapidly. Within days, he provided the detectives with addresses and phone numbers of Lipscomb's fellow drill sergeants. Fortunately, many of them still lived in the area.

The next week Bevans and Guidry went to San Antonio to talk with Sergeant Raymond Martin, the man who had been Lipscomb's commander while he was stationed at Lackland. They had scheduled a breakfast meeting with him.

Both detectives liked the tall, lean sergeant's candor. He seemed as interested in getting to the bottom of the case as they were.

"It's good to talk with you two," Martin told them. "I've had some questions myself about this thing. You know how Bill Lipscomb rose up in the ranks so fast—a real hotshot. He was doing fine, then about a month before his wife's death, he seemed different to me. For example, I was a little surprised at how close Bill got to me—kinda hung around asking my advice, you know, treated me like a father figure."

"You hadn't been particularly close before that time?" Bevans asked.

"No. It was strange because we really weren't good friends, but he frequently came by my house and told my wife and me about his personal problems. He voiced his irritation over Kathleen's interest in her career. It supposedly was much more important to her than he was. Apparently he didn't want to get a divorce and I think he appreciated that we've been married a long time."

"What about the day his wife disappeared? Did you see him then?" Guidry asked.

"Actually, he called me Sunday night and said his wife wasn't at her apartment, so he still had the kids."

"That was the night of the murder," Mike said. "How'd he sound?"

"Kind of drained. But he just wanted to alert me that he'd possibly be late for work the next morning. I didn't see anything strange in that, because it was typical of Bill to be so conscientious.

"He called me again Monday morning to say that she still wasn't home. To me, Bill sounded on the verge of tears. He had those kids with him. Me and the missus told him to bring the children over and they could spend the day with us. Cute little kids. Real easy to have around.

"Then about eight the sheriff called and told him they found a dead woman who looked like Kathy and wanted him to come in and make a statement. When he heard those words, he just slumped. Got real teary-eyed. I went with him."

"You did?" Guidry's eyes lit up. "We hadn't heard that before."

"Yeah. He was pretty shook up. He needed to have someone along," the sergeant said over a second pot of coffee. "I didn't give a statement or anything. Just waited in the entry. I was only there for moral support."

"Sergeant Martin, do you know that he's a suspect in the murder?" Bevans asked.

"Somehow that doesn't surprise me. I know it should be hard for me to believe when I think about all his success in the Air Force, and how impressive his career has been, but somehow I can accept he had something to do with his wife's death."

Listening to the sergeant, Mike knew his words sounded familiar. They were the same words the detectives had repeatedly heard from others they had interviewed. If everyone agreed to this possibility, how come Bill has been slippery enough to evade capture all this time? "What made you feel he could be a suspect?"

"For one thing, my wife was afraid of him. She couldn't put her finger on it, but he made her nervous. When he stayed with us, she insisted on keeping our bedroom door locked at night. And there was another thing that bothered me."

They leaned closer, not knowing what to expect.

"His closest friend seemed to be on a different career path. Bill was going this way, and his friend was like this," he said, moving one hand up and the other down." I couldn't help but wonder, what's the connection?

"Of course drill sergeants can be a pretty intimidating lot, and some of them strut around like a bunch of SOBs in their own little fraternity. But this one was even caught smoking pot."

"Do you remember his name?"

"I believe it's either Roger or Tony Barrelo. It was one of those deals where he goes by his middle name, but the Air Force uses his first name. Heck, half the time I didn't know what to call him. Anyway, I don't believe he was allowed to re-enlist. When he left, he had no idea where to go. I know we didn't have a forwarding address. He pretty much just disappeared."

"He'd be an interesting person to talk with," Bevans said as he wrote down Barrelo's name, but he knew someone who had "disappeared" would take a lot of time to find.

They all stood when the sergeant left. He started to salute, then laughed. "That gets habitual," he said as he reached for the detectives' hands.

They thanked Martin for his cooperation, and he agreed to be available whenever they needed to talk.

On the way back to the sheriff's office, Guidry said, "We gotta find this Tony Barrelo. Obviously, he's a big player in the game."

Bevans nodded. "We'll do that, right after the next thirty interviews we have lined up."

"Literally?"

"Mike, do you realize how many people Bill and Kathleen worked with? We're also talking to neighbors, as well as several more family members."

Four of the interviews would be conducted that afternoon with the four drill sergeants who had worked with Lipscomb. Three of them were still his friends.

Guidry and Bevans questioned each sergeant individually, but they may as well have conducted one interview for quadruplets—Sergeant Ricky Rios, his twin brother, Sergeant Raul Rios, Sergeant Guy Caldwell, and Sergeant Norman O'Reily. The twins were slightly built, contrasting with Caldwell's muscular body. O'Reily, the most outgoing of the four, embodied the identifying red-haired, freckled coloring of an Irishman.

As each man walked in, the detectives saw that their uniforms had been pressed to knife-edge perfection, and all eight shoes gleamed. Four haircuts, skinhead short, capped postures so erect, the detectives imagined boards had been shoved down the back of the men's shirts. As a final touch, every ribbon the men had ever earned was pinned on their jackets.

Bevans and Guidry were dressed in black, priding themselves on their investigative ability, rather than their appearance. Bevans has said "When we finish an interview, we don't leave a piece of information in the room." Even though the investigators introduced themselves, all four sergeants seemed confused as to who the two black-garbed men were. Since the OSI wore no uniforms, the sergeants may have assumed that was who they were dealing with, and the detectives weren't about to set them straight.

The detectives had choreographed their questioning. Guidry started and asked the men about their relationship with Lipscomb, their knowledge of Kathleen, and then delved into the WAPS scam.

As the interviews progressed, Guidry became more and more intimidating. He strutted around like a little general barking orders, making impossible demands, and issuing threats he had no power to carry out.

"You come clean with me," he screamed at each man, "or when the OSI hears about this they'll pull all your WAPS tests and make you take them again."

The sergeants said they knew nothing about the testing scenario, but they all hedged their answers and their eyes darted back and forth between the two investigators. They were understandably nervous over questions that could lead to a court martial. Each had spent nearly 15 years in the Air Force. Five more and they could retire with a percentage of their pay and all of their benefits. Any involvement in a cheating scam would mean forfeiture of everything.

Guidry asked every question he could think of, even calling out specific test questions he found in an old study guide he had bought from an airman for $10. Guidry didn't have the answers, but he frowned as the sergeants searched in bewilderment for the proper reply.

Bevans absorbed the proceedings, kept the tapes running, and thought of other possible questions Guidry hadn't explored. When Mike felt his mental well was running dry, he'd tug on his tie. That was Bevans' cue to jump in with questions. He would run his list, then give his tie a tug, and Guidry would take over again. Their questioning continued until every drill sergeant was sweating profusely and had become limp with exhaustion, but they did not provide much information.

Generally, of the four, Ricky Rios seemed to be closest to Lipscomb, while his twin, Raul, patently didn't care for the egotistical Lipscomb. The detectives surmised that if Raul had gotten any testing help, it had come through his brother instead of directly from Lipscomb.

The only question they adamantly answered was, "Did Bill

Lipscomb kill his wife?'' They all responded with a resounding, "No."

For whatever reason, they behaved as Lipscomb's protectors and would apparently fall on their swords for the man. It would have surprised no one that Lipscomb received at least three calls that night telling him what had happened.

A week later, Bevans drove out to Angela Rios' house in the San Antonio suburbs. He and Guidry were grasping at straws to find out who had kept the kids the night of the murder. Angela seemed a likely suspect, but he anticipated little cooperation because of her husband's closeness to Lipscomb.

If she had any knowledge of the WAPS scam, she refused to admit it to Bevans. However, on everything else she was the picture of accommodation. Thinking about all the hair he had taken from Kathleen's T-shirt, Tom asked her for a snip of hers. Her fingers automatically flew to her hair and she gave Tom a quizzical look.

"My hair?"

"Just routine," he said, casually. "There were some unidentified hairs on Kathleen's T-shirt, and if you would just give me a sample, we can write you off as a suspect and stop pestering you."

Angela finally nodded and obliged him by snipping off a few strands from the back of her head.

Bevans pressed on. Still working on Lipscomb's time schedule for the night of the murder, he knew it was crucial to find the person Lipscomb had chosen to care for his children. He asked Angela if she had seen the children that June night. She said she hadn't because she distinctly remembered meeting some friends with Ricky at San Antonio's Riverwalk---a tree-covered, downtown restaurant and boutique area snaking parallel to both banks of the San Antonio River. They had stayed late to eat dinner. The next day she recalled being tired when

Ricky phoned her from work to say Kathleen Lipscomb was missing. She offered to supply the names of their friends.

Angela told the story in such a direct and spontaneous manner, Bevans found it totally believable. As he stood to leave, he casually turned to ask one last question, thinking she would simply brush him off.

"What do you think about the idea that Bill might have killed his wife?"

She didn't hesitate. "I've considered that because he was so controlling," she said. "Ricky knew better than to push Bill. Yes, Bill definitely could have."

Bevans had trouble hiding his surprise as he left, but he was now more frustrated than when he had arrived. He still had to find the person who had taken care of the Lipscomb children that night.

The day after Tom Bevans returned from San Antonio, he received a phone call from Dr. Pearle's attorney telling him the doctor would cooperate only with the sheriff. Francis claimed that someone from Bevans' office had called Dr. Pearle and threatened him with all kinds of legal hell if he didn't cooperate.

Bevans glared at the closed door of Guidry's office, but decided not to push it. If the doctor wouldn't communicate with them, then that was it. They had given Pearle their best shot with Darlene. Now they'd have to obtain information through the sheriff.

It would soon be the middle of November. The detectives had investigated the case since August and were no closer to convicting Bill Lipscomb than when they had begun. Bevans and Guidry had the resources of their own office, in addition to the sheriff, the San Antonio Police Department, the OSI, and the FBI. Abundant interviews had been taken from Kathleen's friends and neighbors, in addition to most of the people Lipscomb had worked with. All of Kathleen's friends thought Lipscomb was guilty, while most of Lipscomb's friends held to his innocence or refused to give any information at all.

Whenever Bevans reached a standstill like this, he would trudge back to the Bexar County Sheriff's Department to sift through the case file and rummage around the evidence room. There could be a clue he had missed, or some item he had overlooked. At least it gave him a feeling of doing something.

As he entered the office, he stopped by the serologist's lab to see if she had the DNA report back on the semen sample, and learned they hadn't sent it yet. He hung around until he received a promise that it would go out first thing in the morning.

By now Bevans had become a permanent fixture at the sheriff's office, and when he showed up at the evidence room, the deputy on duty automatically handed him the bag labeled "K. Lipscomb." Again he took out the clothes, and shook his head remembering all the hair on the T-shirt.

At one time he rechecked the medical examiner's report and saw a notation that 23 hairs had been taken in total from Kathleen, Dr. Pearle, and the male nurse. The report indicated that only 15 came from Kathleen's shirt. Bevans had found five times that number from the same shirt, but he still waited for the FBI report on them. The medical examiner had found that two of the hairs he had examined had belonged to Kathleen, one from her head and another from her pubic area. Six had been taken from clothes and bathrooms at the male nurse's apartment, and one had been obtained from Dr. Pearle's head and another from his mustache. None of the hairs from the two suspects had matched any on Kathleen's shirt.

Reaching for Kathleen's date book, Bevans sat down at a desk next to Lt. Ramon, and began thumbing through it again. Kathleen had jotted down one general statement for the month of January, 1986: "Numerous calls and nights out passing information around concerning WAPS testing. Bill has all questions for the test.''

On February 14, she had noted that her car had broken down. ''It was three quarts low on oil and the alternator had all but fallen off.'' He remembered Darlene telling him that Kathleen thought Bill had punched a hole in her oil pan. On February 25, she had recorded that Bill had taken the WAPS test. The next night a banquet had been held on base, but Kathleen hadn't gone because she wasn't able to find a babysitter.

Bevans turned to March. There were several notations concerning Lipscomb's whereabouts and Bevans learned that Lipscomb had spent an inordinate amount of time with his fellow drill instructors. On March 15, a Saturday, Kathleen had written that Bill had been at Sonny's pouring concrete all day. The following Tuesday, March 18, he had gone to a softball practice, then to Caldwell's and hadn't gotten home until 12:45 a.m. On Palm Sunday he had again visited Caldwell, returning home at 10:30 p.m. On another day he had helped Ricky until 1:15 a.m. All of the men mentioned were sergeants who had taken the WAPS test and were buddies of Lipscomb's. And all of them had been questioned.

On March 22, Kathleen had penned: ''Softball tournament. Shannon Gilbert there.'' Bevans stopped and reread the statement. Glancing up at Lt. Ramon he asked, ''Who the hell is Shannon Gilbert?''

Ramon thought a minute, then shook his head. ''She's no one we've brought in.''

The name somehow sounded familiar to Bevans. Had Darlene mentioned her? Had he seen her name on another document? He couldn't recall, but he was positive no one had communicated with a Shannon Gilbert. Knowing Lipscomb's softball team consisted of Air Force personnel, Bevans wondered if Gilbert could also be Air Force related. He reached for the phone book and found the number for Lackland's base locater.

"Do you have a Shannon Gilbert listed?" he asked casually, not expecting to hear she still lived in the area. After a short wait he was astounded to be given a number. He dialed it and a woman with a southern drawl answered.

"This is Tom Bevans and I'm an investigator—" was all he could say before she interrupted.

Her voice immediately stern, she cut through her Alabama accent. "If this has anything to do with Bill Lipscomb, I want an attorney."

Chapter Thirteen

Tom Bevans could not suppress his excitement over his conversation with Shannon Gilbert. He wasn't sure what he had struck, but it smelled like pay dirt to him. He asked Dalton Baker to bring Shannon in immediately for questioning. Then Bevans called Rich Fife and suggested that he do a background check on her.

A few days later, Bevans received Fife's bio on Shannon. The report revealed that she was a single mother with one child, and a staff sergeant. In addition, she was a drill instructor. Thinking back to her sexy, Southern voice, Bevans couldn't picture it.

It took two weeks before the sheriff's office could orchestrate an interview with Sergeant Gilbert. On December 1, 1988, the tall attractive woman with her dark hair pulled back into a bun, walked into their office dressed in full military uniform, nervously clutching her black leather shoulder bag. Her attorney, Phillip Overhill, accompanied her.

Bevans, Sergeant Baker, and Fife all reached for Shannon's hand at the same time.

"We're really anxious to talk with you," Bevans exclaimed.

Shannon couldn't hide the fear in her eyes. "If I tell you what I know, Bill Lipscomb will kill me."

"Tell us how we can help." Fife said.

"First, I must be granted immunity from prosecution," she said, twisting a gold ring on her right hand. "Then I'll have to disappear into the Witness Protection Program. It's the only way."

"Just what do you know?" Fife asked.

Overhill stepped forward, and his somber expression made it clear that he didn't want his client giving away free testimony. He reminded the investigators that Sergeant Gilbert needed to have her requests addressed.

"I need to get a general idea of what she can tell us," Fife argued. "I'm with the OSI. It's up to the Air Force to grant immunity."

"I know that Bill hired someone to kill his wife," Shannon blurted out, then broke down crying. "I knew. I really knew. If only I had warned Kathleen. She might be alive today."

At that point, Overhill raised his hand, halting her confession. "Before Sergeant Gilbert continues, we definitely need to be clear on the immunity and protection issues. Believe me, gentlemen, she *is* your smoking gun."

Rich Fife slipped his notes back into his briefcase and said he'd confer with the Air Force about immunity and protection. Then he'd get back to her lawyer as soon as possible.

The next day, a jubilant Tom Bevans joined Darlene for lunch to bring her up to date on the case. He said that Agent Fife had confided that "no doubt" the Air Force would cooperate and give Shannon immunity, and probably anything else she wanted.

"I can feel it," Bevans said, grinning and raising his fist in the air. "Bill is going to be behind bars in a week!"

Darlene didn't feel as sure. It seemed too good to be true that after two and a half interminable years, Bill finally would be brought to justice. She had been on so many roller coaster rides with this case, she didn't allow herself to get overly confident.

"I'm curious about something. What color is her hair?"

"Dark brown. Why?"

"I thought it might have been red. I was thinking that maybe she could have helped Bill. They were having an affair. It's not too much of a stretch."

"Good point. But remember, there were four red hairs. Not one of those hairs had a root. They had all been cut, probably from a red wig. Those strands were placed on the T-shirt to throw off the investigation."

Darlene was silent for a moment. "He thought of everything, didn't he?"

Bevans nodded. "Everything."

"Has the WAPS test scam been forgotten?" she asked.

"No. The sheriff's department still thinks Ricky Rios is involved and he'll probably be arrested for withholding information. The Air Force is discussing a court martial for everyone found cheating on the WAPS test. Things are happening fast now. This is how it's supposed to go."

Darlene had to smile at Bevans. He looked like a big kid who had just won a prize.

Rich Fife became impatient because he still didn't have the sperm test results he had been promised months earlier, so he phoned Sergeant Baker.

"I've been meaning to call you on that," Baker told him. "We've looked high and low, but it appears that sample just isn't here."

''What do you mean, it isn't there? You sent it off, didn't you?''

''Well, to tell you the truth, it didn't get sent because we couldn't find it. Sorry to have to spill that on you, but it looks like we lost the sample. But, hey, we'll keep searching.''

Fife hung up and shuddered.

The following week, Fife called Bevans. ''I just got off the phone with Gilbert's attorney. The Air Force granted her immunity and has agreed to send her to any country she chooses for as long as she wants. Her lawyer has agreed to have her at Lackland's OSI office on December 15th at 9 a.m. Can you make it?''

''Can you keep me away?'' Bevans asked.

Promptly at 9 a.m., Shannon Gilbert and her attorney arrived at Lackland's OSI office where Special Agent Herb Shipman directed them to one of the two soundproof interview rooms. Shannon again wore her full military uniform and an anxious expression.

Tom Bevans and Rich Fife sat eagerly with a tape recorder when she walked in. She placed her written script before her and cleared the tight knot in her throat. Then, after glancing around, she began her testimony.

''I met Bill Lipscomb in 1984 when he was my military training instructor. Then I met his wife in August of the following year, when they bought a cocker spaniel puppy from me. I knew then that their divorce was pending.

''During this time Bill confided to me on several occasions that he wanted to have Kathleen killed.'' Upon giving that crucial piece of information, she looked up at her listeners, and the anxious expression on her face told them she realized the gravity of her words.

"These conversations occurred at my house in Bexar County, Texas. The tenor of his remarks was that he had great concerns for his children and wanted custody over them. Eventually, however, he agreed to let his wife have custody. Nonetheless, the whole matter of his children became an obsession to him. He came to my house and actually physically cried when he talked about his children. He said that the kids should not have to live without him.

"During these conversations, he expressed several acts that I would characterize as vindictive." She bit her lip before giving the first example. "He punched a hole in the oil pan of Kathleen's car. I think he wanted the car to break down." She moistened her finger, then flipped to the next page of her testimony.

"The real clincher came when he expressed a desire to have her killed."

Pulling a tissue from her purse, Shannon dabbed at her eyes. Between sniffles she resumed. "He told me this on more than one occasion. He kept saying, 'Just wait and see. You'll read about it in the newspapers.' He also said that he made a down payment for the murder with his grandmother's ring."

She glanced up at the investigators and spoke without looking at her written statement. She confided that Lipscomb's lawyer had told him that he would need $10,000 for a custody fight, so he had borrowed $12,000 from his parents. "I thought maybe he could have used this money to pay for her killing. When he told me all these things, he was sober and not under the influence of drugs."

Her eyes returned to her script. "During this time, Bill confided that he was compromising the WAPS testing. He also told me that his wife had threatened to report him and his friends to military authorities for cheating on the test if he wouldn't drop the custody fight. Shortly thereafter, Bill stopped his custody demands.

"I first learned about the murder of Bill's wife as follows.

I telephoned Bill at his apartment and asked him how he was doing. He said, 'Okay, I guess.' I asked him what he meant by 'Okay, I guess,' and he said, 'Haven't you heard?' Then he told me that his wife had been murdered.

"After that phone conversation, I began to cry and cry. He had told me all along that he was going to have her murdered and now she was dead. I felt that I should have forewarned her, but I had not. I felt very bad."

Shannon told of taking her son and buying a bottle of liquor, then telephoning Bill from a pay phone at a convenience store. "I was distraught and crying at the time. Bill came down to the store and saw me. There I said to him, 'You told me you were going to have your wife killed and now it's happened.'

"Bill stated, 'my hands,' meaning his hands, 'did not do this.' Bill repeatedly said that what I was saying could get him into a lot of trouble.

"I went home. There I telephoned Wilford Hall Medical Center and told them what had happened and that I was upset over it. The next day I went to see a Dr. Proctor with the Medical Health Clinic at Wilford Hall. I told him what had transpired and how upset I was.

"After seeing Dr. Proctor, I read newspaper accounts of the murder of Bill's wife at the base library. I later called my family and my brother came to San Antonio to be with me.

"Thereafter, Bill came to my office, telephoned me, and came by my residence on various occasions, much more often than before his wife's death. At one time, he sent his children back to Virginia and invited me over to his house. I was reluctant to go. Bill questioned that I must be scared of him. I told him no, but in reality I was scared and wondered if he had cords in his house. On one occasion he told me that he would receive over $200,000 in insurance on his wife's life and that the Air Force was giving him a humanitarian reassignment back to Virginia."

She took a deep breath and looked very tired. "It was my

Kathleen Adams Lipscomb shortly before her murder.
(Courtesy Nadine and Darlene Adams)

As a teenager, Kathy Adams was an officer of the National Honor Society. (*Courtesy Nadine and Darlene Adams*)

Kathy Adams was chosen Most Likely to Succeed her senior year at New Caney High School in Texas. (*Courtesy Nadine and Darlene Adams*)

William Lipscomb played offensive guard for the New Caney High School football team. (*Courtesy Nadine and Darlene Adams*)

**Bill Lipscomb Sr.
Offensive Guard**

Kathy married Bill Lipscomb and her sister Darlene married Gary Sanford in a double wedding ceremony. (*Courtesy Nadine and Darlene Adams*)

Bill Lipscomb with his infant daughter.
(*Courtesy Nadine and Darlene Adams*)

Training Squadron at Lackland Air Force Base in
San Antonio, Texas where Lipscomb turned airmen
into drill sergeants. (*Author's collection*)

Sgt. Bill Lipscomb was General's Flag Bearer during a
military parade at Lackland Air Force Base.
(*Author's collection*)

(Left to right) David Adams, Nadine Adams,
Darlene Adams Sanford, Charles W. Adams.
(*Courtesy Nadine and Darlene Adams*)

Photo of Bill Lipscomb taken by the sheriff the night after Kathy's murder. (*Courtesy Bexar County, Texas Sheriff's Office*)

Bill Lipscomb's former apartment where Kathy was murdered. (*Author's collection*)

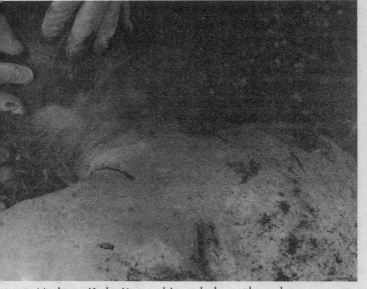
Marks on Kathy Lipscomb's neck show where she was strangled. (*Courtesy Bexar County, Texas Sheriff's Office*)

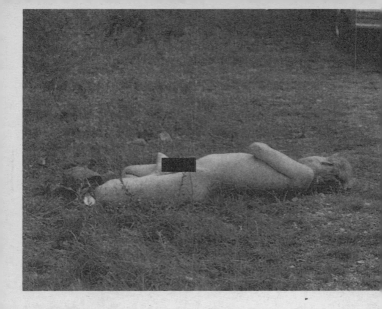

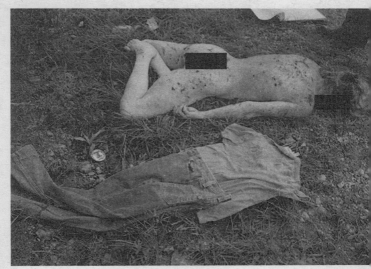

Kathy Libscomb's legs were bent when she was found
with her clothing neatly rolled beside her.
(*Courtesy Bexar County, Texas Sheriff's Office*)

The house Lipscomb built for himself with Kathy's insurance money. (*Author's collection*)

KATHLEEN ADAMS LIPSCOMB
BELOVED WIFE AND MOTHER
SEPT. 1, 1956 – JUNE 8, 1986

Kathy Lipscomb's gravestone in Haughton, LA.
(*Courtesy Nadine and Darlene Adams*)

(Left to right) OSI Special Agent Richard Fife, OSI Special Agent Barney Stegall, Prosecution Attorney Capt. Bruce Ambrose, Asst. Prosecution Attorney Brett Coakley, Asst. Prosecution Attorney Capt. Joseph Townsend. (*Courtesy Nadine and Darlene Adams*)

Private investigator
Mike Guidry.
(*Courtesy Mike Guidry*)

Dr. Charles P. McDowell,
Air Force OSI's Chief of
Homicide Investigations.
(*Courtesy Charles P.
McDowell*)

Bill Lipscomb at Fort Leavenworth Penitentiary in November, 1996. (*Author's collection*)

opinion that he was not distraught over his wife's death and he did not project any grief.''

With her last words, she bent her head and broke down crying—exhausted and relieved at the same time. The information had haunted her for over two years and giving the testimony had served as a catharsis.

The investigators still had no physical proof that Lipscomb had murdered Kathleen. At no time had Shannon placed Lipscomb as the murderer. On the contrary, her testimony had explicitly stated that he had employed another person to do the job.

Fife looked hopefully at her and asked, ''Sergeant Gilbert, you said that Lipscomb hired someone to kill his wife.''

''Yes, sir,'' she said, still crying.

''If he did hire someone, would you have any idea who that person might be?''

Shannon took a deep breath and struggled to maintain composure. ''Yes, sir,'' she said quietly. ''I'd suggest you find Tony Barrelo.''

Over the next month, Shannon Gilbert continued to help the authorities, but she grew impatient to leave the country. At one time, she suggested being hypnotized to assist her recall, but the OSI voiced no problem with her memory.

Frequently she, Bevans, and Guidry would go out together and talk about the case. They learned about her rocky marital history and two divorces. One of the marriages had produced a son, now seven years old. As a child, Shannon had been sexually abused, and was still in therapy to cope with her trauma.

At one of these get-togethers, the investigators decided to have her call Lipscomb. Bevans explained how he would wire her phone to a recorder and promised to be there to feed her questions.

The detectives chose January 12 as the date to make the call, two days before she was to leave the country. After that, all of her records anyone had access to would be erased. The Air Force had placed her under strict orders not to tell anyone which country she had chosen. There would be a P.O. box number in San Antonio where friends could send her mail, and she would write to that box, then the Air Force would send the mail on in each direction. Tightest secrecy would be observed— and only her parents and a couple of close friends would know her phone number.

On the 12th, Bevans and Guidry arrived at Shannon's house to find she had been drinking. The thought of speaking to Lipscomb appalled her and she had sought refuge in alcohol.

Shannon suggested that the master bedroom contained the easiest access for wiring a phone. Two of her female military friends who had come to help her pack were in the room.

As Bevans connected the recorder to the phone, Shannon started crying. Bevans tried to lighten the situation. "Save those tears for Bill. They'll make him feel guilty."

No one breathed as Lipscomb's phone rang, then he picked up the receiver.

"Bill, it's Shannon. Listen, I need to talk to you. Can you talk to me?"

He had to be surprised to hear from someone he hadn't spoken with for two and a half years, yet his voice remained calm, albeit unfriendly.

"The OSI called me in today and they're going to call me back in tomorrow, and I'm kinda scared."

"Of what?"

"Of what? Of everything you told me. They're going to ask me about everything you said."

"About Kathleen?"

"Yes. They showed me all kinds of stuff and you know she

told the psychologist about you and me. She told everybody about everything. They've got her diary with my name in it. They've got names and WAPS test scores and everything. The WAPS regulation is perfectly clear, and my ass is going to hang for you. I know about everything and I'm going to get in trouble over it.''

''There was nothing wrong with anything that we did.''

''Bill, there was too, and you know it. I want to tell you something right now, Bill. They told me they could order me to say whatever I know, and I don't want to tell them what you told me.''

''What have I told you?''

''Do I have to say it?''

''Can you say it, or is your phone bugged?''

She looked at the detectives for direction, and Bevans nodded for her to tell.

''You know, how you were going to have her killed.''

''No, no.''

''You never told me? Is that what you're saying?'' Shannon sounded incredulous.

''If I told you that, it was only how I felt at the time—how we were both feeling when I went through the divorce, but it wasn't true. Just tell them about the WAPS tests and don't tell them anything else.''

Just as Bevans had orchestrated Darlene Sanford during her call to Lipscomb, he furiously wrote notes to Shannon: ''Get emotional, cry, swear!''

''You don't remember that night I called you when I found out about her death, and later when I called you from the convenience store?''

''I don't remember any calls.''

Shannon's hand flew to her mouth in disbelief.

''No,'' Lipscomb continued. ''My mind went blank and lots of things happened that I don't honestly remember. Why are you going to have to say anything?''

"Because, Bill, if they start asking me questions I'm going to have to come clean because I don't want to implicate myself."

"You're not going to implicate yourself. Why don't you just talk to the OSI? You haven't done anything."

"Oh, bullshit, I have too. Bill, you told me all that stuff several times. That you were going to have her killed and I would read about it in the newspapers. You told me you used a ring as a down payment. You said you punched a hole in her oil pan. Don't you lie to me." Now she needed no prodding. Her emotions flew freely.

"No. I didn't do any of this."

Shannon became furious. "Then you lied to me an awful lot, didn't you? You're going to let me fry over something stupid that you did."

"Listen, Shannon. There are some private investigators, and they've been harassing everybody until now they apparently have found someone they can harass that I was close to at that time when I let my emotions go and said things I didn't mean. Those were things that anyone would say in that situation."

"No, not anybody, Bill. I've been through two divorces, and I've never threatened to kill anybody."

"Shannon, I don't know where you came up with all this stuff."

"You told me all this stuff, goddamn it, and you know it. Don't fuck with me, Bill. Just don't fuck with me."

"I didn't tell you she had a boyfriend."

"Yes you did. You told me you found her birth control pills."

"Shannon, you were a very close friend and I confided in you, but you have to believe that I didn't do it, because I didn't."

"I can't, and I need a lawyer."

"You want me to hire a lawyer for you? I don't see how a lawyer is going to help you."

"If I have to go in and tell all this stuff without a lawyer, then I'm going to get into trouble too, and I can't afford to lose my military job."

"I don't have the money to give you."

"Then I'll just have to go in and tell them everything."

"It sounds like you're blackmailing me."

"I'm not blackmailing you."

"We broke off our relationship a long time ago. Now I've got to go."

"Breaking up doesn't change what you told me," she said, swallowing hard. "More than ever I believe that it's true, because you're covering up everything that you ever said to me."

"I've got to go, Shannon."

Her voice became stronger. "Bill, call me a liar on everything else, but don't call me a liar on things that you've told me."

"I've got to go."

"Why do you have to go, because I'm bringing back all the memories?"

Everyone in the room heard the click when Lipscomb hung up. Although they had only heard Shannon's side of the conversation, it didn't take much imagination to discern what Lipscomb had said.

Shannon looked at the detectives. She knew that she lacked the fine art of argument, nevertheless, she felt she had left Lipscomb with the chilling and unmistakable fear that she would cooperate with the authorities.

"I think you were able to get him to wiggle and squirm a little with that," Bevans figured, as he started unplugging the wires. Begrudgingly, he said, "I still have to admire Lipscomb's ability to admit as little as possible." Bevans removed the tape to have it transcribed for the OSI file.

Two days later, Shannon left.

*   *   *

As the year changed to 1989, so did the authority over Kathleen Lipscomb's murder. On January 20, the United States Air Force's Office of Special Investigation took full jurisdiction of the case, and the Bexar County Sheriff turned everything over to them.

As the OSI hunted down Tony Barrelo, Tom Bevans called Sergeant Martin, Bill Lipscomb's supervisor and the first person who had mentioned Barrelo to the authorities. Raymond Martin sounded genuinely interested as he inquired about the progress of the case.

"You said that Tony was Bill's best friend. What made you think that?" Bevans asked.

"Well for one thing, I knew they were sharing an apartment part of the time, and they spent a lot of their free time together. At work, they were forever talking to each other."

"You're not the only one to tell us about Barrelo. Apparently there's a good chance that he's the tie-in to the murder."

"You might want to check with the apartment people where they lived," Martin suggested. "Possibly they could add something to this. Let me look up Tony on our records that we've filed away. I might still have his last address." A few minutes later, Sergeant Martin called back with the information.

On his next trip to San Antonio, Bevans searched out the last known residence for Sergeant Barrelo. It was an older brick apartment complex. The manager, a tired-looking woman with gray streaked hair, sat behind a desk laden with papers. When she looked up and saw Tom, she said, "Sorry, no vacancies."

Bevans flashed his investigator identification.

"Now what?" the woman said, appearing irritated.

"About three years ago a Sergeant Tony Barrelo lived here with a roommate, and I thought maybe if you had some records—"

"Even on a good day, I couldn't forget Tony Barrelo. He had to be one of the *worst* tenants I ever had in my life. Never paid his rent on time. I'd have to bitch at him every time I saw him, and he kept saying, 'Wait until the end of the year. I'll come in and pay you off completely.' Then that damn guy would push his greasy motorcycle up to his second-floor apartment and take it apart on the carpet. Believe me. I won't soon forget Tony."

"Did you finally get paid?"

"Every penny. I'm a pack rat. I keep all those records. You never know when the IRS will start hounding. Come with me. I should have all that stuff in a closet."

Bevans followed her down a dark hallway and into a closet brimming with tattered boxes of old leases that were stacked in a haphazard fashion. Bevans couldn't imagine finding anything there.

The manager started pushing and pulling on boxes, then found one with "1986" printed at one end. "Here it is," she said, pulling out a file with "Barrelo" typed on it.

Bevans sorted through the folder and found a letter from Barrelo stating that he was going to come into some money later in the year, and promised to pay all back rent at that time. Barrelo had paid more than two thousand dollars in November. "Cash" had been printed in the payment column.

"He paid in cash?"

"Yeah. It was kinda funny. He had this big wad of money and proceeded to pull out bills. But he paid in full. I kept his deposit to replace the carpet, though. No way those cleaning people could get out all that grease."

Bevans hurriedly left and called Rich Fife. They discussed how the payment to the apartment manager coincided with the time Lipscomb received the insurance money, and Bevans and Fife came to the same conclusion: "Tony's our boy!"

Chapter Fourteen

The very next week, the OSI located Roger Anthony Barrelo, living in Hampton, Virginia, only three miles from Langley Air Force Base and nine miles from Lipscomb. Encircled by sparkling water, Hampton and the base are located on a peninsula jutting out into Chesapeake Bay that streams into the Atlantic Ocean.

Special Agent Barney Stegall, Rich Fife's counterpart at Langley, presided as the superintendent of the OSI there. All OSI personnel are referred to as "agent," whether enlisted personnel, officers, or civilians. Never wearing uniforms frees every agent to investigate personnel of any rank. Stegall was a 1974 graduate from the OSI Academy who had joined the Air Force five years before that.

Rich phoned Stegall and said, "Dr. McDowell tells me you are going to help us on a murder we have in Texas that's older than dirt."

"That's what I hear. We're wondering why you Texans are so damn slow at investigating."

Rich Fife laughed. ''I think it's been a hot potato that each law enforcement agency keeps tossing to the next higher level. This case involved a nurse who was killed almost three years ago, and her murderer's been a superman at escaping the law. At least he's been too clever for anybody to catch.''

''What do you want me to do here?''

''There's a guy in your area who's an ex-sergeant and possibly could have been hired to do the job. We have zero authority over him since he's a civilian, however this murder took place when he was in the Air Force—a training instructor at that.''

Stegall shook his head and wrote down the information Rich gave him.

''For now, just get background,'' Fife told him. We want to know where Barrelo works, what he does, who he sees, and especially if he sees a M.Sgt. Bill Lipscomb.''

As soon as Stegall got off the phone, he assigned an agent to make a computer run on Barrelo's employment record since moving to Virginia. Of the many strings to grasp, that seemed the logical first choice, and the record might reveal a pattern that could shed some light on the possible murderer.

In the meantime, Mike Guidry's relationship with Nadine Adams and Darlene Sanford was nearing the breaking point as his ''no more than $7,500'' price tag had billowed to $26,000. Nadine was still trying to sell her house, but the large ranch home in the country proved to be a slow sell. The women were paying Guidry a few hundred dollars whenever they could.

Since Tom Bevans had been the messenger with Guidry's original estimate, he felt guilty. He talked Guidry into writing off $3,000 of the total bill, but the remaining $23,000 still represented an insurmountable sum for the family. By letter, Darlene told Guidry in mid-February that they appreciated all he had done for them, but with the OSI acquiring the case, his company's services would no longer be needed. Guidry dropped the case and advised Tom to do likewise. However, Bevans' heart remained committed to the family. He had developed a personal vendetta to find the murderer, and knowing that taxes should have paid for the investigation and not the family's hard-earned money, Bevans vowed to work for free.

Five months before she died, Kathleen had gone to the Air Force's Mental Health Clinic at Wilford Hall Medical Center seeking support in dealing with her husband. Kathleen had told her family about the counseling. Darlene had disclosed this information to Sergeant Baker and urged him to contact the clinic, but Baker reported that the clinic wouldn't cooperate. When The Guidry Group took the reins, she supplied them with the same information in addition to a release to obtain Kathleen's medical records. Guidry wrote the doctors and soon received a letter from Captain Jaggi at Wilford Hall revealing that immediately after Kathleen's death, they sent word to the sheriff that they had information that might be helpful to them regarding the husband's threats.

As Wilford Hall was an Air Force medical center, OSI Agent Rich Fife volunteered to interview the doctors himself, hoping that a shared military experience would give an advantage. He believed the doctors would be eager to reveal information they had kept bottled up for over two years. Most of Kathleen's reports had been signed by the Chief of Outpatient Services, Col. James R. Spadoni, who had vested 15 years in psychiatry and headed the women's therapy groups.

Located at Lackland, the 10-story Wilford Hall Medical Center towered as the largest structure on base.

Col. Spadoni sat at his desk, his dark eyes intent even when he smiled. He offered Rich Fife a chair.

"I've taken the time to look over Kathy's file since you called," the doctor began. "I do remember her. She was bright, but also very angry. Kathy first came to us in early January of

1986. She told us she wanted to end her unhappy marriage. Apparently her husband had a dominant and controlling personality.''

"He taught drill sergeants." Fife laughed. "What can we expect?"

Dr. Spadoni smiled. "That's right. But that control resulted in physical problems for her." He turned to his notes. "Here are some of her symptoms: insomnia, uncontrollable crying, and loss of appetite. Obviously this guy was getting to her. But she wanted to be emotionally and financially prepared, because she planned to leave him and feared that he would try to stop her.

"We decided to place her in a women's therapy group, and it worked well. Being in a group of about fifteen put her in contact with other women who were in a similar situation and they gave each other support and feedback."

"Did anything come up that particularly stuck in your mind?" Fife asked.

"Yes, several times she expressed fear of her husband. One day she crept into the session very quietly—not at all like Kathy. The other women wanted to know what was wrong. Kathy told them she had fought with her husband over their divorce because he intended to pay family members and friends to lie about her in court so he would gain custody of the children. Apparently he had received some money from his father to battle for child custody.

"As I recall, she told him, 'If you tell lies about me, I'll tell the truth about you, and we'll see which one is deemed the more acceptable parent.' ''

"Did she ever say what the truth was?"

"A couple times she used the term 'illegal activities.' Once she said her husband copied pornographic videos and sold them, but she seemed hesitant to relate more."

"Copied pornographic videos?" Fife had to laugh again. "This was one busy guy."

"Kathy looked pretty nervous about discussing his illegal activities, so we didn't push it."

"Let's get back to Kathleen telling the truth about him," Fife said. "Did he say what he'd do to her?"

"I've got that in my notes. He told her, 'I'm not the only one who would be unhappy with what you'd say. There would be other very unhappy people.' I remember precisely the phrase she used next: 'Are you telling me I'll end up on a slab?'"

"And her husband said?"

"I guess he didn't refute her words. I felt she might need a restraining order or something, so I advised her to get a good lawyer before she did anything. I didn't want her putting herself into jeopardy."

A tap on the door interrupted their conversation, and Capt. Christine M. Jaggi entered the room.

Dr. Spadoni introduced the psychologist to Fife, and explained, "Capt. Jaggi became involved toward the end of Kathy's therapy."

"Were you able to help her?" Fife asked them both.

"Yes," Spadoni said, "right away we saw progress. Kathleen stopped being so nervous and seemed to develop a new self-confidence."

Dr. Jaggi nodded. "As time went on, she grew less anxious and more determined. Then by mid-March she became angry again when she told us about her husband's girlfriend. Apparently the woman felt free to call him at home."

"I know she wanted to get out of her marriage then and there," the doctor recalled, "but she still felt her husband might use their children, as she said, 'to get to her.' He had apparently tried that when she filed for divorce the year before."

"I have Kathy's log here," Dr. Jaggi said, taking papers out of a folder. "It was April 8th when she revealed her romantic involvement with someone. She was hesitant to discuss it, fearing others in the group would 'throw stones,' as she put it. But after the group had listened to her husband's antics for four months, they were supportive. We saw Kathy grow stronger and become more independent after that. But the staff and the entire group were disturbed when Kathy told us about threatening to divulge her husband's illegal activities. I think she did this to force him into giving her child custody, but we thought it seemed a very dangerous thing to do, and cautioned her against doing it again. Kathy could tell we were afraid and I believe she thought it was justified.''

"I'm looking at the same log," Dr. Spadoni said. "Since her divorce would be final near the end of May, we had to terminate our services because she'd no longer be an Air Force dependent. My notes say: 'Kathy will need a lot of support—especially through the month of June.' ''

The room grew quiet and the three stared at each other.

Rich also interviewed Dr. Proctor, the counselor with whom Shannon Gilbert had spoken on the day Lipscomb had told her about Kathleen's murder. Shannon, anxious to prove her story, had given the OSI a release to obtain her medical records.

Dr. Proctor pulled up his computer file on Shannon Gilbert, and told Rich Fife, "I see here that she called June 15th, 1986. She sounded like she had been drinking, at least she was very agitated. My notes aren't clear for that day, but neither was Shannon. She babbled on about someone being murdered and cried throughout the entire conversation. Then the next day she came in and we visited for over an hour. At that time she was attending one of our therapy groups, but she explicitly didn't want the group to hear what she had to say."

The doctor went on to detail everything Shannon had told him, which essentially supported her statement to the OSI.

Later Fife called Darlene to ask if she knew about the pornographic videos.

"Absolutely, I knew," Darlene told him in a disgusted voice. "Bill had a big satellite dish outside his house that gave him access to the Blue Max cable channel. He made copies of the videos to sell. This revolted Kathleen, especially when he watched them with other people in the room. But the WAPS scam was far more dangerous, so that's what she worried about most.

"It always blew my mind how the Air Force saw him as being so perfect. I know his on-the-job performance made him seem wonderful, but really, he had to be two separate people."

The next week, OSI Headquarters in Washington D.C. notified Agent Fife that they were being given a 'Special Interest Case' designation. That meant the case would have top priority, and be assigned two full-time criminal specialists. This was in addition to the OSI's top criminal psychologist, Dr. Charles P. McDowell, Chief of the Analysis Division of the Directorate of Criminal Investigations, planning the search. In two weeks McDowell would visit San Antonio to lend his own brand of investigating—establishing a profile of the murderer.

Fife made a quick call to Sergeant Baker to see if the sperm sample had shown up. Baker told him it hadn't, and they were now looking for the serologist who lost it.

OSI Agent Barney Stegall organized four agents from his office to help with the case. Rich Fife had often referred to Sergeant Lipscomb as one of the main players in the murder scenario, so Stegall pulled up the sergeant's reviews and found that uncommon praise continued to be lavished on him as the Vehicle Operations Manager at Langley.

Capt. Linda Goodbrake said that "Bill's dedication and attention to detail were instrumental in his branch being selected 'Best in TAC for 1988.'" Lt. Col. Michael Becker commended

Lipscomb's "management of vehicle support as absolutely superior. Promote now." Col. Richard Myers designated him as "One of the top NCO's in the Air Force." And Maj. Gen. Henry Canterbury observed Lipscomb as, "Articulate and always organized, and that the appearance and mechanical condition of the vehicle fleet at Langley are superb. Promote—he will produce."

When Agent Stegall used OSI contacts to track down Barrelo, he found a very different situation. It seemed that Barrelo had had several jobs after arriving in Hampton, Virginia, in September 1987. He hadn't worked anywhere the first two weeks, probably sitting around his parents' house trying to pull himself together. Then he ran into an ex-Air Force colonel who bought and sold classic cars. Barrelo worked with him for several months, then briefly for a local Montgomery Ward. At Ward's, Stegall talked with a fellow employee of Barrelo's who recalled his getting a phone call around late January. According to the employee, when Barrelo talked, he had whispered and shielded the mouthpiece with his hand. After the call, Barrelo had confided that it came from a friend whose wife had been murdered in Texas.

While Stegall kept tabs on Barrelo in Virginia, Rich explored Barrelo's career at Lackland. According to Barrelo's annual reviews, he had been one of the youngest NCOs to be promoted to the prestigious position of Training Instructor, but after mid-1986, small infractions arose. The first hint that he was beginning to slip came in the weekly log: "Sergeant Barrelo frequently is late reporting for duty." Later, a report read: "Sergeant Barrelo is suspected of substance abuse; he is continually insubordinate, and suspected of having financial problems." Rich knew that Barrelo's bosses would scrutinize him closely after hearing about drug abuse.

Even with all of his problems, it surprised Rich Fife to read that Sergeant Barrelo voluntarily requested to be relieved of his TI position and demoted to a basic training instructor. The next to last of the reviews included a statement concerning Sergeant Barrelo's "dereliction of duty" for completely failing to show up for a class. After that, Barrelo had apparently resigned from the Air Force, leaving at the end of his tour of duty. His file stated: "Not Eligible for Re-enlistment."

With the Air Force less than enamored with Barrelo, Rich knew there had to be more to the story. He called the sergeant who had signed the last report. The man remembered the promising NCO who seemed to fragment before his eyes. The sergeant likened Barrelo to a time bomb, reporting that on one occasion he had the nerve to go to the 3734 Squadron Commander to tell him he had to take some of the stress out of the TI program. The commander said, "Who in the hell are you to tell me how to run my place?"

The sergeant related that when Barrelo resigned, he said, "Lipscomb set me up, then he hung me out to dry."

Rich found his information compelling. One of the most dramatic indicators of a person's guilt is a stark change in his post-offense behavior. Barrelo had been a poster boy for the Air Force before Kathleen's death. Now he was a disgrace.

As the OSI promised, their chief murder expert, Dr. Charles P. McDowell, flew into San Antonio's Lackland Air Force Base. He had been with the Air Force since 1963, but had left in 1969 to pursue his Ph.D. in criminal justice at North Texas University. After working full-time as a college professor, he had accepted a position as a civilian OSI special agent in 1981, and had become their specialist in death investigations. McDowell reviewed the case with Fife.

"I read the facts of the case and, frankly, I'm a little dismayed. Correct me if I'm wrong, and I hope I am, but this is what I understand," he said, loosening his tie. "The victim was a military dependent and hence a civilian, and the killing appeared to have taken place off base. This places the matter out of the OSI's jurisdiction and into the hands of the Bexar County Sheriff's Department.'' He looked at Fife. ''You know, I was never aware of this murder until two and a half years after it happened.''

''None of us were,'' Fife told him. ''I sent you that spot report about it around December 1988.''

McDowell returned to his notes. ''No suspect had been developed so far, and that's why the victim's mother hired Mike Guidry, who went to the OSI for help.''

''I don't think OSI had any intention of actually investigating the murder until Guidry turned up Shannon Gilbert,'' Rich told him. ''She looked like she could implicate Lipscomb, so we had a place to start.''

''Right, that's how I see it. At this point it seemed likely that Lipscomb played a direct role in the murder by either hiring a killer or doing it himself.'' Then Dr. McDowell turned to Fife. ''Do you realize how stale this case is?''

Fife nodded. ''No crime scene and the passage of lots of time. To complicate matters, we suspected that Bill had been fed information on the investigation by someone in the sheriff's department. The Bexar County D.A. told the sheriff that they didn't have enough solid information to secure an indictment, and after Lipscomb moved to Virginia, they had no jurisdiction to go after him. That's how it landed in our lap.''

Dr. McDowell's main task was to put the pieces of the murder back together. He had to place himself into the mind of the murderer, and by using the available facts and the clues from the crime, reconstruct a broad scenario.

The fiftyish investigator looked professorial with his glasses and mustache. He was bright, empathetic, and very easy to talk with. Even suspects tended to forget the pivotal position he held, and spoke openly to him. All the detectives and agents respectfully called him Dr. McDowell. Because of McDowell's expertise in murder, Tom Bevans dubbed him ''Dr. Death.''

Dr. McDowell visited the site where Kathleen's body had

been placed, but now it was spring. What had been straw-like stubble that Kathleen had been thrown on now grew soft and green. Brightly colored flowers pierced the landscape and the area looked serene.

He left Scenic Loop to go back into the city, where he visited both Kathleen's and Lipscomb's apartment buildings, then circled back to Luby's Cafeteria, where her car had been parked. He methodically examined each area and grasped a feel for the case through the physical experience of being there. He asked that Lipscomb's telephone and bank records be pulled, and requested a copy of the complete case file to take with him. As he tucked papers into his briefcase, he promised to return the following month, and with a smile said, "Well, I must confess. I love a tough case."

At Langley, the headquarters of the Tactical Air Command, Bill Lipscomb's multitude of responsibilities included being the Squadron Career Advisor, an additional job he had volunteered for over and above his occupation. It was that extra effort which demonstrated his gung-ho dedication and endeared him to his superiors. As a career adviser, he customarily received the personnel files on everyone in his squadron.

One day while he worked in the squadron office filing the April reports, he was shocked to see a "2J" code on his own file. He knew it meant "under investigation by civilian or military officials." He sensed a storm was brewing.

Ricky Rios had called Lipscomb continuously to keep him apprised of the efforts of the private detectives and the OSI, but this code indicated a serious turn of events. Its discovery led Lipscomb to go to his squadron commander, to whom he explained that his ex-mother-in-law in Texas was trying to frame him on some trumped up charge, and he wanted to know what was happening.

Wanting to help the highly decorated master sergeant, the

commander immediately called OSI, who advised him that the investigation only covered a question on the WAPS test, and it was no big deal. In fact, they advised the commander to tell Lipscomb to "just blow it off."

Unsatisfied with that response, Lipscomb went to the legal office for aid. He talked the Air Force lawyers into calling Special Agent Franklin, who headed OSI, to find out what information they had on him, and learned that Franklin wouldn't reveal anything on the case. Even when pressured by Langley's legal department for more information, Franklin refused to elaborate.

Now Lipscomb was scared.

The OSI hoped that in Lipscomb's present state of panic, he would reveal something about his role in the murder. Shortly after Lipscomb discovered the "2J" code, the OSI detected that Shannon Gilbert's previous work station at Lackland began to receive calls from a Major Coleman, insisting on talking with Shannon. The receptionist there thought she recognized Lipscomb's voice.

The phone records Dr. McDowell had ordered were like a road map guiding the OSI and the detectives through all the calls Lipscomb had made from his home. The records exposed that soon after Shannon had called Lipscomb, he had phoned Barrelo at work. The OSI concluded this might have been Barrelo's first warning that a murder investigation was under way.

April 25, 1989, would become "interrogation day" at Lackland. Before Dr. McDowell's scheduled trip back to Texas, he had asked Darlene for all the latest photographs she could get of her sister, Lipscomb, and their children. By now Darlene didn't question. She appreciated OSI's creative approach and willingly did anything required of her.

Sergeant Dalton Baker called Rich Fife. "I have good news for you. We found those lost body fluids from Kathleen Lipscomb. It appears they've been frozen all this time under the name 'Jane Doe.' Apparently nobody checked the number written on them. We'll get those off for you right now."

Fife replied quickly, "Don't do a thing! I'll be over immediately to pick them up and I'll send them for testing myself." Then he notified the OSI at both Lackland and Langley to start drawing up the paperwork to pull body fluids from Lipscomb, Ricky Rios, and Tony Barrelo.

Dr. McDowell walked briskly into the OSI office at Lackland with Bevans and Fife. He had landed 30 minutes earlier from Washington D.C. and had told the men he had spent hours profiling the case.

"Here's the way I see it," McDowell began. "Every murder has three dynamic components: the victim, the subject, and the crime scene." He tapped the table with his pen at the mention of each component. "If I have any two of these, but a third is missing, I can usually solve the missing part based on what we *do* have. In this case we only have sketchy information of the scene. Remember, we don't actually have the crime scene. What we have is the dump site. But the dump site is particularly important because it tells what I believe to be a false story, and false stories are always more instructive than true stories."

"A false story is better?" Bevans asked, sounding surprised.

"Right, it always tells more because of what's being covered up. For example, the sheriff found her car at a different location from her body. Usually abductors use their own vehicles. If they don't have one, then they take the victim's. This means that the abductor had to have gained control over her in or near her car, removed her from it, and then taken the car to where they recovered it. Somewhere in the middle of all this he'd have killed her and taken her to Scenic Loop. This is too complicated and unwieldy. It just doesn't match reality.''

''So what is reality?'' Fife asked.

''Think about where she was dumped—an isolated area out on a stretch of Scenic Loop. When the kill site is different from the dump site—like this out-of-the way place—it suggests that the murderer wanted to mask the true location of the crime. And there's usually a reason for that. The real crime scene had to be a place familiar to the victim, or a place where the victim might normally be found.''

''But the medical examiner said she had been raped and sodomized,'' Bevans interjected.

''I know what you're saying, since she was found nude. A nude, dead female normally tells a story of a rape-murder following an abduction, but this picture didn't feel right. First of all, she was too clean. Normally rape-murder victims are a real mess. They don't look anything like Kathleen looked. They're usually severely beaten, their faces smashed in, and often there are defense wounds and other physical indicators of how the perpetrator imposed his control over her. None of these were found on Kathleen.

''The Regional Crime Lab found vaginal sperm estimated to be twenty hours old, so she probably had consensual sex prior to her murder. The anal swabs were negative for semen, which means she either sustained a foreign object penetration or a protected penile penetration. I believe Lipscomb intended to kill her and make it look like a sex crime. Who would have suspected the estranged husband of raping his wife? That's where he was clever, because that would draw attention away from him. Anyway, the story the dump site told at first blush was that of an abduction, rape and murder—but since it did not match what we know about such crimes, I rejected that story.

"The placement of the body, fully exposed and face-up, with her clothes nearby, strongly suggested that someone dumped her who was not close to her. For whatever reasons, intimates tend to either cover their victims or at least conceal their faces. Also, we have coined an interesting phrase—'finder by proxy.' People who murder usually prefer the crime to be discovered by a third party—in other words, a stranger. Clearly, Kathleen's body was placed in such a manner that it would be discovered— and discovered quickly—by an uninvolved third party. And that's exactly what happened.

"After mulling this over, I concluded that Lipscomb was responsible for her death, but I don't know if he actually killed her. I was certain, however, that someone else dumped her body, and that's good news."

"Right. That shows he had help," Fife said.

McDowell nodded. "Whenever you have more than one principle in a serious crime, you have a golden opportunity to drive a wedge between them and entice one into implicating the other. I'm also certain that if Lipscomb didn't actually kill her, he had to have been physically present for her murder, in light of his extremely controlling personality."

"He watched someone kill his wife?" Bevans asked.

"Could have," McDowell nodded.

"The bastard," Bevans said, folding his arms across his chest.

"That might not have happened, Tom. That's only one scenario. What I really think is that he most likely is the killer and he had an accomplice who dumped her body and disposed of her car. So, gentleman, that's my profile of the crime. Now we've got to weave that into some kind of working hypothesis so we can get on with solving this thing."

Fife said, "Doc, I know we've all been thinking how purely

circumstantial this case is. We have so little to go on because we can't even be sure of our physical evidence.''

''The evidence hasn't been handled properly,'' McDowell said, ''and the age factor is bothering everybody. But the problem is putting this all together. That's where Ricky Rios comes in. I don't think he's involved in the murder because he's such a wimp. But maybe we can use him as our Judas goat to lead us to someone who was involved. In order to make it work, we have to completely scare him, then gradually ease up as he cooperates. We're interviewing him tomorrow, and the Air Force is offering him immunity for his help. Let's hope he'll go for that.''

''And if he doesn't?'' Bevans asked.

''It will be a much harder battle.''

McDowell looked at his watch. ''We have an appointment to meet with the base commander in fifteen minutes. When you first involved OSI last year, the commander only knew about the WAPS scam. I don't think we've updated him since. I thought we should tell him what we know about the scam and fill him in on the murder.''

''We're going over there now?'' Bevans asked.

''Yes. In just a few minutes.''

''That's the headquarters building where Ricky Rios works.''

''I know.''

''He'll see us.''

''I hope so.''

Bevans whistled. ''This will paralyze him.''

A few minutes later, Dr. McDowell, Bevans, Fife and three other OSI agents dressed in dark suits paraded down the hall of the Lackland Air Force Base Headquarters. They could have taken a more direct route to the commander's office, but they chose the one that marched them past the commandant's office where Ricky Rios worked. With perfect timing, they neared the commandant's office as Rios stood by the doorway. Astonishment flashed across his face when he saw the imposing group. Bevans knew that Rios would remember him as one of the two detectives who had interrogated him. Bevans' companions, with their military carriage and civilian attire, would be recognized by Rios as OSI. Bevans put on his gruffest expression, but later admitted it was hard to keep a straight face. He suspected that Rios would soon place a phone call to Langley.

The next day, Fife helped Dr. McDowell set up a small interview room in the OSI building. The cozy atmosphere was part of McDowell's plan. Fife looked quizzically at the photographs until he heard Dr. McDowell's explanation.

"Put those pictures of Kathleen in her wedding dress on the table right in front of where Ricky will sit. Next to that let's use one from her autopsy. Okay, we'll place the children and Kathleen here."

They continued displaying the short life and long death of Kathleen Lipscomb until they had constructed a psychological nightmare.

"These are my favorites," McDowell said with a mischievous grin as he picked up two easels. "They will hold phony 'Things To Do' lists, such as 'Pick up transcripts of Rios' telephone taps', and 'Coordinate with FBI and the U.S. Attorney General.' We'll throw in some fabricated leads, too."

When they had finished, the room was stuffed with a graphic display of Kathleen's life, death, and the outline of an effective investigation that looked like the OSI was only hours away from nabbing the murderer.

Dr. McDowell cordially escorted Rios into the room, then excused himself to take a phantom telephone call. McDowell went to a two-way mirror to watch Rios and smiled as he got up and walked over to the "Things To Do" board and read about the rapid OSI progress.

When McDowell returned ten minutes later, Rios had turned ashen. McDowell had two agents with him that he had flown in from Washington D.C., Dave Stoll and David Walker, whom he introduced as being from OSI Headquarters. These agents were there strictly for window dressing. For the government to go to that kind of expense, Ricky, who was already shaking, had to realize that the OSI considered this a very important meeting.

Dr. McDowell changed his cordial manner. Without being rude, but with a new edge of firmness to his voice he said, "Ricky, I'm going to tell you two things. Do not screw with me, and do not lie."

Rios' eyes, already large from what he had been reading and seeing in the room, now anxiously searched the agent's stern face.

"I'm going to ask you some questions, but I already know the answers to them, so again, don't lie to me."

Rios stirred uneasily in his chair as McDowell told him they were investigating the murder of Kathleen Lipscomb, and thought he could shed some light on it, even though they didn't think he killed her.

Dr. McDowell started the six-hour interrogation easily at first with innocuous questions about how Rios had met Lipscomb, then built to a crescendo that left Rios soaked with both tears and perspiration. He admitted to calling Lipscomb daily to tell him the progress of the case and what Bevans had on him. As predicted, he allowed that he had called Lipscomb about the procession of people visiting headquarters the day before.

Rios' cooperativeness receded as he calmed down, and McDowell sensed he was losing him. Choosing a picture from Kathleen's autopsy, McDowell slapped it down with gusto in front of the sergeant and said sternly, "Do you think this is a joke? I had hoped we could take care of business here without my having to involve your wife. Maybe I need to go to her school and interview her."

Rios tightened up and became very upset. He avoided glancing at the picture. He revealed that he thought Lipscomb could be responsible for the murder and, at the very least, had hired someone to do the killing. However, McDowell didn't sense that Rios had been involved with the actual strangulation because the sergeant, when pressed for information, didn't appear to know the small details of the death.

"What I want you to do," McDowell said, "is to go to Virginia and talk to Bill while you're wearing a wire."

"Oh, no! I'll do anything, but don't make me do that." He stiffened at the agent's suggestion.

McDowell had been successful at convincing Rios that Lipscomb was using him, but it became obvious that he was also very frightened of Lipscomb. McDowell actually wanted the sergeant to call Lipscomb to help spook him about the investigation, and give Lipscomb the idea that the walls were closing in on him. When McDowell suggested that Rios only make a phone call that the OSI would tape, he relaxed and slumped in his chair. He readily agreed because it seemed so much less stressful than being wired and actually facing Lipscomb.

Lipscomb was accustomed to getting calls from Rios so this call didn't set off any alarms. At the time, Lipscomb was at work, and for that reason, their conversation remained brief.

"Bill, it's Ricky. I got called in by the OSI today, and my ass is smoking from it. It was hell, man. They're even worse than those two investigators. You should see all the people working on this case."

"Who's involved now?" Lipscomb asked.

"They've even pulled in the goddamn FBI."

"Oh, shit," Lipscomb said, before hanging up.

At the close of his interview, Dr. McDowell asked Rios if he had any questions.

"What do you have on the WAPS?" he asked. He spoke tentatively, apparently worried that there could be something.

Placing his hand on the sergeant's shoulder, McDowell said, "We have your number on the WAPS. We've pulled all the tests taken the first half of 1986 and have compared them to your other exams. We see that you all of a sudden got real smart over the last year. In fact, it's too much of a jump to think that you didn't have help. But for your cooperation, the Air Force is willing to offer you immunity from prosecution. I know you're concerned about your career, and if you tell us what we need to know, we'll let you keep it. The first step is for you to take a polygraph. Agree?"

"Agreed," Rios said.

Rich Fife retraced many of the steps Tom Bevans had made in order to get his own firsthand impression of the facts. He knew that Kathleen had moved into her apartment only a week before her death. However, he felt it important to talk with any residents who still lived there who had been there at the time of the homicide.

The manager gave Fife the names of seven people. Three were men who remembered Kathy as a great-looking woman, but couldn't recall more than a casual greeting. Two other people didn't remember her. The investigators had told Fife to avoid Hector Salquero, who they felt had been thoroughly checked out. However, one woman, Claudia Hansel, remembered Kathy well.

"I called the sheriff, but no one seemed interested in taking my statement," she told Fife. "It made me feel that what I had to say probably wasn't all that important."

"What were you going to tell them?" Fife asked.

"I wanted them to know that Kathy and I went swimming in the apartment pool that Sunday. It was early in the afternoon. She mentioned she had been without her children all weekend and how much she missed them. Her ex-husband had called. I can't think if he had car trouble or . . . no, I remember, she told me that he said if she'd go over and pick up the children, he'd give her some family pictures she wanted. That was it. I guess if she went there, she could choose the photos.''

"What time was she to get her children?"

"She didn't mention a time. I just remember her saying 'later on.' Since it was already in the afternoon, the way she said it made me think she meant around dinnertime. Anyway, I had to leave about three that afternoon and noticed Kathy's car still parked by her apartment. It was dark when I returned, and I didn't see her car then.''

Fife left Claudia's apartment thinking, damn, what great information she had and how incriminating it could have been if known immediately after the murder. Fife now contemplated the possibility that Kathy could have been killed in Lipscomb's apartment.

Chapter Fifteen

Agent Barney Stegall secured the go-ahead from Dr. McDowell to become visible around Tony Barrelo, even though the FBI had not finished checking the ex-sergeant's background. McDowell drove over from Washington, D.C. to orchestrate Stegall's moves and plan the psychological assault on Barrelo.

In order to launch the plan, the OSI first had to make Barrelo aware of their presence. The ultimate goal of securing his cooperation would be a monumental task since he was the suspected murderer. Judging from his 20 years of OSI investigation, Dr. McDowell estimated that it would take approximately 30 days to undermine Barrelo's self-control. With no OSI jurisdiction over him, and only the word of Shannon Gilbert that Barrelo and Lipscomb were involved, this case had to be unraveled using smoke and mirrors.

Dr. McDowell's strategy for the first day, May 4, dictated an overt surveillance. They started by meeting Barrelo's neighbors. Stegall drove to Barrelo's apartment early that morning and found a U-shaped complex of three brick buildings facing a communal parking lot that allowed each building to look upon the other. He brought along Special Agent Mike Beech, an OSI reserve agent and a special agent with the Virginia State Police. Stegall told Beech to carry his state ID.

The first person they interviewed was a man sitting on the hood of his car playing a guitar. Stegall introduced Beech as a special agent with the Virginia State Police. When questioned, the man acknowledged knowing Barrelo, and pointed out Barrelo's apartment to the investigators. With a minimum of prompting from the officers, he told them what time Barrelo left for work by (7 a.m.), when he usually returned (about 6 p.m.), how often he traveled (rarely), and whether or not he had many visitors (a few). Not surprisingly, the man's interest was piqued and he wanted to know the reason for all the questions.

Stegall scanned the parking lot as if to make sure no one else could hear. Then in a hushed tone, he leaned toward the guitarist and confided, "We're not at liberty to say, but believe me, it's serious. And do me a favor," he added gravely, "don't tell Barrelo."

During the day they questioned over a dozen other apartment neighbors using the same routine, and received basically the same answers, combined with curiosity.

Per Dr. McDowell's strategy, Agents Stegall and Beech arrived at 6:30 the next morning and sat outside Barrelo's apartment in their unmarked OSI car equipped with tall radio antennas and a front seat full of surveillance equipment. McDowell had told Stegall to keep the red light on the dashboard of the car so Barrelo would see it. Also, whenever he was in sight, Stegall was to constantly stare at him.

Even though the men wore no uniforms, anyone who had been in the Air Force would recognize them as OSI from their specialized communication gear. At six-foot-one and 245 pounds, Stegall made a big impression. The OSI reserve agent,

Mike Beech, was a lean, quiet man. He had become accustomed to Stegall doing the talking.

They waited.

About 6:45, Barrelo strolled down the stairs of his apartment and out to the sidewalk to pick up his newspaper. Bare-chested, dressed in gym shorts, and wearing a pair of rubber thongs, he wasn't expecting company.

Barrelo's appearance surprised Stegall. For someone who had been on drugs and done the bidding of a controlling friend, Stegall had expected Barrelo to look emaciated and weak. Instead, he had a strong muscular torso and handsome dark features.

Barrelo glanced over at the car containing two men in suits, coats, and ties, who sat staring at him.

As he turned to go back to his apartment, he stopped to talk with one of his neighbors the investigators had spoken with the previous day. They both rotated to look at the OSI car. The neighbor nodded, and Barrelo returned to his apartment.

Forty-five minutes passed. Barrelo came out dressed in a shirt and tie and climbed into his car, trying to ignore the men who had parked nearby. He left his parking lot and took a right. The OSI agents pulled out and also took a right. Barrelo drove down one block and took another right, this time into the parking lot of another apartment complex, where he pulled into a parking space and stopped. The agents stayed close behind and parked also. However, Stegall and Beech were surprised when Barrelo got out of his car and walked directly toward them. Stegall rolled down his window.

"Good morning. I'm Tony Barrelo. How are you?"

"I'm just fine, Tony. I'm Barney and this here's Mike."

Barrelo couldn't have missed the radio equipment on the front seat now that he stood looking into their car, but he asked, "Is there any particular reason why you're following me?"

"No, not really. Actually, we don't have anything better to do," Stegall told him in a conversational tone.

"Well, if you guys need to talk with me, like if there's anything wrong, I'll be more than happy to have you come into my apartment."

"We appreciate that," Stegall said, "but we really aren't prepared to talk with you right now."

"Okay, but if you want to, I'd be more than happy." Barrelo fished out a business card from his pocket and handed it to Stegall. "You can call me there if you want." Looking disgusted, he turned and walked away.

The agents returned to the OSI office and an hour later, Barrelo called and asked to talk with someone in charge.

"I'll take the call," Stegall offered.

"Hi, Tony, this is Barney Stegall. How are you?"

"Not too well. With you guys following me like that and coming out to my apartment complex, well, that's just not good business." He swallowed hard, then continued. "It looks bad for me when you're asking my neighbors questions. It's making them nervous."

Stegall hadn't detected any nervous neighbors, but he did hear a stammer in Barrelo's voice. "I understand where you're coming from. Have you talked with Bill lately?"

"Ah, Bill, er, Bill, ah . . . You mean, ah, Lipscomb?"

"That's right."

"Yeah, I talked to him. It's been a month or several months since I've spoken to him. It was just to say, 'Hey, how are you doing?' We were stationed together at Lackland."

"Are you sure that's the last time?"

"Well, maybe I called him the first time you guys were out to my neighborhood asking questions."

"Why did you feel you had to talk with him?"

"I heard from a friend in San Antonio that OSI was investigating Lipscomb for something to do with the WAPS compromise. Why?"

"No special reason. I just wondered." Stegall let a silent moment go by, then asked, "Tony, does the date June 8th,

1986, mean anything to you?'' Stegall spoke calmly, but let the force of his words carry the punch.

There was dead silence on the other end of the line.

"No, no, should it?" Barrelo finally sputtered.

"Oh, I just think it's a nice date."

Stegall felt sure that the OSI's strategy of getting Barrelo's attention had hit its mark. He ended their conversation, although he had been tempted to take Barrelo up on his offer of a chat, but at this point he felt unprepared. Before they talked to him again, the FBI had to finish its background check, and the OSI would fly in an agent from Lackland who was well versed on the facts of the case. All this would take over a month, and Barrelo was forced to spend that time stewing in the realization that the OSI wanted him.

The investigation also started to build steam in San Antonio as Ricky Rios flew through his polygraph with flying colors. But two weeks later, Rios was called back for yet another OSI interview, and on this occasion he was a totally different person.

"WAPS? What do you mean? You've got to be kidding. I don't know anything about a testing scam." Now he couldn't remember anything about cheating on a test, or whether anyone else had either.

Agent Rich Fife told him to think about it over the weekend, but on Monday if he didn't cooperate, they would put him through the same process they had a couple of weeks earlier. The room filled with photographs proved to be enough of an incentive, for in just three days, Rios' memory had greatly improved. That following Monday, he confessed to everything on the WAPS. He said they had compromised the test, and he also remembered Lipscomb telling him that Kathleen had threatened to turn him in on the scam. Rios offered to cooperate by divulging the names of everyone else who had been involved, and volunteered that most of the questions and answers came from a source in the Records Center at Randolph Air Force Base. He also told them that when he had talked to Lipscomb about being questioned, Lipscomb had told him, "You do not know anything about anything."

Despite all of Lipscomb's problems, he still carried on his fight with Nadine Adams over her visitation rights with the children. Even as late as mid-May, Lipscomb refused to let the family talk with the children over the phone. When pressured, he promised Nadine she could speak to the kids later, but when she phoned at the appointed time, Nadine received a busy signal. When her irritation reached the boiling point, she'd have the operator check, and invariably be told that there was no conversation on the line. This prompted Nadine to instruct her lawyer to send Lipscomb a letter regarding her court-ordered rights as a grandparent.

But before that letter reached Lipscomb, Nadine was alarmed by information Philip Garrett told her. Garrett, a friend for many years, worked for the Lutheran Brotherhood Insurance Agency, where Nadine had bought a $5,000 policy for each of her four children in 1974. Bill had taken out a policy on Kathleen for $50,000 on August 26, 1985, about nine months before her death, and had requested a policy that awarded double indemnity in case of accidental death. Garrett notified Nadine that Lipscomb, that very morning, had increased his children's life insurance from $5,000 to $36,000 for each child.

"He's going to do it again," she said to herself and her lower lip trembled as she tried to quickly punch in Rich Fife's number. Fife immediately notified Dr. McDowell.

Now that Tom Bevans was helping without remuneration on the case, he was accepted as family. Darlene felt like a sister and contacted him daily, even if it meant calling him on his cellular phone on the golf course, which she did frequently.

On the same day, Bevans relayed McDowell's report on Ricky Rios. He told her of the sergeant's cooperation and the fact that Rios had decided to no longer discuss the status of the case with Lipscomb. Lipscomb complained to Rios that when his tour of duty was up, he wouldn't be allowed to re-enlist. The news devastated Lipscomb; outside of delivering newspapers as a boy, the Air Force had been the only job he had ever known.

Tom Bevans smiled when he summed up the situation. "I guess Bill is finally beginning to feel the pressure."

"I can't imagine how Bill's coping with a situation he can't control," Darlene said. "I saw him act anxiously only one time, and that was when Kathleen and I wanted to visit our grandmother's grave and we asked Bill to drive us. The sun was setting as we drove out there, and Bill said that he didn't like the idea of going to a cemetery, especially when it was getting dark. I thought he was kidding. By the time we reached the cemetery, it was evening and Bill wouldn't get out of his car. He said knowing there were dead bodies in there gave him the creeps. I truly think he's afraid of ghosts, because around every June 8th, he acts kinda strange. One time when I asked him what was wrong, he said it was the 'remembering season.' Isn't that odd?"

A couple of weeks later, Nadine received a call from Agent Fife with a strange request. Nadine had become accustomed to these appeals, as had Darlene.

"Did you happen to take any pictures of Kathleen in her casket?" he asked her.

"Goodness no, we couldn't stand looking at her."

"How about her tombstone? Any pictures of that?"

"I have a cousin in Shreveport who could take one for you."

"Okay, do that. Have him scatter some leaves over 'Wife' so it only reads 'Mother.' Also, get me the address of the cemetery, as if you were mailing something to the caretaker's house. We need that."

"What's this all about?"

"Dr. McDowell's at it again. I think it has something to do with Lipscomb's fear of ghosts. He's going to start receiving letters from 'Kathleen' showing the cemetery as the return address. I'm not sure, but they'll probably say something like: 'Why did you do this to me?' Bill's at the cracking stage, Nadine, and we just want to give him a little nudge."

The lines around Nadine's eyes crinkled. She found the resourcefulness of the OSI to be perversely entertaining.

"What did Dr. McDowell think of the children's insurance being increased?" she asked.

"It bothered him, but he said it would be more serious if Bill had raised the policies to $100,000, or $150,000. We won't sweat that right now. Please just get me the stuff on the cemetery as soon as you can."

By the time the hot, steamy summer smothered San Antonio, Rich Fife finally received word from Atlanta regarding the long delayed test results of the body fluids. Being three years old, then frozen and thawed—no one knew how many times—the specimens proved useless. Fife was disappointed. Now they had nothing but the pubic hair to go by, and the only thing they knew for sure was that it wasn't Kathleen's.

Fife didn't have the heart to call Nadine about the fluids, so he told Darlene.

"So what's left?" she asked, sounding depressed.

"We can pull pubic hair from Bill and Tony and test that. I'd bet my bottom dollar one of them will be a match. Meanwhile, we're moving ahead with Barrelo. We're sending an agent from Lackland to give Agent Stegall a hand during the interview.''

''Is this going to be the break we've been praying for?'' Darlene asked, finally allowing herself to hope.

''Remember,'' Fife cautioned, ''Barrelo was Bill's good friend, so we better not get too enthusiastic. He has probably called Bill every time something's happened on this case. And besides, OSI can't touch Barrelo because he's a civilian.''

Darlene's optimism drained. ''It seems we know for sure that Bill had Kathleen killed, but it looks like he's going to get away with it. I don't know which is harder—not knowing for sure Bill killed her, or knowing he did and not being able to do anything about it.''

''We're dealing with a very sharp man, Darlene. He's been able to pull off the impossible. Bill's found out where we sent Shannon Gilbert and called the hotel where she's living. That just doesn't happen. Now we'll have to move her again. The hotel had been instructed to take calls from only her family and a couple of close friends, but the desk clerk didn't recognize this man's voice, so he refused to forward the call. It had to be Bill.''

Special Agent Janice Pegram, a tall black woman with a very pretty face and a no-nonsense personality, had been an OSI agent for 10 years. She had been on duty at Lackland's OSI when Tom Bevans first presented the case to them. Having familiarized herself with all the facts of the murder, Janice was chosen to fly to Virginia on July 5 to assist Agent Stegall when he questioned Barrelo at a 7:30 meeting that evening.

At three in the afternoon, Barrelo called the OSI office and canceled. He claimed he needed to sell his car.

An hour later, Stegall phoned Barrelo and said, ''this meeting is a lot more important than selling a car. Here's what it boils down to. You can meet with us this evening, or you can talk to the FBI sometime down the road.''

Barrelo decided it wasn't so important to sell his car that night after all.

Agents Pegram and Stegall drove to Barrelo's apartment. They had agreed that Stegall would do most of the talking, while Agent Pegram would jump in with questions if Barrelo strayed from the known facts of the case.

Barrelo's congeniality looked forced when the agents entered his apartment, and by the time they had settled on his sofa he displayed a good deal of nervousness.

''Tony, I have no jurisdiction over you,'' Stegall admitted. ''This is a noncustodial interview. The OSI can't investigate you because you're a civilian. I can't arrest you, so I can't read you your rights or anything of that nature. I'm here to talk to you about something very important, but if you think it's the WAPS compromise, you're wrong.'' He paused for an instant, staring directly at Barrelo, and then let the full brunt of his words hit the young man. ''We're here to talk to you about the murder of Kathleen Lipscomb.''

Barrelo's Adam's apple bobbed.

''We want to learn what exactly happened that night. What part did you play?''

Before he had a chance to respond, Stegall told him, ''Let me give you a scenario—a hypothetical explanation of what we think happened. We assume you're the one who killed Kathleen. Not that it was your idea. Bill probably hired you to do it.''

''No, no,'' Barrelo began. ''I can clear up this whole thing.''

''Okay,'' Stegall said, and leaned back to listen.

''I first met Bill Lipscomb in early 1983 when we were both stationed at Lackland, and even though we played on the same softball team, I didn't know him well. Then one day, I happened to be taking pictures of a military parade. Bill had been a general's flag bearer at that parade, and I had taken a picture of him, so I drove over to his office and gave him the photo and we talked some. Later we both were TI's, and became close friends. At least he seemed like he was my friend. He'd tell me of ways he was helping me after we were both instructors. For example, he said he ordered a plaque for the wall showing some honor I received. That would make me look good, right? I was excited about that. It made me feel that Bill is really a great guy. When the plaque came in, I found out it was for him. He'd do that type of thing." Barrelo looked off into space as he remembered the deed, and his dark eyebrows slanted in an angry frown.

"About the end of April, Bill came to my apartment and told me that Kathleen had filed for divorce and he didn't want to lose his children. He became real emotional. I kinda felt sorry for the guy. But I thought he was crazy."

"Why?"

"He asked me to kill his wife."

Chapter Sixteen

Agents Stegall and Pegram listened for an hour and a half to Barrelo's re-creation of the murder. Then Stegall sat forward and glared at him.

"I don't believe you. You know too damn much about that night, about the cords and everything else to *not* be the one who murdered Kathleen Lipscomb."

Barrelo couldn't believe his ears. "No, sir," he gasped. "I did not kill her—Bill only asked me to. It's hard enough to live with what I did. But I can prove this to you. I'll take a polygraph. I'll wear a wire and talk with Bill so you'll know I didn't do it."

"We're not going to talk about doing any of that right now," Stegall said. "But we need to get those words in writing. How about going over to the office with us tonight and giving a statement?"

"I'll do that," Barrelo told them eagerly.

On the way to the office, he asked in a timid voice, "What's going to happen to me?"

"That depends on what the Bexar County Sheriff wants to do," Stegall told him. "They're the only ones with jurisdiction over you. The next move is up to them."

As they drove, Stegall alluded to what a frantic evening that must have been for Barrelo if he had done everything he said he did.

"Yeah, it made me feel real dirty—inside and out. I got home about 1:30 in the morning and took off my sneakers, jeans, and everything else I had on and threw them all in my apartment complex's dumpster. I knew I'd never wear those clothes again.

"But it didn't end then," he continued. "A few days later Bill gave me the chest he had put her body in. He told me to get rid of that, too."

"How come you had the chest if it belonged to Lipscomb?" Stegall squinted his eyes, giving Barrelo that same cold look of disbelief.

"No, this is how it happened, honest," Barrelo insisted, having trouble forming his words. "Bill had the chest in his bedroom closet, and that's where he put Kathleen while his kids were in the next room taking a bath. He only gave me the chest to get rid of it."

"Okay, let's just say for a moment that I believe you. How did you get rid of the chest?"

"I kept it. It was too good to throw away—besides, I needed more storage space."

"You still have the chest?"

"Yeah, it's at my apartment."

"Can I have it? It may have some blood or semen. Some trace evidence we could tie to Lipscomb."

"Sure."

Stegall screeched the car's tires, made a fast U-turn and sped back to Barrelo's apartment. They carried the chest down the stairs and Stegall took it back to the OSI building where he tagged it and locked it in the evidence room.

"This is great, Tony. The way DNA is starting to develop. It's possible we could find dried body fluids of Kathleen's and Bill's. This would add credibility to your story."

Barrelo glanced nervously at Stegall. "You really don't believe me?"

"If we're going to jump on Lipscomb, we need more evidence. All you've done is tell us this. We need some kind of proof on your part or admittance of guilt from Bill. All we've got are your words and a chest that you had in your possession."

Tony looked troubled for the remainder of the trip to the OSI office. But once there, he was quite verbal, and with the help of Agent Pegram, threw himself into dictating several pages of testimony that duplicated what he had told the agents earlier.

After that, a lab technician ushered him into the medical examining room to pull pubic and head hairs, and take blood and urine samples.

While Barrelo was with the technician, Stegall called Rich Fife at Lackland to brief him. Fife became ecstatic with the news, and promised to coordinate the new information with Dr. McDowell at headquarters. They only hoped Barrelo's account could be proven.

Stegall went back to where Barrelo had just finished signing his statement. "Basically, Tony, what you told me is a little hard to swallow. You did all the things you told us and that was your only involvement? Are you sure you actually didn't kill Kathleen?"

"I swear, honest. I didn't kill her!" He was near tears. He wondered how many times Stegall would ask him that. His confidence had shrunk to zero.

"Well, Tony, there is a way you can prove it."

"How? What? I'll do anything, just tell me." He was trembling.

"I've been an OSI agent for many years, and it's kind of like, in God we trust, everybody else we polygraph."

"I told you I'd take a polygraph. I'll do it right now. Come on, give me a polygraph."

"Actually, I'd have to get approval first and that will take a couple days." Stegall leaned against the wall and watched Barrelo shake.

"And like I told you before," Barrelo reiterated, "I'll wear a wire and talk to Bill, and ask him about the time he killed Kathleen. You'll have everything recorded. I'll do whatever you want. I have no allegiance to Lipscomb. You should have seen him that first day when everyone found out about the murder. He moped around, got tears in his eyes. He acted like he was the victim. But around me he didn't seem the least bit remorseful. Everyone was all, 'Poor Bill.' I thought, my God, what an actor!"

Stegall looked at Barrelo's eager, desperate face, and wondered if Tony realized he didn't have to say a word. "Why are you doing this, Tony? Why now? When I went to your apartment tonight, you could have just told me to get the hell out of there."

Barrelo stood silently for a few minutes and Stegall thought he might cry.

"I met this girl. A very nice girl. Her name is Gloria. She's a school teacher, and a really good Southern Baptist. She's opened my eyes. She really has." He gave Stegall a tentative glance as if wondering if this also needed proof.

"I've accepted Jesus Christ." He moistened his lips. "I've got to make this right with the Lord. When I go to church with Gloria I feel so guilty. I can see God looking down on me, saying 'Repent. Confess your sins.' I know what He's talking about. You've got to let me do this, Agent Stegall. You've got to let me repent."

Agent Stegall kept in constant communication with both Agent Fife and Dr. McDowell. Together they formulated the next stage of their plan. Since Barrelo had offered to wear a wire and meet with Lipscomb, the OSI had decided to let him do just that. Stegall particularly liked the idea because it had been Barrelo's suggestion, and not originated by the OSI.

For the taping, Dr. McDowell flew down from headquarters, and the OSI summoned their technical agents, who brought body wires, recorders, and a myriad assortment of speakers, radios, and monitors. The agents decided to hold the interview in a shopping center parking lot so there would be enough activity to divert attention from the four OSI agents crowded into a van monitoring the conversations.

On July 7th at one in the afternoon, Barrelo met with Stegall and Dr. McDowell in room 228 at the Red Roof Inn in Newport News.

"You know you don't have to do this, Tony," Stegall told him.

"Yes, I do. I have to do this for all the shit I've been living with since the murder."

"Well, remember, this is your decision, but I do want you to know how much we appreciate it. Besides, these tapes will be used as evidence in court if we get that far."

Barrelo nodded. "Let's hope we get that far."

Under Dr. McDowell's direction, Barrelo phoned Lipscomb's work station, but he wasn't there. Barrelo's frustration grew with each call, until finally he reached Lipscomb on the third try.

"Bill, this is Tony. I need to talk with you today."

"What's up, guy?"

"We need to talk. Can you meet me at 4:45?"

"What's up?"

"I don't want to talk about it over the phone. Meet me in the parking lot behind Steak and Ale."

When Lipscomb finally agreed to the meeting, Stegall could see that Barrelo had begun to squirm.

"You're doing great, Tony," he told him. "It takes balls to

do this. We've got a couple hours before he gets here. Let's go over a few things.

"First of all, you aren't an agent of the OSI, but we still have to worry about entrapment. Don't ask Lipscomb incriminating questions such as 'Did you kill Kathleen?' If I, as an agent, were to ask questions of that nature, I'd have to read him his Miranda Rights, and that would raise one hell of a red flag. Now I want you to act natural. Well, as natural as possible under the circumstances."

Barrelo paced the floor and nibbled on his nails as he listened.

"Essentially, your story will be that the OSI wants you to meet with them next Monday, and you're very concerned about that meeting. I don't think you'll have trouble showing that you are nervous and apprehensive.

"The idea is to try to obtain some sort of supporting comments from Lipscomb. Stay in your car and don't get into Bill's van. And for heaven's sake, if for some strange reason you find yourself in his van, don't, I repeat *don't,* let him drive you anywhere."

Barrelo nodded anxiously and fidgeted while the agents wrapped a wire around his waist so he could be monitored from the van. As a fail-safe measure, an additional recorder had been installed in his car.

By 4:30, the OSI agents were in the restaurant's parking lot, and had the ability to speak with Barrelo as he sat in his car. Their taping began as he started his car to head for his meeting because they had to record his consent prior to the interview. The jittery Barrelo could feel the constricting wire wrapped snugly around his waist.

A voice said, "Okay, Tony, read from that card we gave you."

"I, Tony Barrelo, voluntarily give my consent on this seventh day of July, 1989, to be taped and monitored by the Air Force

OSI. I have not been subjected to coercion, nor have I been promised a reward or immunity.''

His nerves were getting the best of him as he stuttered through his declaration. He called for Stegall.

''I'm here.''

''So you want me to drive around and stay out of the way until I see his van pull up?''

''Right. Make sure you let him park. Then drive up to his van and motion for him to join you. Once he's in, drive a couple of spaces away from his van and park.''

''Okay, I'm out of here,'' Barrelo announced. ''Let's hammer him. I'm not wearing my seat belt, sorry. God, give me strength. Please continue to love me, and I won't let you down. I've done some bad things, and I'm doing what I can to rectify them. Amen.''

The tape went silent for six minutes.

''There he is. He just pulled in. Well, here it goes. Lord, answer my prayer.''

At precisely 4:45, Bill Lipscomb entered the rear parking lot, steered into a space and parked his van. Barrelo gave him thirty seconds, then drove in from the opposite direction. He pulled alongside Lipscomb, unlocked his car door, and signaled for Lipscomb to get in. Looking cautiously around the lot, Lipscomb walked over.

As soon as Lipscomb sat down, he said, ''Hey, man, what's happening?''

''Remember those two OSI agents who were talking shit at my apartment?''

''Yes, that Barney guy.''

''Yeah, I guess that's his name. Well, I got a call from him this afternoon and he wants to talk to me first thing Monday morning. He said it was about the WAPS compromise. They mentioned your name, and I'm worried. Bill, why would they fuck with me over the WAPS? You know what I'm saying? I think they're going to ask me other questions, and the only thing that I can think of is that they found something."

"They're just going to ask about WAPS," Lipscomb said, remaining calm.

"Screw the WAPS, I can handle that. No problem."

"We had nothing to do with anything else. That's all you have to remember."

"They're not worrying about the WAPS." Barrelo raised his voice. "I'll guarantee you. Just from what the guy said on the phone."

"Why do you have to talk to him?" Lipscomb sounded genuinely puzzled.

"Well, I'm worried if I don't. Right now it's my ass hanging on the line."

"Why?" Lipscomb shifted uneasily in the car seat.

"It just sounds like it with the way this guy's been talking to me. What I want to know is, was there something that happened that night after I left?"

"No."

"There's gotta be something, Bill. I just need for you to help me out a little bit, because I'm the one they're fucking with, man, and I'm scared. I just want you to go over that real quick. There are some gray areas there for me."

"I don't want to talk about it, really."

"But Bill, man, I need to know."

"There's nothing there. Guarantee it."

"What about the duffel bag? They've got to have dug up something. Maybe the duffel bag can be traced back to you."

"Let's walk and talk," Lipscomb suggested.

"Man, this car is about the safest place I've got."

"Let's walk and talk," Lipscomb said, opening the car door.

As he watched Lipscomb leave, Barrelo unconsciously glanced back at the OSI van hoping for some sort of signal. He had to make a swift decision. He couldn't let Lipscomb get away from him, but he had been told to stay in the car. Quickly, he opened his door, and called out, "Hey, Bill, wait." But Lipscomb didn't stop as he headed for his van.

The tape went blank for almost 10 minutes. The agents in the van checked their equipment and increased the sound level, but they could hear nothing. Everyone became wet with perspiration even though the air conditioning hummed on.

"Oh my God, we should have factored in that we're dealing with a control freak," Dr. McDowell admitted.

"I just hope the guy doesn't get himself killed," Stegall said. "He's our best bet for nabbing Lipscomb. Wouldn't you know, all this planning, and Lipscomb figured a way to out-fox us."

Suddenly, Barrelo's voice came back on the tape, accompanied by a lot of static from his clothes rubbing against the antenna.

"When the guy says something to me about jail time, I get nervous because WAPS doesn't involve jail time."

"Yeah, it does," Lipscomb assured him.

"Not for me. I'm out. I've done my homework. There's something like the statute of limitations."

"They're trying to find something to pin on me as a motive. That's why they're using WAPS."

"Man, Bill, just answer one question, okay? I'm trying to deal with this the best I can, but how in the fuck are you able to deal with it? I keep asking myself why it had to happen."

"I don't know why it happened, Tony. God, I can't tell you why."

"But you should hear all the things they're saying to me."

"Tony. Tony, they're going to come at you with that attitude. They're going to bluff you, they're going to lie to you, they're going to tell you whatever they want."

"Bill, there are certain parts of what happened that I'm worried about. Can't you understand that?"

"Yeah." Lipscomb's eyes scanned the lot. "I don't like that guy sitting there. Man, I don't like that."

"Who? That guy in the Mercedes?"

"I don't like that," Lipscomb said, shaking his head.

"Well, that's why I feel better in a car than out in this open parking lot."

"Let's go drive then. I'll drive."

"No. I've got to split soon," Barrelo said nervously. "Gotta get back to work. Bill, I'm telling you. I sit in church with the girl of my fucking dreams, and I've got this shit all resurfacing. It's all I think about and I'm trying to keep this from her. But I need to go over the details of that night so we can get our stories straight."

"I don't like to talk about this with anyone. Let's get into my van. I don't like what I'm hearing from you. It makes me very suspicious."

They stepped up into Lipscomb's van.

"How do I know you're not wearing a wire?" Lipscomb said, as he placed his hand on Barrelo's shoulder then moved it down his back to feel for a recorder.

Barrelo shook off his hand and fought to stay calm. "Come on, Bill, who do you think you're talking with here?"

"I know, I feel bad for asking, but lately I don't trust anyone. I don't like talking in parking lots with people sitting in their cars around me either."

"Bill, why did it have to happen?"

"I don't know. I guess the Lord took her. She was screwing around on me and she was a bad person, so God took her."

"I heard she had sex prior to her death," Barrelo stated.

"They found Dr. Pearle's sperm inside her, and proved she had uncontested sex earlier on Sunday. He confessed to this. Dr. Pearle probably killed her."

"Come on, Bill. I need the truth. I'm so fucking nervous now. I don't even sleep. You know what I mean?"

"Tony, it will pass, man. It's the season. It's the remembering season. It will pass."

"But, Bill, if the OSI's found anything, they can put my ass in jail."

"They don't have—Tony, wait a minute. Time out. Time out. If they had something on you, they would go right down to the damn jail and get a warrant for your arrest and they would come on out. Think about it. They're not going to spend all this time talking to you if they really had something. That's bullshit. They don't have anything on you, do they?"

"I've still got that chest in my house. What if they search my place?"

"Get rid of it."

"Okay, but I need to talk to you now."

"Did you see it happen, Tony?"

"No, I didn't see it happen. But I know in my heart, and you know, I didn't kill that girl."

"I know you didn't kill her, Tony."

"Then will you talk to me Monday after I see these OSI guys?"

"We can talk if they're not planning to come after me on Monday. I still don't see what's getting to you," Lipscomb said, frowning.

"It's just that because I have knowledge. It's plain eating me up."

"The only knowledge that you have, Tony, is that the girl got killed. That's the honest to God truth, isn't it? What's happened to you? What happened to your edge? Don't lose it."

"How are you able to deal with this, man?"

"I was a different person. That was a different time. I just put it out of my head."

"Bill, my religion tells me no matter what happens, I'll face the music for what I did. Man, disposing, you know what I'm saying? I'm paying every day. I lost my career."

"Yeah, I'm losing mine every day. I don't work like I should, Tony. I'm just there. I don't have a career anymore. I just exist.

You don't think I get all the eyes looking at me? Everybody that knows about the investigation questions my credibility. I have no credibility. I have absolutely nothing, and all you have are these little guys wanting to talk to you and you're schizoid about it. If you go in there and don't like their questions, tell them you don't want to talk to them and go get a lawyer.''

"Shit, I can't afford a fucking lawyer, man. But I don't want your money, Bill. I don't want your money. I'm just trying to cover all the angles because I know they're going to be asking me some serious questions. They're going to try to get me for murder for hire.''

"Do you have an alibi for that night?''

"Yeah, sorta. I don't know.''

"I have my kids," Lipscomb said.

"Do you think your kids remember me taking them to McDonald's?''

"I don't remember you taking my kids to McDonald's.''

"Okay, good," Barrelo said. "I just wish I never had come back here to Virginia.''

"Why did you?''

"My parents live here. You know that. Where the fuck did I have to go? I had no job. I had no car. My parents are the only fucking reason I came here.''

There were a few seconds of silence on the tape. Then Barrelo's voice came back on.

"Have you ever told anyone what you did?''

"Nah, never. Have you?''

"No, I can't. That's why I need to talk to you now. Can't you understand?''

"I can understand that, but Tony . . .''

"I mean, I know you don't want to talk about it. It's not something I want to talk about, but help me put my soul to rest, buddy.''

"You can never put your soul to rest unless you can learn

to deal with it inside. I look at it that Dr. Pearle is the one who killed Kathy. Dr. Pearle did that, Tony.''

''Well, he might have killed her mentally.''

''Tony, did you see it happen?''

''No, I didn't see it happen, Bill. But promise me you'll talk with me Monday after I talk to them,'' Barrelo said as he opened the van's door.

''Yeah, let's talk on Monday,'' Lipscomb agreed. ''We need to decide what we're going to do. I need to get away. I can take a day of leave. If nothing else we can go out in the country. Go do some fishing and talk. Have you met my grandfather?''

''No.''

''Good, we could go to his farm. We'll tell him you're somebody else. Now don't worry,'' Lipscomb called as Barrelo walked back to his car. ''They don't have shit.''

Chapter Seventeen

Dr. McDowell ached to get a tailored confession out of Bill Lipscomb, but he knew that's not what they had achieved with Barrelo's interview. He called for all the agents to go back to the hotel and regroup.

Later, as the agents sat around the hotel room, they debated what they'd have to do to receive the confession they had hoped for. The agents pondered whether Barrelo would allow them to put him out on a limb again, but knowing he wanted to clear his neck, they thought he'd cooperate.

Dr. McDowell suggested tightening the screws to add more pressure on Lipscomb. This time they would choose a different place than a parking lot. They all had seen Lipscomb's continuous glancing around the lot. He had looked scared. Maybe he'd feel more free to talk somewhere inside at night.

This time, Dr. McDowell would have Barrelo tell Lipscomb that he didn't feel good about their meeting. That he wasn't put at ease, and he was still concerned that he had to meet with the OSI. They would have to talk again. McDowell chose

Barrelo's office as the meeting ground and they would wire the whole place and monitor the taping from the office next door.

McDowell reached for the phone and handed it to Stegall. "He should be back at his apartment by now. Give him the good news."

Barrelo answered on the first ring.

"You did great, buddy," Stegall told him. "You really stuck you neck out there."

"Hey, Barney, did you hear Bill say, 'I know you didn't kill her,' did you hear that?"

"We heard, and that sounded good. But you know something else, Tony, you are the only person in this entire world who can help us nail Lipscomb. You're the guy, and we're going to need some more help. But it's your decision, because we're not pressuring you."

"I know. I'm the man. I'll do whatever. I told you that."

"McDowell thinks that just a little more pressure and Lipscomb will pop. We can wire your office and have you call Lipscomb again and get him to meet you there. We'll be right next door. How about tonight?"

"Tonight?" There were a few moments of silence. Barrelo sounded hesitant when he said, "Sure, sure, I'll do it. I'll do it for you, Barney."

"That's the attitude. How about if we meet you around 7:30 at your office? You can call Lipscomb from there."

"Right, 7:30."

McDowell had listened to Stegall's conversation and sighed. Two recorded interviews with Lipscomb in the same day. He just hoped Barrelo could handle it.

Barrelo had bought a professional resumé writing franchise almost a year earlier. His sparse waiting room contained a table, two chairs, and a video game. A connecting door led into his

12-by-12 office which held a desk, a computer and printer, in addition to two more chairs. It was through his business that he had met his girlfriend, Gloria, when she had come in for a resumé. Barrelo had started talking to the pretty woman and that conversation had led to his inviting her to lunch. He had been delighted when she had accepted.

The OSI met with Barrelo at his office, and Dr. McDowell had already planned the scenario Barrelo would set up for Lipscomb. Around 9:15, McDowell instructed him to call Lipscomb. Fortunately for Barrelo's nerves, Lipscomb was at home and answered immediately.

"I just can't take it any longer, Bill. Knowing what we did to Kathleen. I just can't hide it. I've been sitting in my office since our meeting wondering if I should kill myself. Then I came to the conclusion that instead of killing myself, I'll get this off my chest best if I just report the information to the authorities, and take whatever action is due me."

Lipscomb's voice was strained as he pleaded, "Don't do it, Tony!"

"I just can't deal with it any longer, Bill. I have faith now, so whatever happens to me happens. I'll be in my office if you want to talk."

"I'll come right over. Where are you?" Lipscomb's voice was tinged with urgency.

Barrelo gave Lipscomb his address and directions, and waited.

After Barrelo hung up, the agents resumed their wiring. Nine men wiring both offices crowded the small place. They had brought the same equipment they had used earlier, this time installing the transmitter recorder in Tony's office so he wouldn't have to wear a wire. In order to have a back-up system, the waiting room housed another transmitter that also sent a radio signal to the recorder located in the office next door. Dr. McDowell and the technicians left Barrelo's office to go next door, leaving Stegall alone with the high-strung man as he paced back and forth across his small office.

"Barney, he's going to try to kill me. I can just feel it."

"Look, we'll do everything we can to protect you. We'll have nine agents next door and after Bill gets here, two of them will be stationed in the hall outside your office door."

"I bet Bill goes out and buys a gun if he doesn't already have one. Just how fast can your men get in here if he pulls a piece on me?"

"They'd be in here like lightning. Couple seconds, maybe."

"It would only take him one second to shoot me."

"That's true."

"So, fuck, Barney, what should I do?"

"Duck," Stegall said, smiling, and gave Barrelo a couple, "You can do it" pats on his arm. But it was no laughing matter. There literally wasn't anything the agents could do. Stegall went next door to join the others.

One of the agents spoke over the recording system to check the equipment. "This is Special Agent Izzo and Special Agent Johnson. There is a consensual eavesdrop in place. You understand the eavesdrop is in place?"

"Yes, sir," Barrelo told him.

Barrelo decided to find out just how much space existed under his desk in case he had to duck. While getting down on his hands and knees to investigate, he began talking.

"You all get the bastard if he kills me. I think you will. He's a crazy sonofabitch. I hope you can hear this because I don't want to go through this shit for nothing."

A fly, that had been buzzing around the office landed on him.

"Get the fuck off of me. I'm still a fucking neat freak," he said, as an explanation to the listening agents.

"There's not a lot of room under his desk, fellows. This bastard might try it, man. The more I think about it, he might just fucking try it.

"All right, Barney, this is for you, buddy. You are going to believe me one way or another. I just hope I'm here to see you when it's over. This is not a fun feeling. I hope you boys are quick. Barney, you said I had balls, but I think I'm showing you a different side. Oh Lord, please give me the strength and ability to do this.

"Okay, I'm back up in my chair. Damn, I just knocked off a pencil, if I don't stop shaking, I'll clear the whole desktop. Shit, Bill should have arrived ten minutes ago. There's no sign of him."

Barrelo continued his monologue for a few more minutes as he fussed at his desk.

"Wait. I see a vehicle creeping up from the highway, could be him. I don't know. This nightmare has gotta get over. Shit, they drove on. Something's wrong. It shouldn't take that motherfucker this long to get here."

Stegall called Barrelo and told him to phone Lipscomb's home. Barrelo talked to Bill's wife, Francine, who told him that Bill wasn't there.

"She said he's not there, Barney. He's not here yet either. Where in the fuck could he be? If he got lost, he would have called. You guys better be checking the airports."

A full hour went by without any sign of Lipscomb.

"Dang, what I wouldn't give to have a piece of chewing gum. Come on, Bill, show your ass. Let's go. Let's get this behind us, man. He could have bought a gun and got some ammo by now. I feel like a duck during duck season. Nothing good comes easy. Where is this bastard?

"I didn't do it, Barney, no matter what. If the worst happens tell my mother what I tried to do. It's important to me."

After Stegall called again from the office next door to pacify him, Barrelo remained quiet for the next 16 minutes, until the ringing phone broke the silence. It was Bill.

"Hey, man. Where are you?" Barrelo asked.

"I'm home now. I drove down Jefferson trying to find you."

"No, I'm on J. Clyde, on the right past the brown two-story shingle building. I'm upstairs and to the rear. Are you coming?"

"I'm coming." Lipscomb said tersely, and hung up.

"It doesn't make any sense, Barney. He has my number. He could have called. So he was out somewhere. Bring me a beer, man. An hour and a half driving around doesn't sound right."

Ten minutes passed and Barrelo fidgeted restlessly.

"I see a van. He's here. God, Barney, this is it. Oh, shit, let's go."

The tape rolled on silently for five minutes, then Bill appeared in Barrelo's doorway.

Barrelo greeted him with, "Hey, man, I'm falling apart. I just got to let you know in case you want to dash." Then he stopped and unbuttoned his shirt. "Here, do you want to check for a wire?"

"No," Lipscomb said, falling into the chair in front of the desk.

"No," Barrelo echoed, "because they don't need a wire, buddy. I'm sorry Bill, but I'm gonna tell them myself. I got to. You asked me to kill this girl twice. I didn't. Then all of a sudden she's dead. I feel like I did it. I feel responsible."

"Why, Tony?" Lipscomb seemed angrily puzzled.

"Bill, there's nothing else I can do, 'cause this is just destroying me. Why was it me that you picked? I'm history. I'm sitting here contemplating killing myself or turning myself in. It's not worth it, Bill. I'm going to take what comes. Man, I'm sorry." Tony pounded a pen on his desk for emphasis.

"Tony, what is it that—"

"I can't deal with it, Bill. I'm not like you. How do you feel knowing you strangled her?"

Lipscomb sat silently, looking at the floor. Then he raised his head and stared at Barrelo with eyes that had begun to moisten.

"At least I deserve some answers. I'd like to know before

I go to them, and I am going to them. How does it feel knowing you strangled her?''

"I was lost.'' Lipscomb hung his head, and sat looking at his hands. ''Tony, there's got to be something, some way we can deal with this. There's got to be.''

"There's only one way. I'm sorry, man.'' Barrelo felt resolve build in him, knowing the agents were clustered next door.

"Please, Tony. Tony.'' Tears rolled down Lipscomb's cheeks. He bent over to cover his face with his hands, and his shoulders started to shake.

Barrelo had never seen him so devastated.

"Bill there's only one way to cleanse this for me, man. If I've got to spend five, ten in the slammer, at least I'll be able to fucking sleep.''

"God, Tony, please don't. It's not worth it. God, it's not worth it.''

Lipscomb's answers were garbled and they became difficult to understand. Then Lipscomb reached into his pocket and Barrelo froze. He quickly looked down at the knee space, wondering how fast he could get there. A split second later, he saw Lipscomb pull out a handkerchief to blow his nose.

Barrelo took a deep breath. ''Bill, you killed a girl and I dropped the fucking body. How do you think that makes me feel?''

"Man.'' Lipscomb sat shaking his head.

"Did you or did you not kill her, Bill? I mean, let's face facts, man.''

The temperature increased in the adjoining room. The OSI agents blanched as they stared at each other. Barrelo's tactics went far beyond their guidelines on propriety. But the agents were frozen in place. At this point no one felt compelled to crash through the office door and protest.

"I didn't kill her,'' Lipscomb shrieked. ''I'm telling you the truth that I didn't do it.''

Barrelo's eyes opened wide. ''That's bullshit!''

"I didn't do it," Lipscomb continued, looking down at the floor to avoid his friend's eyes.

"You fucking called me up and said, here take the kids to McDonald's, now dump the body, and now throw away the cables and all the rest of the shit."

Lipscomb sat shaking his head.

Barrelo racked his brain wondering what he could possibly ask Lipscomb to get him to admit the truth. "I have to do what's right. There's no alternative for me. I'm going to rot in hell as it is and you sit there and tell me you didn't do it. Goddamn. This is a fucking nightmare."

"It's going to get worse," Lipscomb told him.

Barrelo stared at Lipscomb. He couldn't imagine the lies Bill so easily told. "I sit here and beg you for answers and try to justify in my mind not saying anything, and you still sit there and tell me bullshit. If you didn't do it, who did?"

"Ah, I can't tell you who did."

"Bill, you're going to go fucking down. I went to your house and you asked me if I wanted to see the body. Remember that?"

"There was no body, Tony."

"What the fuck are you talking about?" Barrelo's voice was becoming more shrill by the second. Now he was screaming. He continued to bite on one nail until it bled. "I go to your house. You're broken out in a cold sweat. Are you that sick, man? Are you that sick?"

"Tony, why can't we just live through this?"

"I can't take it on the inside. I need the truth, Bill. This is your last chance to talk to me as a free man. This is it," Barrelo said as he thumped out the words with his fist.

"Tony, think what's going to happen to the people who love us. Look at it that way. Are those people not worth it to you—your mother, your brother, your girlfriend?"

Lipscomb's words were meshed with strong emotion, and his prolonged crying began to fluster Barrelo. Barrelo took a deep breath. "It's because I love those people that I have to tell the truth. They deserve that."

"I'm talking about my wife, Tony, my parents, my children," Lipscomb stammered. "My life may be fucked up but theirs isn't. But it will be. They will have to live with it the rest of their lives."

"I've got someone who loves me a great deal, Bill, and this is going to fucking tear her up."

"She doesn't know?"

"No, she doesn't know. Is she going to know? I'm sure she will as soon as they come and throw me in the slammer. It's going to kill her, man." The mention of his girlfriend made Barrelo realize how much he could lose. He had become so fatalistic about this interview that he had talked Gloria into going to Sears to have a formal photograph made—something his family could remember him by after his death.

"Tony, it's got to stop. Think about it."

"I've thought about it for three years. I lay awake at night and this has fucked with me for three years."

"We are going to die in jail."

"Bill, I'd rather die in jail than live the living hell I've had here. I mean that."

"God, Tony, no."

"I can't, Bill. I'm trying to tell you, man. I'm finally getting my life straight, but you know what? Until I get rid of this I can never have my life straight."

"Don't, Tony, I'm begging you. I've never begged a day in my life, but I'm begging you now."

"Bill, don't beg me, just answer a question. Why did she have to die? I ask that over and over. You know the question I ask myself? Did she deserve to die? And my answer is 'no.' Why did you do it? Why did she have to die, Bill? Fucking why, man? I'm going insane asking myself this question."

"Tony, I didn't kill her."

"What kind of shit are you pulling on me now? I don't

understand this. What kind of mind games are you trying to play? Did you not tell me that you killed her?'' Barrelo's mind flashed to the listening OSI agents, and he speculated what they were thinking with Lipscomb refusing to substantiate his story.

Lipscomb immersed himself into a litany of ''I didn't kill her,'' repeating it at least a dozen times. While Bill carried on, Barrelo worried that he had run into a brick wall. A wall that would prevent him from hearing the truth for the rest of the evening. Undaunted, he pursued a new course.

''If you didn't kill her, who did?'' he asked.

Lipscomb only stared back through wet eyes.

Barrelo didn't want to hear a repeat of the doctor killing her. ''It wasn't Pearle. That's a horseshit theory. Bill, you're going down, buddy, I'm sorry. I can't live with this.''

''Tony, I love you.''

''I love you too, Bill, but damn it, man.''

''Tony, someone else killed her.''

''Are you protecting someone that I don't know about?''

''Would it change anything?''

''Don't, Bill—you killed that girl. I can't fucking deal with it any longer. You want to skip the country? I'll give you to morning.''

''No, why don't you?''

''I can't, Bill. I'm broke, number one. I can't get up and run away. I can't run away from what's in my heart, man.''

''Tony, what do you want?''

''I don't want money, Bill.''

''Do you want to leave? Tell me, man.''

''What are you going to try to do, buy my soul? What, a couple hundred thousand?''

''I don't have that much right now, but I can give you $2,000 on Monday.''

''I don't even want a hundred thousand. I want the truth. You told me that when the first cord broke, Kathleen said, 'Oh my God, Bill, no!' Do you remember that? Do you know how that fucking phrase has haunted me day and night for three years?''

"Tony, I'm begging you. I'm pleading with you. Don't do this. You don't want to go to jail.''

"I'm in jail right now, Bill. I've been in jail for the last three years.'' Barrelo thought back to Dr. McDowell's words when he first met him: 'Someone is going to ride Old Sparky, and at the moment, I have you.' Barrelo realized he had to get a confession out of Bill to keep himself out of the electric chair, but his chances were getting slim.

"You're going to ruin our lives, Tony.''

"It's the only way, Bill. I've got to get it off my back.''

"I don't want to die, Tony.''

"I don't either. I suspect that Kathleen didn't want to die. Did you ever think of that?''

Mopping his eyes with the backs of his hands, Lipscomb kept on bawling. His wet clothes stuck to him and his face glowed red from the heat of the small room.

"If you're covering for someone, tell me, Bill. It could make a difference.''

Lipscomb's eyes held a hint of promise. He paused a few moments, then said, "Shannon Gilbert killed her.'' He looked directly at Barrelo. "I was downstairs with the kids and Shannon killed her.''

Barrelo felt his head spinning with Bill's words. "Come on, Bill, what about the body in the duffel bag?''

"There wasn't a body in there, that was trash. I just made it look like a body so you wouldn't know about Shannon.''

Barrelo had heard enough. "Go home, Bill.''

"I need to know what you're going to do, Tony.''

"Just fucking go home before I kick your ass.''

"I'd rather you kick my ass.''

"Bill, leave, man. Go, just go, Bill. Get out of here.''

"I didn't lie, Tony.''

"Go home, Bill."

"God."

"Go!" Barrelo screamed.

Lipscomb stood up and stared at Barrelo through red, swollen eyes. Saying nothing, he walked toward the door. After the door shut, Barrelo fell back into his chair. He looked down, and his clothes were almost as wet as Lipscomb's. The shaking had stopped, but he was numb. It was over. At least this part was over, and he hoped to God it had been the hardest part.

A minute later the door burst open and nine OSI agents rushed in.

"You did a great job. That must have been tough putting up with all his lies," one of the agents said as he patted Barrelo's back.

Stegall came over and shook his hand, "Thank you, Tony, good going."

Dr. McDowell said, "Fine job, young man. Although we didn't get that tailored confession, we got a lot of admissions. First, there's Lipscomb's concern about his family finding out what he did. Secondly, his pleading for you not to tell. Then, he just cried when you confronted him about killing Kathleen, and he didn't deny you dropped the body for him. Of course, once he collected himself, he came out with all those lies, but I'm sure we have enough to take him to court, thanks to you. You can be proud of yourself."

Barrelo didn't feel proud. He felt drained.

It was after one in the morning by the time the agents pulled the wires and equipment from the two offices, and Barrelo left for his apartment. He glanced around the parking lot, his heart in his mouth, wondering if Lipscomb were waiting for him. Then, he headed for his car that stood alone under a dim light.

Chapter Eighteen

The day before the covert taping, Barrelo warned Gloria about his clandestine efforts for the OSI. He tried to downplay the risk involved, but she hadn't believed him. Afterward, she had impatiently waited for his promised phone call. She wasn't expecting a visit at 1:30 in the morning.

Her sleepy eyes opened wide when she saw him standing at her apartment door. "Oh, thank God, you're alive! I was so worried about you." She hugged him.

He led her over to the sofa, motioned for her to sit down, then swallowed hard and tightened his determination.

"There's something I need to tell you," he began, and conceded that he had hidden an unbearably dark secret from her. Although he had told her snippets over the past several weeks about that night, he hadn't told her the entire story. Even now he danced around its periphery, but finally admitted to helping Lipscomb commit a crime.

Gloria listened patiently, shock and disbelief creeping over her face until she began to cry.

Barrelo anguished over how he had been eaten with remorse since that macabre night and how it had devastated his life, including, most painfully, his military career.

Through her tears, Gloria reminded him that one of the main tenets of their church was that God forgives. She vowed to forgive, too, and promised to stand by him.

Then after she heard his fears of what Lipscomb might do if he stayed in his own apartment, she suggested that he spend the night with her. His hopes turned to dismay as he watched her carry a pillow and two sheets into the living room to make a bed for him on her sofa. He realized that she embodied all the pure things he never was, but had hopes of being, and gratefully, accepted the couch.

When Barrelo returned to his apartment the next morning, he was shocked to see broken glass that had been punched out of the door to his kitchen's rear entrance. He thought instantly of Lipscomb. A random robbery would have been less terrifying, but he disregarded robbery even before he found a $50 bill that he had left earlier in plain view on his countertop. He phoned Stegall.

"First, we toyed with the idea of putting a tail on Lipscomb last night," Stegall told him, "but in his paranoid condition, a tail would be the first thing he'd have noticed. It's got to be one of two things. He either intended to finish the job you thought he'd do during the taping, or he went to pick up the chest you told him about yesterday. Now that he's been there and found no chest, you need to convince him you're hiding it somewhere else.

"I've got an idea. We'll plan to have an escort spend time with you today. Pack your bag. You're going to be our guest at the Holiday Inn tonight."

Stegall's words dissipated some of Barrelo's concerns. With the OSI watching, Lipscomb couldn't hurt him, could he? But he was now alone in his apartment, and the OSI several miles away. Quickly he shoved underwear and toiletries into his suitcase, and hurried out to his car.

At the OSI office, Stegall directed Barrelo to the evidence room where they pulled out the chest. Stegall folded the front page of *The Air Force Times* so that the date showed clearly, then placed it on top of the closed chest. He took two close-up Polaroid shots, one of the newspaper and chest, and one with the chest opened. When the image came into view, the date left no question as to when it had been photographed.

"Here, Tony," Stegall said, handing him a notepad. "Write something in the vernacular you'd use, and make it strong."

He wrote:

"If you think I'm fucking around with you, here's proof I still have the chest. Had I taken a better picture, you would see the stains in the bottom. If you don't help me, I can't get out of the country, and I'll have to talk to those people. This is your last chance. Tony."

Around 3:30, an agent took the envelope containing the Polaroids and note to the Transportation Squadron where Bill worked, put it under the windshield wiper of his van, hid in an unmarked car, and waited.

After work, Lipscomb noticed the envelope on his van. He casually looked around the lot, then picked up the envelope and got inside. Tearing it open, he read the note and took a few moments to stare at the photos.

As Lipscomb left the lot, the agent followed him, having been told that Lipscomb would probably head for the closest pay phone to call Barrelo. Lipscomb stopped to call no one, and instead drove directly home. Perhaps suspecting a trap, he made no effort to contact Barrelo.

Dr. McDowell listened to the agent's report, and shook his head, admiring Lipscomb's shrewdness. That meant that the

OSI had to go on the offensive again. It bothered everyone that, despite all their efforts, they still had no current physical evidence tying Bill to the case. McDowell's mouth watered thinking how damning a cash outlay from Lipscomb to Barrelo would be in court.

To accomplish that end, the next day, Sunday, July 9, Dr. McDowell instructed Barrelo to call Lipscomb at his home and push for money to leave the country.

Compared to his demeanor when taping Lipscomb, Barrelo was relatively calm when he made the phone call, no doubt bolstered by the two OSI agents standing beside him.

"Bill, this is Tony. I want to tell you I've decided to take you up on your offer to leave the country instead of going to the OSI. I need your help, though."

"I don't think I can do anything," Lipscomb told him with resignation.

"You made me an offer," Barrelo said, raising his voice, "and I need your help to get out of the country."

"Call me back. I'll see what I can do."

An hour later, the OSI agents escorted Barrelo to a pay phone at a convenience store where he phoned Lipscomb again.

"Bill, I'm at a pay phone and I really don't like the idea of standing out here in the open. How long is it going to be before you know something?"

"I don't know. Why don't you just go to the OSI?"

Lipscomb was back playing his mind games.

Barrelo told him, "I have a plane reservation to fly out of the country tonight and I need $5,000. I can tell you later what time to meet me at the airport to give me the money."

Hearing only silence on the other end, he reiterated the story about the chest, mentioned that his apartment had been broken into, and again asked for financial help. Finally, he threatened to call Bill's wife.

"I'll try to do something." Lipscomb sounded irritated. "Call me tonight."

Barrelo spent the entire day in the protective custody of the OSI agents. They didn't know Lipscomb's whereabouts. As the hours ticked on, Barrelo became more and more grateful for the OSI presence.

The last phone call Barrelo made to Lipscomb was late at night and brief. Lipscomb told him he couldn't give him any money because it would show association. Barrelo hung up and never spoke to him again.

As early as ten on Monday morning, July 10, humidity and heat rose in waves across OSI's parking lot. Agent Stegall, Dr. McDowell, and the other agents involved in the case sat in the OSI office pondering their next move.

The agents working on the case were alerted by the sergeant at the front desk that Bill Lipscomb had just walked into the OSI office. They looked at each other, astonished and elated at the same time. "For God's sake, he's going to turn himself in," one said.

Special Agent Pete Ober, the OSI detachment commander, had been immersed in the case for the last several days and had offered to talk with Lipscomb. The handsome, almost boyish-looking agent, was both an attorney and a physician's assistant. With such a diverse background, Ober had often helped the OSI in many areas. Moreover, he possessed a natural ability to put people at ease when he talked with them. But today he questioned if those talents would help him under these unusual circumstances.

Ober approached the front office as Lipscomb stood at attention. Knowing the facts of the murder, Ober almost expected to see the man wearing horns. Knowing about his late-night taping, he also expected Lipscomb to be exhausted. Lipscomb stood ramrod straight in his crisp uniform. He looked defiant and determined

"What can I do for you, Sergeant?"

Stone-faced, Lipscomb said, "I have been made aware of a serious problem that needs your immediate attention."

Ober could barely camouflage his puzzled expression. "What problem is that?"

Lipscomb removed the note and Polaroid photos from his wallet. Unfolding the note, he slapped the three pieces on the agent's desk.

"This was left on my windshield. I think it's obvious that this man 'Tony' is blackmailing me. He gave me these two pictures of a chest—whatever that's supposed to mean—and wants me to give him money. His inference is clear from his note. His name is Tony Barrelo and I can give you his address and home phone number. I think you should conduct an investigation of him at once."

"Of course," Ober said, concealing his emotions. He wrote down the information as Lipscomb dictated it, and left to make copies of the note and photos.

Lipscomb still stood at Ober's desk when he returned. "What I propose is that the OSI set up a sting operation. I could meet with him and you could tape the two of us. Then you'd hear him demand money from me . Should be no problem to catch Barrelo in this scheme of his."

Ober could only look on in astonishment. He managed a nod.

Lipscomb tucked the items back into his wallet, saluted, and left.

Even Dr. McDowell shook his head. "That really took balls," he said. "He's a rare bird. I run into a lot, but this guy is off the charts in craftiness."

"You should have seen the SOB," Ober said. "He straight-faced the whole thing. Didn't look one damn bit nervous."

"He's got to be aware of our investigation," Stegall added.

"But he's acting like we don't know a thing. That's just disgusting."

The agents sat stunned for a few moments, still dazzled by Lipscomb's grit.

Dr. McDowell broke the silence. "Let's add up what evidence we have."

"We've got the written statements and tapes from Barrelo and Gilbert," Stegall said. "The way it turned out, they were in separate cities when they talked to us, so I doubt the defense could say there was collaboration."

"We already have the chest that Kathleen's body was in," Agent Izzo said.

"And we have the word of those psychologists at Lackland that Kathleen admitted being threatened by Lipscomb," Ober offered.

Dr. McDowell sat fingering his mustache while he listened to the agents add up the evidence, nodding each time they ticked off a new piece.

"Here's the best reason of all to arrest him," Stegall said, sitting forward in his chair. "After Barrelo stuck his neck out for us to help make those tapes, his life might not be worth a plugged nickel with Lipscomb running around free."

"That's the clincher!" McDowell said, hitting his desk with his fist. "Now it's time. If anyone gets hurt while we try to gather more evidence, it wouldn't be worth it. Let's draw up the warrant for his arrest."

"I agree," Stegall said, and stood up to get the forms and start the paperwork.

All of the agents in the room concurred. It was time.

Lipscomb's pillared house overlooked Chesapeake Bay in Poquoson, Virginia, about 10 miles north of Langley Air Force Base. His wife, Francine, had chosen this night to host a baby shower for her pregnant sister who was visiting from Seattle.

The big house was filled with more than 20 women watching the visitor open her gifts. The men in the family had been sent out to eat pizza.

As a courtesy, Stegall notified the Poquoson police that the OSI would be arresting one of their citizens. They also told the police that they didn't know who would be at the house and solicited them for back-up in case there were any problems. The police agreed and met the OSI agents at the police station a little after seven to formulate a plan. Then with Agents Stegall, McDowell, and Ober in one car, four more OSI agents in another, and two patrol cars, each filled with four Poquoson police, they all headed for Lipscomb's house.

The large home stood in the center of a quiet cul-de-sac on a tree-lined street. The mayor of Poquoson lived nearby. When the law enforcement people arrived, they found an assortment of cars gathered in front of the Lipscomb house.

Dr. McDowell shook his head and said, "We sure picked the night didn't we? I had hoped we could apprehend him quietly."

"Too late for that now," Stegall said.

Both agents walked to the front door, while two Poquoson officers went around to the back in case anyone tried to make a quick escape. Stegall knocked, and a petite brunette answered and said that Bill wasn't there. Stegall introduced himself and McDowell as OSI agents. Seeing the police cars crowded with officers sitting in front of her house, the woman look startled and stepped backward.

"We're having a baby shower," she explained nervously, as if that would be enough to turn away the agents.

"I beg your pardon for interrupting at this time, ma'am, but would you mind if we just came in and looked around?"

Francine appeared distraught as she opened the door for the men. Stegall and McDowell walked in and were immediately the center of attention of the women. The men walked upstairs, entered every bedroom, opened each closet, and finally satisfied themselves that Lipscomb was not in the house. They walked back down and ran into Janice Lipscomb, Bill's mother, who appeared unruffled. Stegall looked into her eyes and didn't see a glimmer of tenseness or concern, and wondered if she were in shock.

The agents walked out the front door, and were headed for their cars when Lipscomb drove up with his father, his son Billie, and Francine's son, Joel. By now neighbors had come out to their front yards to see what was causing all the commotion.

Stegall walked up to Lipscomb as he stepped out of the car.

"Are you Sergeant William Thomas Lipscomb?" Stegall asked.

"Yes, sir." A deep swallow was the only reflection of nerves Lipscomb allowed to escape.

Stegall introduced himself and said, "You are under arrest. You are to walk up and place your hands on our vehicle."

Lipscomb stared at the agent, wide-eyed, and his face blanched to chalk. As they walked, Lipscomb looked at the sidewalk, and the back of his shirt began showing perspiration.

After Stegall completed his pat-down, he turned and looked at the front porch. Stegall thought it pathetic, but now all of the women from the party had walked out to the Lipscomb's porch to watch Lipscomb be arrested for the murder of his former wife. Stegall read him his rights, and warned him not to make any comments that could be held against him. They locked handcuffs on him and opened the door of the OSI car.

Francine and Bill's father rushed up to Bill. Sobbing uncontrollably, Francine tried to get into the car with Lipscomb, and the agents had to restrain her.

"When is he coming back?" she screamed.

"He's not." McDowell told her.

At the same time, Lipscomb's father kept shouting, "What on earth is this all about? Why are you arresting him? What's the charge?"

As sympathetically as he could, McDowell turned to the older man and explained, "He's been arrested for murder."

Nelson Lipscomb turned to look at his son, now seated in the backseat, and his eyes grew icy and hard as he stared in bewilderment. After a few seconds he said in a shaky voice, "I'll get him an attorney."

Lipscomb tried to look away from his father. Lipscomb's white face had flushed to red and looked like a crimson mask. His jaw was set strongly in defiance.

Then Stegall drove away, leaving the other agents to cope with Lipscomb's wife and parents.

Using a cover-up that even Dr. McDowell could appreciate, Bill Lipscomb had been able to evade the law for three years, one month, and two days, almost to the hour.

Chapter Nineteen

The yellow sports car screeched to a stop half a block from the Lipscomb house. Tom Bevans sat at the wheel, hot and uncomfortable in the small car. Darlene Sanford was next to him.

"Shoot. The police are gone. Looks like we missed them again," Darlene said.

"Sure does," Bevans agreed.

Rich Fife had called Darlene on Saturday after Barrelo's taping to tell her of Lipscomb's imminent arrest. Darlene couldn't wait to tell her mother, but just for the sheer satisfaction of it, she eagerly told her husband. Upon hearing that, Gary finally became convinced that Lipscomb, after all this time, had to be guilty. As the story spread to her brothers, relatives, and friends, they too accepted what they felt had been the impossible.

Darlene had rushed to her mother's house. They hugged each other and the tears they had cried for three years were now tears of culmination. They planned for Darlene to fly to Poquoson, accompanied by Bevans, pick up Mary Ann and Billie, and bring them back to Texas. It would be a wonderful reunion—almost like having Kathleen back again. Both women were ecstatic.

Bevans and Darlene made plans to meet the OSI agents in a Poquoson school yard after the agents connected with the police there. However, Poquoson had two grade schools and the Texans waited an hour at the wrong school. Finally realizing their mistake, they dashed over to Lipscomb's only to arrive after he had been escorted to Langley's OSI Office.

"I guess I should go up to the door and ask Francine for the children."

"I'll go with—" Bevans started to say when a late model Cadillac tore down the street, careening between cars parked on each side.

Darlene had heard the many stories of Lipscomb's friends and their intentions to take out anyone who could hurt him in court. This obviously was one of them. The two sat frozen as the burly-looking man hurriedly pulled himself out of his car, slammed the door shut, and began peering into each parked car.

"Let's get out of here," Darlene urged.

"I'm way ahead of you," Bevans said, as he tried to start the car. The engine of the rented vehicle chugged over and over, but wouldn't come to life. The closer the man came, the harder Bevans tried. The engine emitted an anemic click as it died.

At that moment, the man stood a mere car away, so making a dash for it was fruitless. When he came upon their car, he stared at Darlene and walked around to her side.

"Darlene Sanford?" he asked.

Meekly, she nodded as the stranger opened her car door.

The man stuck out his hand and grasped hers. "I'm Frederick Lipscomb. Bill's older brother. I just wanted to meet you."

Darlene exhaled in relief. Frederick explained that he had

been told of Bill's arrest and he had come to comfort his parents. Frederick knew of her overt role in the investigation, and assumed she would be there. He accompanied them to the Lipscomb home.

Bill's mother, Janice, opened the door. She reached out and hugged Frederick. She glared at Darlene. Janice also knew of the role Darlene played, and highly disapproved of her family having hired private detectives. Darlene looked past the older woman and asked to speak with Francine.

Red-eyed, Francine came to the door and listened to Darlene's request for the children. Then she told her, "You may have them this evening, but under no circumstances can you take them back to Texas."

Darlene was thunderstruck. "But they're my niece and nephew. We're their family."

"They are *my* children," she said coldly. "Last year Bill had me adopt them."

Placed side by side were two interrogation rooms in the OSI building. The agents ushered Bill Lipscomb to one, while Tony Barrelo sat perched on a wooden chair at a table in the other. Barrelo's head bobbed every time someone walked down the hall as he anxiously waited for Lipscomb to be brought in. He didn't want to talk with him. He only wanted to know when the arrest had taken place. The evening had been tense at the OSI office, but everyone had stayed in contact through Stegall and McDowell's car phone.

Dr. McDowell walked into Barrelo's room and pulled up a chair next to him, grateful that Barrelo had helped make the arrest possible. "I know you are going through a lot of introspection right now. You are doubting that you're a good person. You are hating every moment that you fell under Bill Lipscomb's spell."

Barrelo nodded without raising his head.

"Let me tell you something, Tony. Never in all my years have I come across anyone as canny as Bill. You were set up from the moment he suckered you into his WAPS scam. He bought your friendship with that, and used it to manipulate you without your ever knowing it was happening."

Barrelo sat slumped over with a worried expression. "I'll never forgive myself for not going to the police when he approached me about murdering Kathleen."

"Let me assure you of one thing. It wouldn't have mattered. With that cult that followed him around? He simply would have chosen someone else."

The OSI brought Bill Lipscomb in at 8:09 p.m. and both Agents Stegall and McDowell interviewed him. Stegall, who outweighed Lipscomb by 60 pounds and had five inches on him, read Lipscomb his rights under the Military Code. He stood there tall and angry, and barked out, "I am investigating the murder of your former spouse, Kathleen Lipscomb, of which you are a suspect." He told Lipscomb he could remain silent, and select either military or civilian counsel, or both. "Do you want to seek legal counsel now, or are you willing to talk to me?"

Much to Stegall's surprise, Lipscomb said he would talk.

They were eager to hear what Lipscomb had to say, but first they had to search him. Then while Lipscomb waited for several minutes on a hard wooden chair, the agents went to another room and looked through the contents of his pockets. In his billfold they discovered Barrelo's note and the two Polaroids of the chest. They took the photos for evidence, then went back to talk with Lipscomb who still sat erectly with military bearing.

Dr. McDowell began, "Bill, do you want something to drink?"

He shook his head.

"Come on, Bill, even the bad guys get thirsty. How about a Coke?"

Lipscomb said nothing.

Seeing that his prisoner preferred to ignore him, McDowell pursued a different course. "I suspect you feel a sense of relief now that it's all over with."

Lipscomb's frigid blue eyes stared right through him.

"The worst that you have dreaded for three years has just happened, so you might as well relax. You'll have no more worry that the next phone call or knock on the door will be the law coming to get you."

McDowell paused to gauge Lipscomb's reaction, but he saw that he would have no part of this approach, so McDowell jumped to more tangible matters. "The purpose of this interview is not to determine if you played a role in your wife's death. As far as I'm concerned, that's already been answered. But sometimes there are mitigating circumstances. I know you were undergoing a very stressful divorce. A normal person under those circumstances could have overreacted to some sort of provocation, which resulted in your wife's death. Or on the other hand, this might have been premeditated murder. This is what we want to clarify." McDowell's attempt to find an "explainable" motive for Lipscomb to have killed Kathleen was part of his master plan to coax Lipscomb into an admission of guilt.

Lipscomb still remained silent.

Stegall tried his hand. He said, "Do you want an attorney?"

Lipscomb said, "No."

Stegall sat on top of the table, pointedly looking down at Lipscomb. He told him that their investigation would entail learning the when, the where, the how, and the why of the murder. Then, locking eyes with Lipscomb, he said, "We know *when* you killed your wife. We know *where* you killed your wife. We also know *how* you killed your wife, but what we don't know is, *why* did you kill your wife?"

Absentmindedly, Lipscomb said, "I don't know why."

Then, in shock, realizing his blunder, he sat up, crossed his arms around him as if he were cold, and bellowed, "I did not kill my wife. I did *not* kill my wife!"

Stegall moved in quickly. "Bill, you're a liar! You not only wrapped that fuckin' cord around her neck once, you wrapped it around twice and strangled her," he roared.

"That's it!" Lipscomb demanded, slapping the table and giving Stegall a hostile glare. "I'm not going to say another word until I talk with a lawyer."

The agents knew the meaning of those words: the interview was over.

Agent Stegall jotted down the time, stood up to get the paperwork to book Lipscomb, and asked him if he'd like something to drink. Lipscomb again shook his head. Dr. McDowell stayed in the room with Lipscomb and stared at him. Lipscomb stared back. Neither man moved nor blinked.

Fifteen minutes later, Stegall entered the room with the proper forms and a glass of orange juice. The two men were still silently staring at one another, a gaze broken only by Stegall's presence.

"Here, I brought you something to drink in case you changed your mind," he said. They filled out the forms and left Lipscomb alone.

Both McDowell and Stegall went to a two-way mirror and watched Lipscomb. His arms remained folded across his chest, and he eyed the juice. But he never touched a drop.

"Did you stare at him the whole time I was gone?" Stegall asked.

"Absolutely. I had to show him who's in control," McDowell answered.

They both glanced back at Lipscomb, still sitting defiantly with his full glass.

"I'm not sure he got your message, Doc," Stegall said, with a hearty laugh.

The two agents stood there for another moment watching. Stegall said, "To think this all started with that one clue that Kathleen left about Shannon Gilbert in her date book."

"That's right," McDowell agreed. "It was like getting a clue from the grave. After three years, Kathleen ends up helping us solve her murder."

"It's ironic," Stegall said, "the one person Lipscomb wanted to control ends up controlling him. If this turns out like it should, he'll get the death penalty or spend a good part of his life at Leavenworth. You talk to those people up there, Doc— do you think Leavenworth will change Lipscomb?"

"They have a hefty complement of psychologists. I have long suspected that an inmate has a remarkable ability to mold himself to the therapeutic model 'suggested' by his keepers. Thus, in prisons run by preachers, the inmate finds God. In those dominated by mental health professionals, he finds insight. The benchmark words at Leavenworth have the inmate admitting that his conscience is bothering him and he wants rehabilitation so he can re-enter society. That's how they determine if the prisoner is ready for parole."

"That ought to be a snap for Bill," Stegall observed.

"I've had jailers up there tell me they didn't care what the person did to get in, didn't even want to know because it might prejudice them, they're just intent on getting him out."

They continued staring at Lipscomb. "What do you think he's thinking?" Stegall asked.

"He's probably cussing Kathleen for making a diary out of that date book. And if he regrets anything, I'll bet it's getting caught."

Stegall talked to the Staff Judge Advocate who determined that Lipscomb would not be released that night. Instead he would spend it with the Security Police. Then he would be placed in pre-trial confinement. Lipscomb would have to be taken to court in 90 days, or set free. However, if for any reason he asked for a delay, the clock would stop.

Lipscomb's father hired Kenneth Merrow, a thin, cocky lawyer who seemed to know his way around the jail. He had a fiery voice that more than compensated for his small stature. Bill Lipscomb paid him a retainer of $25,000 from Kathleen's insurance.

On the day after Lipscomb's arrest, Merrow sent his private investigator, Odis Pirvany, to interview Lipscomb. After a very nervous, sleepless night, Lipscomb found it comforting to talk with someone who thought everything would turn out just fine.

A guard took Lipscomb to a visitor's room to talk with Pirvany, who came across as a bad guy who had gone straight, a ploy that had served him well in gaining acceptance by those he interviewed. He was tall and broad-shouldered, and dressed better than he spoke. His street-smart voice and mannerisms didn't fit the silk suits he wore.

No one had brought Lipscomb a clean uniform, and although he hadn't slept in it, it wasn't the crisp, precise clothing he had become accustomed to. He tried to smooth wrinkles from his pants as he sat down at a table with the investigator.

"It's time you got to tell your side of the story regarding June 8, 1986," Pirvany said in a very non-threatening manner. "I'm on your side, Bill, and you know everything you say is held in confidence."

Lipscomb looked off in the distance. Then he leaned back in his chair. "June 8, 1986. That date has been engraved on my mind. I suppose it always will be. Kathleen and I were separated and it was my weekend to have the kids. She came over around 6:30 to pick them up and look at some of my photos she wanted.

"I remember she parked her car across the street from my apartment and I watched her walk toward my building. I still loved her and it was like slow motion watching her walk. She was wearing blue jeans and her orange USTA T-shirt. She had her shoulder purse and wore white sandals.''

He took a deep breath and looked at the detective. ''These are hard memories. It's like it was just yesterday, but in my mind's eye, it's been that way ever since that day. When I opened the door and asked her in, she immediately wanted to know where the children were. I tried to explain that Tony had taken them to get something to eat at McDonald's, because they had been in the pool most of the afternoon and were hungry. She was really upset at me for letting Barrelo take them. She never liked the guy. I tried to defend my actions, but it was no use, I was wrong and I knew it. She threatened not to let me see them any more if this was what I did with 'her children.' That felt like a knife cutting into me. 'Her children.' They were part of me also, and a very big part. That knife feeling would not be the last that she threw my way that evening. She saw the photo albums on the coffee table and immediately went to them and sat down on the floor in front of the TV. She started to separate and spread the pictures out on the floor.

''I asked her where she was last night because the children wanted to say goodnight and no one answered the phone. She accused me of checking up on her and said that it was none of my business where she was or who she was with. The way she acted, I assumed she was with a man. I asked her who he was and she said, 'I have a boyfriend.' ''

Lipscomb gave a despairing shrug. ''In my mind I could only hear the remarks of the past year about how she couldn't stand any men, and that it would take her a long time to have another relationship. During this conversation she continued to separate the pictures. My group of pictures were snapshots; the professional photos from Sears or K-Mart ended up in her pile, and then her knives—well, not literally—kept striking me.''

It didn't seem to bother Lipscomb that Pirvany said nothing. He sat next to him, listening and monitoring his recorder.

"Kathleen was going to keep a certain picture, but cut me out of it. Keep the wedding pictures, but cut me out of them. She wanted all of the baby pictures because, as she said, 'You can't be trusted with the children, letting Barrelo take them, so how can you be trusted to take care of the pictures?' I couldn't keep any pictures of her family, and she didn't want any pictures of my family.

"All of this drove me wild inside and I started to battle with this little replica of myself on my right shoulder. It was so real, this little me telling myself that she will never change and that she would cut me out of my children's life totally. I couldn't even understand how I had gotten to this point. Why did I deserve this? The little me kept telling me to, 'Shut her up, shut her up, she'll never change.' There was an actual turning of my head to see this little guy on my shoulder, then . . ."

Lipscomb paused and seemed to have trouble continuing with his story. "In my mind's eye it's all so slow. I grabbed a piece of stereo cable—you know, coaxial cable—wrapped it around her neck and pulled her to me. My knees wrapped around her upper body, and after a brief struggle . . ." Lipscomb stopped again and swallowed hard. "Before I realized what was happening, she went limp. I think I finally took a breath and the realization of what had happened hit me like a blast of cold air.

"In the struggle I had somehow tied the cable. I don't remember doing it, or how long it took. Her face was bright red and her tongue swollen. That face lingers in my mind as it will forever. I fell back on the floor as the shock settled in, and I realized that I had killed her. Then I quickly moved over to her and listened for a heartbeat. It was an empty sound. A death-perfect silence. I was terrified. What to do? What to do? I kept asking myself.

"Then the phone rang. It was Tony. He asked if Kathleen

were there. I told him, 'You need to get back here. I just killed her!'

"I quickly picked up the pictures and placed Kathleen in my closet on the floor. The cable remained wrapped around her neck and I was afraid to touch it. All the time my hands hurt. I kept trying to rub off the red marks the cable made and bring back the circulation that had been cut off. When Barrelo came in he was very excited. He's the nervous type. He wanted to know where she was. My children were still in his car, eating. I told him where I had put her and that I needed his help to get rid of things. He agreed to dispose of her car and her body. So that he wouldn't leave prints, I gave him my baseball batter's glove and my racquetball glove. He suggested I go to her apartment and act like nothing had happened, and he would be back later. I asked when, and he just repeated, 'Later.' He took the keys from her purse and asked where the car was, so I pointed it out to him. I gathered up the kid's suitcases and walked out. He stayed behind, going through her purse."

Pirvany interrupted. "Hold on a sec. You mean you left him alone with her? What about the bruises, the rape, the sodomy? This could be important."

"I don't think he sexually attacked her," Lipscomb offered magnanimously. Then he started to speak again and Pirvany held up his hand. "Tape's full."

He flipped over the tape and reinserted it, then signaled for Lipscomb to continue.

"I went back to her apartment. I was so nervous that I could barely concentrate on driving. When I got there, the children jumped out and ran up to the door. It was locked and they wondered where their mother was. I was beat up with guilt and started to panic. We waited by the pool and talked with several people. I finally left a note on her door with the wrong time stating when I was there, and the cover-up began.

"By the time I returned to my apartment, I was literally a

wreck. I told the children to get into the bathtub, and I was concerned that one of them might open the closet door. When they were in the tub, I went to the closet and Kathleen wasn't on the floor. She was gone.''

Pirvany looked surprised. "Where the hell was she?''

"It was then I realized that some of the things were out of the chest. I opened the chest and saw Kathleen lying on her back, naked, with the cord still wrapped, and her clothes rolled up on top of her.'' Lipscomb shook his head. "I was really losing it at this point. I grabbed my military duffel bag and lifted Kathleen out of the chest and untied the cable. A gasp of air came from her that scared me so bad I almost screamed. I thought she was still alive. I listened again for a heartbeat. There was none. I put her body into the bag with her clothes, and draped a shirt over the end. I checked on the children. Then I took the bag downstairs and placed it in the back of my truck. There was a camper shell on the truck.

"Once the kids were in bed, I cleaned the apartment in a frenzy that had me drenched in sweat. I could not find her purse, shoes, or glasses.''

A guard walked by, looked through the glass in the door, but moved on.

"Were you able to find those items?'' the detective asked.

"Not until the next day. But that same night I washed the clothes I wore and let the washer run another cycle with nothing in it. I vacuumed the floor, emptied the bag, and cleaned the vacuum. I took all of the garbage to the dump site in the courtyard behind my row of apartments, and then waited for Barrelo.''

"Now wait a minute,'' Pirvany said, "you actually left your apartment for a few minutes?''

"Just to throw away trash.''

"I've looked at the evidence with Merrow and there's a tape of your daughter saying she woke up and you weren't there. That could have been the time.''

"I wasn't gone all that long. But I started to panic when Tony hadn't shown up by 11 p.m. When he did get there, he was nervous and very high. He didn't want to take Kathleen, but he had to, I couldn't risk my children waking up and my not being there for any long period of time. So he left. He returned a full two hours later. I had grown wild with anxiety over how long he had been gone. He never told me where he placed the car or the body. I didn't want to know.

"I didn't sleep at all that night. I watched a lady in an apartment below me wash her clothes and clean house. Then the next day became one cover-up after another. My boss, the day care center, calling Kathleen's work. It was the beginning of a huge lie that began to swell. So much happened so fast— Nadine calling me the next afternoon, the police calling me down that night. I don't remember the cop who threw a Polaroid of Kathleen at me, telling me she had been beaten up and strangled. With everything else, my grandmother had died that morning. It was my grief for her that they saw that night. As each day passed, the more I felt that I would never be caught. And then a good friend of mine, a one-time neighbor who knew me and my children—in fact, he and his wife were like a second set of grandparents to my kids—he kept me apprised of everything the sheriff's department did on my case."

Pirvany nodded and flipped the tape recorder off.

"Let me turn this over to Merrow," he said, "and we'll be back in touch." He shook Lipscomb's hand and left.

Three days after Bill Lipscomb's arrest, the OSI locked hand-cuffs on him and took him for a 30-minute ride through the Hampton Roads Tunnel crossing under the Chesapeake Bay. They headed toward the brig at Norfolk Naval Base in Norfolk, Virginia, the largest naval base in the United States, where Lipscomb was to serve his pre-trial confinement.

Still in control, Lipscomb refused to sign a waiver to

exchange his uniform with the master sergeant's stripes for that of a prison inmate. If he had decided to shed his Air Force attire, he would have been allowed freedom from his cell to serve on work details and mingle with other prisoners. He could have gone to chow three times a day on his own, watched television, and enjoyed outdoor recreation. Lipscomb's objection to losing his designation stemmed partly from his fear of being supervised by military personnel with a lower rank than his, but he had confided to one guard that he feared what might happen to him if he mingled with the brig's general population. Prisoners have their own way of dealing with wife-killers. So in lieu of changing his uniform and mingling, Lipscomb spent 23 and a half hours a day in solitary confinement in a cell measuring six feet by eight feet, eight inches. He could not sit or lie on his bed from 7 a.m. to 4 p.m. His cell consisted of a bunk, toilet facility, and a wooden chair/desk combination. No books, newspapers, or television were allowed. Lipscomb's only activity involved counting the cars on a freeway that he could see from his cell window.

Each day when his 30-minute allotment of freedom arrived, he spent it taking a shower and walking around the cell block, but the isolation took its toll as one day melted into the next.

The newspapers had a field day. In addition to the Virginia newspapers, the military and Texas newspapers covered the crime as well. *The Air Force Times'* headline shouted: "NCO held in murder and WAPS plot," and as a sub-headline: "Wife knew of alleged scheme." *The Houston Chronicle*'s first page headline trumpeted: "Search for killer uncovers military scandal." *The Humble Echo* declared: "Officer arrested in wife's death," and a sub-headline recognized Nadine's struggle: "Victim's mother pushes for justice." Inch-high letters formed the headline of the *San Antonio Light:* "Brutal death and AF scam merge in 'nightmare.'"

* * *

After Lipscomb's transfer to the Norfolk Navy brig, Pirvany came back for a visit. By now, he had discussed Lipscomb's comments at length with Merrow. The private investigator spent a great deal of his time coaching clients for Merrow, and very possibly, along with Merrow, had created a scenario of the murder, but Lipscomb could never admit that Merrow knew anything about it.

Lipscomb has since revealed his conversation with Pirvany that day. The PI told him, "This is how it's gotta be. Tony Barrelo killed Kathleen and is holding something over your head. We'll come up later with what it is. Anyway, for three years he's been blackmailing you, and you finally decided you had enough, and you're not going to pay him another penny. Now, when you told Tony that, he got mad, and that's why he gave his incriminating statement to the OSI."

Pirvany gave Lipscomb a few minutes to assimilate the concocted story, then he said, "By the way, Bill, what you said to me that I caught on this tape is never, and I repeat *never*, to be repeated. Got that?"

Lipscomb nodded.

The next day Merrow came by for a word-by-word replay of the story Pirvany had told him to say. The energetic attorney listened and smiled. "That's right," he said approvingly. "You play along and we'll get you off," Merrow told him.

"Just like in the movies?" Lipscomb asked, with newly awakened confidence.

"Yeah, Bill," Merrow said. "Just like in the movies."

Chapter Twenty

On the outside chance that Tony Barrelo had snowed them, the OSI decided to give him one last chance to prove his innocence. Up to now, they only had his word. There wasn't much physical evidence to shore up his story, and it was Barrelo, not Lipscomb, who possessed the chest Kathleen supposedly had been hidden in. Also, Lipscomb, at least to the authorities, steadfastly maintained his innocence.

One week after Lipscomb's arrest, Barrelo and Agent Stegall climbed on a plane headed for Bexar County to let Barrelo retrace his steps the night of the murder.

When they neared the Alamo city, Barrelo's tenseness grew as they looked down at the broad flats that were home to San Antonio's military complex. Lackland and Kelly Air Force Bases met as neighbors on the west side, Brooks Air Force Base sat on the east, and Fort Sam Houston, the big army installation, camped in the north.

After landing, Stegall took Barrelo to the visiting officers' quarters where they would spend the night. Barrelo had left

San Antonio three years earlier as a dismissed and disgraced sergeant, and now he was back as a guest in the officers' quarters.

Sharing an adjoining room with Stegall, his companion and guard, Barrelo got ready for bed and flipped on the television to watch the end of a baseball game before going to sleep. Stegall sauntered in.

"Well, that's it, Tony. I'm going to sleep so you can't watch any more TV."

Barrelo looked at him in astonishment. "It won't be long," he pleaded, "and I'll turn down the sound so it won't bother you."

"No, that's not what I mean," Stegall told him, the corners of his mouth curling. "The set won't work because I'm going to remove the coaxial cable."

The next morning, Barrelo sat in an unmarked OSI car with Agents Barney Stegall, Rich Fife, and Herb Shipman. In what was a near hopeless quest, Stegall wanted to find the cable Bill Lipscomb allegedly used because it might have his fingerprints on it. They desperately needed physical evidence, but realistically they knew it would be nearly impossible to locate it.

They let Barrelo do the driving. The plan was to start at Barrelo's apartment, then head to the apartment where Lipscomb had lived. Barrelo's fear resurfaced. The first words Stegall had told him when he had given his statement came back: "Okay, that's your story. Now you're gonna have to prove it to me."

Barrelo first drove to the apartment where he had lived. "This is where Bill came and asked me to murder Kathleen. Initially, I thought he was joking. But he kept talking about it. He said he would take out a $40,000 life insurance policy on her to pay for my getting out of the Air Force and going to college. I told him I just couldn't do it. Then, a week later he came back here again with the same suggestion. That time he gave me a $1,200 ring of Kathleen's. The ring supposedly first belonged to his grandmother. Anyway, he said it was the down payment for her murder.''

Barrelo pulled out of the complex and onto the highway. ''I sold the ring for only $75 and bought some grass with the money. Bill told me what time Kathleen would be home, and gave me her address and directions to her apartment.''

''Take us there now,'' Stegall told him.

''Bill handed me a buck knife to go kill her. He had been to her apartment earlier in the day to help her move some furniture. He had left a window unlocked so I could get in.''

Fifteen minutes later, Barrelo pulled up to the pink stone apartment complex near U.T.'s Health Science Center, and pointed. ''That's her apartment at the end of this building. I parked about four doors down and went to that window over there. I could see Kathleen through the window. I had met her several times—a real nice-looking lady. In fact, I can still picture her sitting in the bleachers at the softball games. Anyway, I watched her for a few minutes. She kept moving around, unpacking boxes, putting things away, and getting her new apartment ready. Well, I just couldn't do it. I hated to go back and tell Lipscomb that, so I told him she was with someone.''

''That adds up,'' Stegall said, glancing around the quiet complex. ''None of the forensic evidence we have on her apartment indicates she was killed here. Let's go over to Lipscomb's place.''

''Right,'' Fife said, ''and stick to the same route you took that night.''

Barrelo thought the atmosphere in the car seemed cold toward him. He had no trouble finding Lipscomb's apartment, where he pulled into the complex of several buildings. He passed by streetlights—large glass balls sitting on tall gray poles. Bird of Paradise trees, with bright orange blossoms, dotted the landscape. Barrelo stopped in front of the gray stucco structure. Lipscomb's apartment was on the second floor.

"Hold it right here," Stegall said, scanning the painted gray metal steps leading from Lipscomb's place. "I want to check out the route he would have carried the duffel bag. He'd have taken her down those seven steps to that landing, then turned, and down those lower seven steps to the parking lot. Looks like the first space his truck could have been parked was about twelve feet from the bottom step. Would he have any trouble doing all that?"

"Nah," Barrelo said, "she was just a little thing. On that Friday before she died, Bill called me and said that time was getting short. In that last week or so, he kept talking about the importance of timing, but not until later with the insurance and all did I realize why. He said that their divorce would soon be final and we had to put together some plans. He wanted me to make myself available to him on Sunday, June 8."

"Why didn't you just tell him to go to hell?" Stegall asked.

"It's all so clear to me now. Today that's what I would have said, but back then Bill had this control over me. He gave me money to buy drugs. No way would he take them himself. Bill knew what he was doing. The drugs weakened me and allowed him to take over."

"Tony, I want it straight. Are you clean now?"

"Yeah. I haven't taken anything for over a year. I'm going to stay clean, too."

Barrelo sensed that the agents were looking at each other, and he felt they still didn't believe him.

"Bill called me that day and asked me to come over about 6 p.m. to take his kids to McDonald's. I'll show you where we went."

After another 10-minute junket, he pulled into the McDonald's parking lot. "Bill said Kathleen would be coming soon and he wanted to talk with her alone. Kathleen hadn't arrived by the time I got there, and Bill gave me some money for

McDonald's and told me to call before coming back. I had a feeling he planned to kill her, but I didn't really think he'd go through with it.'' The agents gave Barrelo little encouragement despite what he had shown them so far. The longer Barrelo talked, the drier his mouth became and he had trouble swallowing. ''Okay if we get a Coke here?''

''Sure,'' Stegall said. ''Use the drive-through to save time. We've still got a lot of ground to cover.''

Everyone ordered a drink at the window and Barrelo pulled through the parking lot and back onto the highway.

''Did you question Lipscomb about what he kept asking you to do?'' Agent Fife asked.

''No, not really. I just kept following his instructions like some dumb shit. He had emphasized that I had to call before I brought the kids home.'' Barrelo slowed the car and squinted. ''I know there's a pay phone down the road here a little ways. Ah, there it is.''

Herb Shipman sat in the back seat with a stopwatch, timing each of the destinations to make sure they matched the time frame Barrelo had given them.

Barrelo pulled up to the pay phone, and Shipman said, ''Four minutes and twenty seconds. Sounds right.''

''I called him from that phone and when Bill answered he was breathing hard and sounded excited. He said, 'I did it. I did it,' and I asked him, 'Did what?' He said, 'I killed Kathleen, so bring the kids back.' Although I knew there was always a chance he might go through with it, those words chilled me.

''When I got back to Bill's apartment, he was sweating like a pig. I even remember what he was wearing. He had on blue shorts and a matching T-shirt, and they were both stuck to his body. He looked like a madman. The veins were bulging on his arms. It's a hard thing to describe, but the look on his face told me he had killed her. Unless you had been there, you can't imagine what he was like.''

''Did the kids see him looking like that?'' asked Fife.

"Yeah, but I don't think they noticed much because he rushed them into the bathroom and started running water in the tub. He told them that they had to take a bath because their mother was coming to pick them up. Then he closed the bathroom door and said, 'Do you want to see her?'

"I followed him into his bedroom and he opened the closet door. That's where the cedar chest was. Bill raised the lid, but I couldn't look. I walked away.

"I went back into his living room and Bill followed me. He said, 'It's not like in the movies. It takes a long time to kill someone. The damn cord broke and I had to do it again.' I couldn't imagine how Bill could have broken a coaxial cable, but he did give me three pieces to throw away.

"Now the story gets sick at this point. He said that when he reached for the second cord, Kathleen got a gulp of air and said, 'Oh my God, Bill, no!' But he finished the job." Barrelo shook his head and his eyes looked moist.

"Then Bill starts telling me, 'You've got to help me get rid of her car. We've got to get rid of everything.'"

Barrelo continually glanced at the agents as he recounted his tale, looking to gauge their level of belief. But he saw only expressions of stoic noncommittal.

"Shit, I didn't know what to do, but I said 'okay.' Bill grabbed Kathleen's purse and got out her car keys, and I think he took out a twenty. I'm not sure how much, but he said, 'Take the car and park it somewhere. Here, take this money and catch a cab, but don't come all the way back to the apartment.' Also, he gave me a couple sports gloves so I wouldn't leave fingerprints. I know one was a pitcher's glove, and I think the other was a racquetball glove. Anyway, I took the keys and the money and drove her car to one of these shopping centers off this interstate."

Barrelo drove less than 10 minutes and turned into Luby's parking lot and hesitated. He started to pull into one place, then stopped. He thought for a moment, then pulled into the third space on his right, and looked at Fife.

Fife nodded. "The exact space."

Barrelo relaxed. "I remember pulling the seat all the way up to make the police think that a real short person had driven it. It was about 7:45 then, and I walked to a Pizza Hut to call a cab. I took it back to a 7-Eleven on Culebra—within a mile of Bill's place. I walked the rest of the way.

"When I got back to Bill's, he told me he had already gone over to Kathleen's apartment and left a note on the door. He had put the wrong time on it to cover his tracks. At that time, he said he wanted me to come back around midnight to get rid of the body. I argued with him. I didn't see why he couldn't do that. I'd stay with the kids. But he worried that they'd wake up and wonder why he wasn't there, so I agreed, I was really scared."

"He had you get rid of the duffel bag and other things, didn't he?" Barney asked.

"Yeah, but that was after I dropped the body."

"Okay, but from what you told us before, isn't this about the area where you threw them?"

"Right. I dropped the duffel in a dumpster not far from here." He turned west and went to an area with several apartment complexes. He drove into one of the parking lots. "It was that dumpster over there where I threw the duffel. Well, at least the dumpster that was there at the time.

"When I went back to his apartment, Bill handed me three cables. One about eighteen inches and the other two about a foot each. He also gave me her purse to get rid of. I put the purse in an apartment dumpster over by Lackland."

"Show us what you did with the cables," Fife instructed.

"I threw the cables in a grassy field past Hamburger Hill. It's back this way."

Barrelo turned the car around and drove toward the vicinity of the field he had told them about, but when he approached the area, he found cars whirling down a six-lane highway built directly across the land.

Tony shrugged and turned to Stegall. "Just go on," Stegall said. "The cables will be long gone."

Barrelo waited impatiently for the traffic to clear, then made a U-turn. It appeared that his subconscious had taken over. He needed the extra help, because the big test lay ahead—Scenic Loop Road. On the way, he continued to discuss the murder.

"I literally had trouble coping with what I was doing. But it was kinda like the trouble I had at work, you know, as a TI. We had an unbelievable amount of pressure put on us. They'd give us these students, and it'd be like they handed us Volkswagen parts and expected us to produce a Cadillac. Our supers were always threatening to pull a stripe if we didn't perform miracles for them and that led me to use a little speed to get through the long hours and all the expectations.

"Like I told you, Bill used to give me drug money. My head was so fucked up then that I didn't realize it was his way of making me vulnerable. This is all so clear to me now. Why, I've asked myself a thousand times, couldn't I have seen it then. Actually at that time, I was developing a problem with crank—you know, methamphetamine. But my drug use then couldn't be compared to how it was after the murder. It doubled, tripled—no, quadrupled. I used it to escape. To forget what I had done. So that night I contacted my source and bought a whole gram. I went home and used half of it. Can you imagine how I was speeding?"

"I can't believe you could have driven a car," Shipman said.

"Hell, I was flying. I didn't need a car. Anyway, I went back to Bill's around 11:30, and Bill looked real nervous, like he'd been worrying I wasn't going to show up. He had already put Kathleen in a duffel bag and loaded her into his Mazda pickup. He told me to drive way out in the country, didn't care where, and just drop her some place. I drove to the edge of town, like I'm doing now, but in my condition then, I got lost."

He interrupted himself to point out a 25-cent car wash. "That's where I took the truck on the way back. I cleaned it off because I had been driving on dirt roads. While I was there, I saw some blood in the back of the truck, so I used the pressure hose and scrubbed it real hard."

"Yeah," Fife said, "I remember seeing the crime scene photos with blood around Kathleen's head and mouth."

"I had wadded up the duffel, so if there was blood on that, I never saw it," Barrelo said. "After that, I took the truck back to Bill's and told him all I had done and I had to get the fuck out of there. That's when he gave me everything else to get rid of." Barrelo seemed to drift away in his memory, then shook his head.

"Now, what was I saying? Oh, yeah, I got lost. I drove through some little town, can't even think of its name, and a police car followed me. I have never been so scared in all my life. If he had stopped me then ... well, I can't even think about it." Barrelo shuddered.

Barrelo had driven north on Highway 10 for 30 minutes, leaving the haze of the city far behind as he approached the low hills that ring the northern outskirts of San Antonio. He exited onto Bourne Stage Road and passed several sprawling ranches. Most of the ranch houses were built of native, light-colored Austin stone, and glittered like white castles in the noon sunlight. After a couple miles, he took a left at Scenic Loop. As his search continued, he regained composure and looked more confident.

"It was right along here that I dropped her, but I swear I never saw the body. No way did I want to look when I shook her out of that bag. I threw the duffel into the truck and left."

Barrelo continued driving down the narrow, two-lane road where he searched the 15-foot strips of rough grass, intermingled with gravel, that bordered each side. He noticed a rustic fence of barbed wire with posts fashioned from tree limbs that ran parallel to the route. He followed it up and down the hilly terrain, trying to recall if he had seen that before. He remembered the gnarled old oak trees, their bent and twisted branches covered with stunted Spanish Moss.

"How am I doing?" Barrelo asked Stegall.

"So far, so good," was the only encouragement he received.

As Barrelo drove on, no agent said a word when he passed the site where Kathleen had been found. He drove another mile, and it became apparent to everyone that he was hopelessly lost. Inside the car, the agents sat dispassionately while perspiration poured from Barrelo. He couldn't mask the redness now glowing on his skin.

"Remember, I've only been here once and it was at midnight. I mean it was blacker than the inside of a cow." A frown etched his face, and he finally said, "Ah, shit, I think I've gone too far."

"Why don't you go back to where you turned onto Scenic Loop, and start over," Fife suggested.

Barrelo followed his directions, and again became ill at ease as he strained his eyes searching for the crucial spot. He drove another mile. This time he slowed down when he approached ground zero. Carefully, he guided the car onto the roadside.

"This is it. I remember it was less hilly here so I had a flat area to pull off the road."

Stegall patted his back. "Well done, Tony. Let's get back to Langley. Now we have the corroboration for your testimony."

Chapter Twenty-One

Kenneth Merrow began the arduous job of preparing for Bill Lipscomb's Article 32, the military equivalent of a grand jury hearing. It would determine whether or not the prosecution had enough evidence for a court martial. However, time rushed away from him as he researched the tapes of Tony Barrelo and Shannon Gilbert. He also had to wade through the variety of statements made by all the people the OSI and the Guidry Group had questioned. Then he spent more time studying the autopsy, as well as the reports from Kathleen's psychiatrists and psychologists.

At first, Merrow agreed to the August 1 hearing, but he requested a delay until August 28, then another postponement until September 26. Finally, on October 18, three months after his arrest, Bill Lipscomb sat in the courtroom next to his only available attorney.

Captains McMinn and Brash, his military lawyers, had scheduling conflicts and couldn't attend any of the three sessions. At the time, Lipscomb felt content to have only Merrow and waived his right to military counsel. Actually, from the beginning, Lipscomb was dubious as to the professionalism of his military lawyers, especially when he heard that Capt. McMinn, a young attorney, had never before been involved in a capital punishment case. The tall, thin, bespectacled captain seemed intimidated by everyone, including Lipscomb, who deemed the military's assigning McMinn to his case to be their guarantee of a conviction. From the beginning, Lipscomb's mistrust of his military lawyers led him to be far less open with them than he had been with Merrow's investigator.

Lipscomb looked around the almost empty courtroom in Langley's legal building that could have accommodated a large gallery of spectators. "Where is everybody? I thought this would be a three-ring circus."

"That's exactly what we didn't want," Merrow assured him. "With all the media coverage and the public hysteria, we asked for and were granted a closed hearing."

Lipscomb nodded his approval. The arrest of the handsome, highly decorated and fast-rising master sergeant, accused of masterminding a world-wide cheating scam and also killing his wife, would attract a great deal of public interest by itself. The fact that he had escaped detection for over three years made the story even more sensational.

Lt. Col. Robert E. Sears from the Fourth Circuit USAF Judiciary, stationed at Lowry Air Force Base, Colorado, served as the appointed judge—in military vernacular, the Investigating Officer. The soft-spoken judge had the power to decide if the case, as outlined by the prosecution, was significant enough to recommend that Bill Lipscomb be court-martialed. But should Sears find that the charges had no merit, he could also recommend that they be dismissed.

Judge Sears kicked off the hearing by formally announcing the Air Force charges against Lipscomb: one, the premeditated murder of Kathleen Adams Lipscomb; two, the obstruction of justice by offering Tony Barrelo money to leave the country so he couldn't testify against him.

The case against Sergeant Lipscomb was not a sure thing. With the lack of physical evidence, nothing but words tied him to the murder. If for any reason the judge threw out Barrelo's tapes or Gilbert's statements, the prosecution's case would be impoverished. And Merrow, no doubt, would put forth every effort to prove that Barrelo had a decidedly vested interest in trying to portray Lipscomb as guilty.

Merrow was anxious over the abundance of taped evidence against his client. He also worried that the Air Force OSI was the driving force behind the investigation. A military judge had already been appointed, and if this went to a court martial, the jury would consist of military personnel.

Lipscomb likened this to working for a large corporation and being charged with arriving late for work by the corporation, then being tried by that corporation and assigned a lawyer who was on their payroll. After that, being sentenced by a judge appointed by the corporation and sent to a corporation-run jail. Also, all appeals would be handled by that corporation's appointees. Fair or not, the military criminal justice system holds a much tighter rein on the defendant than civilian courts do.

The prosecution presented what little physical evidence it had: the crime scene photos of a nude, dead woman by a country road, the autopsy, the transcripts of tapes, and an old chest.

Captain Joseph T. Townsend, a military lawyer stationed at Langley, was one of two prosecution lawyers designated as Assistant Trial Counsel. Even though he was only an assistant counsel, the tall, trim, blue-eyed blond would conduct all the questioning for this hearing. He looked older than his 35 years, and rose to open the case, wasting no time calling the first witness for the prosecution, Staff Sergeant Shannon Gilbert.

Shannon, clad again in her blue uniform suit, had been brought back from Germany—where she recently had been relocated. Townsend summoned her to identify the accused. She nervously pointed in Lipscomb's direction.

Without emotion, he stared back at her outstretched finger.

Capt. Townsend asked Shannon Gilbert if she recognized the statement she had made to the OSI almost a year ago. She scanned the three-page document and nodded. Townsend took the document from her to enter as Exhibit #1, over the objection of Merrow, who called it "hearsay."

Townsend asked Shannon when she had met Lipscomb.

"In September 1984, Sergeant Lipscomb was my MTIS [Military Training Instructor School] seminar instructor. Then after I graduated, he continued to contact me and take me to lunch. We were pretty much friends until June of the next year, when his wife went to Houston and Sergeant Lipscomb invited me out." She talked freely about their relationship, how Lipscomb often spent time at her house, watching television, talking about his upcoming divorce, his tearful dismay at the unfairness of his children having to live without him, and how, most significantly, he planned to have Kathleen murdered.

"Do you remember specifically when you had your first sexual encounter?" Townsend asked.

Shannon wasn't embarrassed by the question, but had to pause a moment to recall. "I guess that was the night I saw him walking down the street. He had a fight with his wife and decided to leave her. He planned to spend the night with Tony Barrelo. I guess that's where he was going when I saw him. I picked him up and took him home with me. He took a shower at my house, then we had sex, and he ended up spending the night. But he went back to his wife the very next day."

"The next day?" Capt. Townsend had already discussed the testimony with Shannon, but he wanted to emphasize that Lipscomb had jumped from her bed right back to his wife's within 24 hours. "Why so soon?"

"I think his parents were coming to visit, and it wouldn't

look right for him not to be there. But he continued to come over to see me.''

Townsend did his best to depict the cold, self-serving mindset of Bill Lipscomb. ''Tell me about your finding out Kathleen Lipscomb had been killed.''

''After Bill told me Kathleen had been murdered, I became hysterical and met him to talk about it. He said, 'these hands,' ''—she extended her hands, palms up—'' 'did not do it.' I reminded Bill that he told me he would have someone kill her. Of course he denied that, but he looked very worried. He made me promise that I wouldn't tell anyone. He kept telling me, 'What you are saying could get me in a whole lot of trouble.' The thing that really surprised me was that he seemed much more bothered over what would happen to him than the fact that his wife had just been murdered. So I promised him I wouldn't tell anyone.''

''Why did you say that?''

''Truthfully? I was afraid for myself and my son. I thought if he actually did it and knowing he had told me, he could certainly kill me without any qualms whatsoever.''

Townsend quizzed her about the last time she saw Sergeant Lipscomb. ''How would you describe it as far as your relationship ending? How did it affect you?''

''It was no great trauma. I mean, we were basically friends, not really platonic, but mostly friends. I guess I was his confidante.''

When it came time for Merrow's cross-examination, he questioned Shannon Gilbert's memory, intending to undermine her answers. To soften the image of Sergeant Lipscomb, Merrow always referred to him as ''Billy.''

.''At the time of your statement to the OSI, you hadn't seen Billy for two full years?''

''No, sir.''

''And now it has been over three years, and in all that time, you can remember these minuscule details?

"Yes, sir."

Merrow spit out one question after another in his fiery, direct manner, challenging her recollections. He had a razor-sharp mind and was good at catching defendants in gaffes. He drilled Shannon on her drinking and how that affected her ability to remember, and on her attending therapy sessions. He forced her to recall her abuse as a child—the presumed source of her emotional problems.

Then the lawyer pressed her about testifying for the reward of immunity from prosecution. "Did you have any sort of understanding as to what may be done with you by the authorities in exchange for your information?"

"I was granted immunity as far as not giving information about WAPS or the murder for the last two and a half years."

"So before you even walked into that room you had a blanket promise of immunity from all the authorities, both military and civilian?"

"No, sir. Not a blanket. It was a very limited grant of immunity. If I had been involved in the murder, it would not have covered that."

Merrow's tone was alternately accusatory and condescending, but Shannon held her ground. He held a copy of a transcript of the phone call she had made to Lipscomb.

"Essentially," the attorney said, "you became an operative for the OSI after December 1988?"

Townsend stood to object. "By using the term 'operative,' it calls for the witness to make a legal conclusion."

Both lawyers knew that in an Article 32 Hearing, objections are noted, but not ruled on. The objections would not affect the questioning process, but gave the attorneys a chance to wedge their opinions into the record.

Shannon explained that the private investigators had suggested the phone call, and that she wasn't aware beforehand of the reasoning behind it.

"Let me get this straight, Sergeant Gilbert," Merrow said,

"the private investigators came to you out of the clear blue sky and asked you to call Billy Lipscomb for a reason that you didn't know?"

"Yes, sir."

"So you just did it voluntarily, out of the goodness of your heart, for no reason and no expectation that it would benefit you at all?"

"Certainly not to benefit me. I was trying to help them with the investigation."

Merrow let that pass and asked questions about the taped phone conversation to Billy, and he scored big. Shannon had to admit that at no time did Sergeant Lipscomb confess to hiring anyone to murder his wife, nor did he even object if Shannon talked to the OSI about it.

"You were doing an acting job, weren't you?"

"I guess," she conceded.

Townsend looked concerned. Shannon was so guileless that she was becoming putty in Merrow's hands.

"And the whole purpose of your acting job, Sergeant, was to try to get him to incriminate himself, true?"

"Yes, sir."

"And you tried to get money out of him for a lawyer, true?"

"Yes, sir, I guess."

"And that's when he said something to you about blackmailing him?"

"Yes, sir, he did."

Then Merrow wanted to hear more about Bill's infidelity.

"That night you had sex with Billy, he was separated from his wife, right?"

"Yes, sir."

"Other than that night, Billy Lipscomb had been faithful to his wife, with you at least."

"There was a time in June 1985, when he came over to look at my puppies and we made out."

"Okay." Merrow gave her a resigned shrug. "Other than that time."

"I would say so."

"Then after his wife was murdered, you saw him regularly."

"Yes. He would come over to my house. He brought his kids over and then every once in a while I would go over to his house."

"And slept together twice."

"Slept together?"

"Had sex, right?"

"Yes."

"And this is the man that you are afraid of?"

"I was not totally confident, sir."

"You described it, Sergeant. Let there be no doubt about it. There is no doubt in my mind. You said, 'I was afraid of this man.' Is that the truth?"

"Yes, sir."

"But you would go out with this man and with your son—you would be with him and his children, and you would sleep with him, sexually, at least twice that we know of for sure, and this is the man that you are afraid of?"

"Yes, sir." Shannon sat wide-eyed. There appeared to be no contradiction in her mind that you could make love to someone you feared.

Merrow stared at her incredulously. She had answered all of his questions calmly, and had agreed that what the attorney had said was true, but had given no argument, no plea for credibility, or excuse that she had been coerced by Bill. He shook his head. "I pass the witness."

The Investigating Officer, Lt. Col. Sears, was more than a judge because he also had the right to question any witness. During the morning proceedings, he had mostly leaned on the bench with his hand on his chin, taking notes and listening. Now he asked Shannon Gilbert, "I got the impression that when you first heard from Sergeant Lipscomb about his wanting to have his wife killed, it was something that you did not take seriously?''

''No, sir, I did not.''

''When was it that you took him seriously and why?''

''The night I called him and found out that Kathleen had been murdered. It was just too coincidental for him to say I would read about it in the newspaper, and then all of a sudden she's dead.''

''Did you at some time come to feel safe with him? Obviously you were with him a number of times after that.''

''No, sir. I never did feel safe with him and there was one incident where we went out to Bandera, Texas, that he stopped along the side of the road and I was so scared that I could hardly talk. It was on a very dark, desolate road. I was extremely scared.''

''Did he ever do anything to you that might make you fear for your life or fear any harm?''

Shannon paused for a moment. ''Not overtly. No, I don't think so.''

''That is all the questions I have,'' Sears said, looking at Capt. Townsend. ''Do you want to follow up?''

Townsend needed to help repair some of Shannon's flawed affirmations.

''Yes, I have one more question,'' he said, standing. ''Shannon, did anything else happen on Bandera Road as far as your being scared?''

''When we came back from Bandera, Bill pulled off the side of the road and we got out to talk. It was real dark. I don't remember what we talked about, but we ended up having sex in the back of the truck. I felt like I had to do it because I was so scared that something bad would happen to me.''

''That's all the questions I have,'' Townsend said, nodding toward Merrow.

Merrow seemed fascinated with Shannon's fear for her personal safety with no apparent justification. He stood to take another crack at one of the prosecution's star witnesses.

"Do I understand, Sergeant, that Billy never said anything to you, threatened you, did anything—you just got scared on your own?"

"Yes, sir, I certainly did."

"Nothing further," he said, and still shaking his head, walked back to the defense table.

Tony Barrelo's hand trembled when he took the oath to tell the truth. This was his first face-to-face confrontation with Lipscomb since the clandestine taping in his office. In a courtroom with military brass in attendance, Barrelo played the role of the star and took the opportunity and the excessive time to recount every detail of his involvement. He even described how far two of his wheels were off the road when he parked the truck to dump Kathleen's body.

Frequently he would request permission to rise from the witness chair and pantomime his actions, showing how he dragged the body from the truck or how he injured his thumb on the truck's tailgate. Everyone listened intently as Barrelo narrated Lipscomb's efforts to coax him into killing Kathleen. Barrelo described Kathleen's ring that was used as a down payment for the murder. Then he itemized every dollar that Lipscomb had disbursed to him during the last three years. He was on the stand for five hours.

Still, during Merrow's cross-examination, Barrelo had to concede that Lipscomb had never admitted on tape to killing Kathleen. He also had to acknowledge that there were many inaudible portions on the tape. Barrelo tried to slip in the fact that those voids were caused by Lipscomb's crying, but Merrow cut him off.

The prosecution highlighted the part of Barrelo's taped conversation with Lipscomb they liked best—Bill's encouraging

Barrelo to leave the country to avoid contacting the OSI, and offering him money to do so. This was deemed the most damaging part, because from it the military could construe that Lipscomb was obstructing justice.

The prosecution heralded Barrelo's trip to Bexar County as a clear demonstration that he knew where everything had taken place, thus serving to authenticate his testimony.

The last witness was OSI Special Agent Peter C. Ober, to whom Lipscomb had reported Barrelo's blackmailing scheme. He testified about the second taping.

"We were in the next room listening to the recording. Also, we could hear their voices through the wall. Parts of the conversation were difficult to hear. Some I remember very clearly. Sergeant Lipscomb was most concerned that Mr. Barrelo not go to the OSI. He was begging him not to go and at times you could hear him crying through the wall, saying that Barrelo was going to ruin his life."

On cross-examination, Merrow asked what Lipscomb had said about killing his wife, and Agent Ober granted that Lipscomb only stated that he did not kill his wife.

The prosecution had not presented an airtight case of Lipscomb being the murderer. However, the presentation by the defense was even less stellar. No witnesses were called, but they were possibly being saved for the court martial. Merrow entered into evidence all of Lipscomb's Airman Performance Reports from October 1975 through January 1989. The reports would do their own talking.

Following three days of testimony and debate, Lt. Col. Sears addressed the hearing:

"After weighing all of the evidence of this case, I conclude that there is sufficient evidence to proceed to trial on the charges of premeditated murder and obstruction of justice. Due to the seriousness of the charges, I recommend the referral to trial by general court martial as a capital case.''

This was the strongest referral that could be made against Bill Lipscomb. The military reserves capital cases solely for the two most serious offenses: murder and treason. There are exclusively two sentences in a capital case: death or life in prison.

The Air Force moved swiftly. The day after Lt. Col. Sears made his recommendation, Lt. Gen. Charles Horner approved that decision and sent the charges to the Ninth Air Force, Shaw Air Force Base, South Carolina. That same day, Lipscomb was served with the charges.

Now the wheels were in motion. If found guilty, Bill Lipscomb could be put to death.

Chapter Twenty-Two

While Bill Lipscomb languished in solitary confinement, the legal proceedings crept along. It was already 1990, and he had been in jail for six months.

On January 19, the next phase of Lipscomb's trial, the Article 39 (a), began. Its purpose would be to iron out legal issues, and the defense would use the opportunity to try to get as much incriminating evidence dismissed as possible.

The military judge, Lt. Colonel Michael T. Callinan, mentioned that he had previously worked with the lead prosecution counsel, Captain Bruce Ambrose, in the same legal office at Nellis Air Force Base, but that it wouldn't prejudice him in any way. Callinan's full head of white hair made him look older than his mid-40s. His broad shoulders and chest loomed massively behind the bench, and he seemed even larger when he spoke in his deep, assertive baritone. His fine reputation was based on the best credibility a judge can have: very few of his convictions were ever overturned by appellate courts.

Lipscomb's civilian attorney and lead counsel, Kenneth Merrow, grabbed every opportunity to offer broad and generic motions, even questioning whether the President of the United States, as Commander and Chief of the military, had the constitutional authority to bestow the death penalty on military personnel.

Judge Callinan took the motions under advisement and denied every one of them. Then he asked the accused to rise and state how he would plead.

Bill Lipscomb stood arrow stiff and in a strong voice said, "Not guilty, Your Honor."

Later the judge asked how he wanted his panel constituted. Panel is the military term for jury, and Lipscomb had the option of selecting officers or a combination of officers and master sergeants.

Lipscomb quickly conferred with his attorney. "I don't want NCOs. Can you imagine what those master sergeants would think of this alleged WAPS scam? They wouldn't understand how I could miss fifteen questions on each promotion test and then miraculously get almost one hundred correct. They just don't know how hard I can work if I really want something."

Merrow nodded. "Since officers don't take the test, they would place less importance on the exam process."

Lipscomb agreed and turned to the judge. "Officers, Your Honor."

Merrow then hammered away for a new Article 32 to be convened. "This case should not have been brought to trial in the first place because there was an inadequate government investigation, no motive that Bill Lipscomb needed the insurance money, and no evidence of prolonged physical or mental pain."

He looked pleadingly at Callinan, but all of his motions fell on deaf judicial ears.

However, the judge surprised everyone by throwing out the current Article 39 (a) Hearing. He stated that the convening authority, Lt. General Charles A. Horner, had been imprecise in his wording, not mentioning that he had a choice of convening the court martial as capital or non-capital.

Callinan contacted the three-star general, who the following year would distinguish himself with his handling of air strikes in Desert Storm. Horner had little patience with being told he had been imprecise.

"I knew I had the option," he barked. "I just chose not to mention it. I called for the case to be convened as capital so that the death penalty is an option, and that stands."

One fax settled the issue and Judge Callinan scheduled a new Article 39 (a).

In the meantime Lipscomb's lawyers were bickering among themselves. Since Lipscomb did not trust his military lawyers, seeing them as part of the regime bringing the charges against him, he gave a less than candid scenario of the murder to Capt. Brash, who had been brought in from Bolling Air Force Base in Washington, D.C. The short, heavy-set attorney compared his notes to Merrow's and learned that Merrow intended to have Lipscomb profess his innocence, even though Merrow was aware of Lipscomb's confession to his private investigator, Pirvany. Brash exploded.

"If you put Lipscomb on the stand, I promise I will get up and testify against him myself." Brash lived up to his name. He was quick with his words, direct in his delivery, and intimidating to the other lawyers.

Merrow rationalized that Lipscomb had "confessed" to his investigator, and not to himself, so therefore he had not actually heard the words from Lipscomb's lips. But Brash knew any lawyer risked his career to knowingly allow his client to stand up and perjure himself.

The turn of events called for a special Saturday meeting between Lipscomb and Merrow. Merrow called his client to say he would be visiting him within the hour, but he didn't divulge the reason. He met Lipscomb in a meeting room at the Norfolk brig, and abruptly announced, "I've got to relieve Brash from this case." Merrow tried to avoid the startled eyes of his client as he continued, "and once I do that, you have to fire me." Merrow didn't explain that he could not stay on with Brash out there ready to pounce if Merrow carried out his plan to have Lipscomb testify.

Lipscomb felt like a knife had been shoved into the pit of his stomach. It had been over six months since his arrest and now he found himself back at square one. Merrow offered to help him choose a new lawyer and to stay on until that lawyer had been fully briefed.

Merrow hired an expensive attorney, J. Cabot Foxmire, for whom Lipscomb again reached into Kathleen's insurance to pay a retainer of $50,000. If any of his attorneys realized the irony that Kathleen was paying for her accused murderer's defense, they didn't mention it.

Foxmire frequently advertised on local television as a personal injury specialist. In his late 40s, he was the oldest of all the attorneys in the courtroom. Lipscomb also received two new military lawyers and hired a second civilian lawyer, Timothy S. Fisher, to handle specific motions because he had prior military legal experience. Even though Fisher had been a military lawyer and now served as a Reserve Major, Lipscomb felt confident of his loyalties since he was paying him.

The new hearing began on March 2, 1990. Foxmire rose to speak and revealed a slow, measured voice that didn't match his flashy appearance. When he addressed the change of attorneys, he looked Judge Callinan directly in the eye and said, "If I were sitting in your chair and I saw the change of counsel come across the way it did, my first thinking as a judge would be, 'This guy has told his lawyers that A, B, C is true, but he is going testify to C, D, and E,' and his lawyers said, 'I'm not having any part of that.' " He pointed at the judge, "I want to state, under oath, that this is not why the defense counsel resigned. It was irreconcilable differences and conflict between military counsel and civilian counsel, and not because Sergeant Lipscomb was going to lie under oath. Had that been the case, I wouldn't be standing here today representing him."

A few eyes rolled in the courtroom, but no one refuted his statement.

Then with great humility, Foxmire begged for a continuance even though he personally believed in a "rocket docket." He cited that since he had just been hired by Lipscomb, had other trials on his docket, and had planned a trip to Italy with his family, he had no time right now. He had consciously thought this case would take about a week, when in actuality it would last more than a month.

Judge Callinan agreed and set the actual court martial for August 20, 1990, but the Article 39 (a) Hearing that would cover a time span of only a couple days continued.

The defense began by calling Lipscomb's counselor from the Norfolk brig, who described him as a "model prisoner." However, when the prosecution questioned the counselor, he had to admit that Lipscomb was only out of his cell 30 minutes a day, so he had little time to get into trouble.

Then Capt. Linda Goodbrake, Lipscomb's supervisor at Langley took the witness stand. As his concerned friend, she twice visited Lipscomb in the brig. Now she gushed to the prosecution's attorney over Lipscomb's job record that she termed: "Excellent, outstanding, and superior." When quizzed about Lipscomb as a person, she described him as "very level-headed, very confident, very detailed, and just a very concerned person for his troops and for the operation itself."

When prosecution lawyer, Capt. Ambrose cross-examined her, she told him, "Knowing Bill from how he performed for me, I could not believe he could do something like this."

Master Sergeant Mary Ann Chatmon also became a friend of Lipscomb's by working with him, and she showed an eagerness to help even after his arrest. Twice during his confinement, he needed to visit a dentist. Sergeant Chatmon willingly escorted him from the brig to his appointments.

Confinement rules dictate that a prisoner be handcuffed when leaving the facility, but just as soon as Lipscomb settled in her car, she unlocked his restraining cuffs and allowed him to enjoy a temporary freedom. She told the prosecution that she had absolutely no fear of the man.

With all the wonderful things being said about Sergeant Lipscomb, Foxmire took the opportunity to ask that Lipscomb be released from pre-trial confinement. After much argument on both sides, Judge Callinan determined that Lipscomb's release could cause alarm to the many people who had already testified against him, and on that basis denied the motion.

Lipscomb and his attorneys had previously discussed the handling of the tapes from his two covert conversations with Tony Barrelo.

"First the damn tapes had been sent to the FBI for 'enhancement' because of their garbled sound quality," Foxmire complained. "Then even after the FBI modifications, several portions of the tapes remained inaudible and what does the OSI do but allow Tony Barrelo to fill in the words on the transcript that he *said* Bill told him."

"I want you to listen to those tapes again," Lipscomb insisted. "Those words Tony put in were just not said. He made up most of that."

"This is a big loophole that should blow the case sky high," Foxmire assured him. "The OSI let Tony pluck words out of his goddamn memory and insert them into an official transcript."

Lipscomb relaxed and smiled at the encouragement.

Back in court, the defense launched a huge frontal attack on the tapes. "Your Honor" Foxmire began, "Any court of law reviewing this case would ultimately throw out any decision against my client because of these tapes. They are nothing but pieces of fabricated evidence. They've been custom-made to show one of the most damning claims, which is attesting that the defendant offered money to Sergeant Barrelo to get him out of town. It would take an imagination better than I could dream up to hear anything of that nature on those tapes.''

Foxmire shouted over objections from Capt. Ambrose, but it didn't matter. Nothing the defense did could convince Judge Callinan that the transcripts should not be admitted. And the tapes became some of the most damaging evidence against Lipscomb.

The chain of evidence of the tapes became comical with the witnesses' sketchy memories after almost a year's lapse. Dr. McDowell couldn't remember if he had placed the tapes in his trunk that weekend after the conversation between Barrelo and Lipscomb, or locked them in the evidence room.

Foxmire called the source of the controversy, Tony Barrelo, to the stand. Barrelo had been comfortable testifying at the Article 32 Hearing, where he had recited the tale of the murder as he had wanted it told. Now he had to undergo examination by the key defense lawyer. He would not have chosen the questions.

Foxmire pounced on Barrelo to tarnish his credibility. ''Were you on drugs when you listened to the tapes?''

''No, sir.''

''Have you ever abused drugs in the past?''

''Yes, sir, I have.'' Barrelo shifted in his chair.

''When did you listen to the tapes for the very first time to try to change what was on the transcript?''

''It was . .'' Barrelo sat nervously stroking his chin and looking into space as if the answer would soon appear to him.

''Do you remember the month?''

''I'm trying to recall, sir. It's been quite some time. July, August . . .''

''Do you remember the season?''

Barrelo sat pondering.

''Do you remember the year?''

''Yes, sir. I'm just trying to recall the facts in my mind.''

"Having trouble recalling?" Foxmire made it look easy to show Barrelo's inability to remember, the man the OSI trusted to plug in crucial information on the transcript from the tapes.

"The initial investigation started around the end of May, the tapings, July—" Barrelo began.

"Your powers of perception diminished because of your drug use?" Foxmire grinned.

"No, sir, not at all." Still, he could not supply the answer.

"How about your powers of remembrance? Are they diminished because of your drug use?"

"I believe it was sometime around September."

"Of what year?"

"Sir, that would be— I'm trying to recall if it was prior to Christmas or after Christmas."

"Well, I think we could all stipulate that September comes before Christmas. Now, what year?"

Foxmire continued to hammer away at Barrelo, knowing he had him completely rattled. He smugly looked at the prosecution table and the worried expressions those attorneys wore.

After badgering everyone about the tapes, the defense called in all the OSI agents to discuss the investigation.

Agent Barney Stegall swore to tell the truth and settled his large frame in the witness chair while his facial expression remained calmly confident. He had testified at hundreds of trials over the years.

Foxmire asked him to detail every aspect of the Dr. McDowell-orchestrated surveillance, which he did with ease. He drilled Stegall on the entrapment issue of using Barrelo to tape Lipscomb, and Stegall came through with flying colors. Then the attorney asked him about the Investigative Form 73 that he filled out the night Lipscomb was arrested.

Foxmire asked, "Was the 'Remarks' section of that form written in chronological order?"

"No, sir, it wasn't," Stegall said in a matter-of-fact manner.

"Do you see the time there, 2009, when you read Sergeant

Lipscomb his rights, and 2010 when he acknowledged he understood those rights? It had been crossed out. Was there a question when this happened or *if* it happened?''

''No, sir, I think Dr. McDowell started to scratch through that.''

''What about the time 2029 that says Sergeant Lipscomb requested an attorney? Would you state, under oath, that he waited nineteen minutes to request an attorney?''

''Yes, sir.''

''Is that normal?''

''Sergeant Lipscomb said he would talk to us.''

''Where did you finish filling out this form?''

''At my residence.''

''At 2208?''

''Yes, sir.''

''Well, how is it that Sergeant Lipscomb is departing at 2202 and you're filling this out at 2208?''

''Agent Watlington called me at my residence.''

''Did you ask Watlington to call you?''

''Yes, I did.'' Stegall's voice remained firm, but he pulled out a handkerchief and mopped his damp brow over the grilling.

''You're lying, aren't you?'' Foxmire accused.

''No, sir, I am not.'' Stegall's posture immediately stiffened and he sat up taller in his chair.

Then, shocking the court, Foxmire insisted that Stegall be sequestered so that Watlington could be brought in to confirm Stegall's testimony. The court ushered Stegall to an empty office where he would remain alone. After a considerable delay, Agent Watlington arrived.

Following preliminary questioning to establish that Watlington worked as an OSI agent with Stegall, Foxmire asked him, ''Do you recall receiving instructions from Mr. Stegall prior to his departing concerning M.Sgt. Lipscomb's case?''

''I just—'' Watlington frowned. ''I may well have or I may not have. I just do not remember.''

''Do you recall calling Special Agent Stegall at home that evening to tell him anything about the interview or anything about the case?''

The courtroom had become quiet. Most would have assumed that Watlington would have come in and immediately verified that the highly respected Stegall had told the truth.

But after some hesitation, Watlington replied, ''I can't say specifically that I did. I just don't recall. Since I have talked to you gentlemen and I have thought about it, it's vague. I can't say 'yes, I did,' or 'no, I didn't.' ''

The lawyers at the prosecution table glanced at each other. They were dumbfounded by Watlington's testimony, but they could do no more than to let the question hang in the air that possibly Agent Stegall had falsified the form regarding the night Lipscomb was arrested.

Foxmire questioned almost everyone involved in the investigation, including the psychologists from Wilford Hall Medical Center, as well as some of Kathleen's friends.

Then it was Bill Lipscomb's turn. After sitting for almost a year listening to other people unfavorably discuss him, he seemed eager to stand up and tell his side of the story.

Lipscomb's attorney walked him through the details of his arrest and Lipscomb admitted he would never forget how embarrassing the arrest had been in front of his entire family. Then Foxmire brought up the disputed issue concerning the night Lipscomb was arrested.

Foxmire asked, ''Did you request a lawyer at any time during your interview [with the OSI]?''

''Yes, sir, I did.''

''How many times did you request a lawyer?''

''Three different times, sir.''

''At what points?''

''Mr. Stegall read me my rights, and then asked me if I

wanted a lawyer. I said I did. But he said, 'Well, let me finish,' as if he was going to continue reading the rights. But he said, 'I want to tell you a story.' He started talking about an airman in a murder case, then he related it to Kathleen and said he wondered why these things happened. And I said I didn't know why, thinking about his story. When I said that, Dr. McDowell came up with his elbows on the table and he said—''

At that point Lipscomb stopped and looked at the judge. ''My testimony will contain some profanity if I relate exactly what they said to me. Is that appropriate?''

The judge didn't move his face from the hand it rested on. ''I've probably heard it all,'' he said. ''Go ahead.''

''Well, Dr. McDowell said, 'Oh, so you're just a cold-blooded, fucking killer?' He shocked me with that and before I could respond, Agent Stegall spoke up and said, 'You even put that cord around her neck twice.' So again I said, 'I want a lawyer.' ''

''So is that the third time?''

''No, that's the second time. They kept coming at me. The next time it came from Dr. McDowell. He said, 'You want to play fucking hardball? Well, we'll play hardball. We've got a tape of a six-year-old girl in Houston that says she woke up and saw your truck gone.' And I said, that's a lie. I want a lawyer.''

''The investigation form indicates that you were read your rights at 2010, but you didn't ask for a lawyer until 2029. Did that much time go by between the time you were first advised about your right to a lawyer before you asked for a lawyer?''

''No, sir.''

''How much time went by?''

''The entire conversation between myself, Agent McDowell, and Agent Stegall could not have lasted more than three to five minutes.''

Then it was Bruce Ambrose's turn at Lipscomb. The attorney for the prosecution tried to make him admit that he had a motive for giving dishonest testimony, but Foxmire objected. Then Ambrose asked, "Can you think of any reason why Agent Stegall or Agent McDowell would have to be less than honest with the court regarding the facts of your interview that night?"

"Yes, because they were incorrect in documenting what actually transpired that night."

"Just because they entered the wrong time?" Ambrose said, his eyes glaring.

"The entire document, sir. The words on both sides of the document."

"Can you tell me why two highly respected OSI agents with almost twenty years experience each would put their entire careers on the line to falsify the document?"

"I couldn't put myself in their place, sir, to give you their motive." Lipscomb remained calm, completely in control of his answers.

"So you have no idea what motive they might have?"

"Well, I'm certain, sir, their motive would be to have something incriminating to use against me."

With Lipscomb's thought-out answers and Foxmire's well-placed objections, Ambrose couldn't catch Lipscomb in anything concrete.

The hearing neared its conclusion and Judge Callinan deliberated on all the motions, evidence, and testimony presented to him. Lipscomb became convinced that the judge hadn't listened to one word his lawyers had said when Callinan announced that all physical evidence, such as the chest, would be admitted to the court martial, as well as the doctored tapes and their amended transcripts. All statements would be allowed and all charges would remain. When everything boiled down, the only thing not admitted was Mary Ann's "my daddy lies" tape, which had been the impetus for the family to bring the case to the detectives in the first place.

* * *

The following month, a very somber J. Cabot Foxmire went to the brig to talk with his client. His news would be devastating.

Chapter Twenty-Three

J. Cabot Foxmire's expression alarmed Bill Lipscomb when he met his attorney in the brig's visitation room. Lipscomb noticed too that the lawyer, wearing a suit and tie, had overly dressed for a Saturday visit with a client.

"What's up?" Lipscomb asked, his eyes wide with curiosity.

The attorney began somberly. "Ambrose just notified me that sixty witnesses are ready to testify against you."

Lipscomb dropped down to a hard wooden chair, looking startled. After a few moments, he said, "Who do *we* have?"

"We can muster maybe a dozen or so people—those you worked with. Maybe your five brothers and sisters will testify that they love you and they have never seen you act violently. But we're talking character witnesses here, not someone saying, 'Oh, yeah. I was with Bill on the night of June 8 and he never went near his wife.' We have nothing like that."

"Well, if Tony would tell the truth, you'd find he was almost as involved as I was. He was mad at Kathleen because she threatened to squeal about the cheating scam. If I hadn't stopped him, he'd probably have killed her himself.''

Foxmire gave Lipscomb an impatient glance. ''You flunked your lie detector test. Remember?''

Lipscomb remained silent.

''You know,'' his lawyer continued in a serious tone, ''the way this case has been convened, I don't have to remind you what happens if we lose.''

Lipscomb's blue eyes squinted as if he'd been hit. He stared at Foxmire. ''Yeah, I know,'' he said in a low, hoarse voice, ''I'd be history.''

''Anything would be better than that, right?''

''What do you suggest?''

Foxmire took a big breath, searching for the right words, as he sat down next to his client at the metal table. ''I suggest,'' he said softly, ''that you plead guilty.''

''Plead guilty?'' Lipscomb frowned at the horror of the suggestion. This was the attorney who had promised to dazzle the jury and get him off on the basis of ''reasonable doubt.'' Now even Foxmire didn't believe he had a chance.

''Think of the consequences, Bill. You could get lethal injection. Let's submit a pretrial for second degree murder and no sentence cap. You'd probably have to serve only ten of that. Beats the alternative.''

Lipscomb sat reeling, numb from Foxmire's words, and tears rolled down his face. ''I never thought it would come to this.''

''Think about it. We'd sit down with the prosecution and draw up a Stipulation of Fact for you to sign. It would mean no more court martial, and no chance of the death penalty. Just think about it.'' He waited a few more minutes, but Lipscomb was too stunned to discuss it any longer. ''I'll call you in a few days.'' He patted Lipscomb's back, and left.

* * *

After three days, Foxmire called Lipscomb, who was still despondent, and suggested they meet with Lipscomb's assistant trial counsel, Lawrence H. Woodward, Jr.

Lipscomb agreed to see the two lawyers the next day, although he had never entirely trusted Captain Woodward. He still hadn't gained any confidence in his military lawyers, because in his opinion, they were working for the enemy.

In a strange twist of fate, Woodward's mother had attended school with Lipscomb's father. The parental connection came up when Foxmire brought Woodward to meet with Lipscomb at the brig. After Woodward discussed Lipscomb's background and his father, Lipscomb allowed himself to open up more to the attorney.

When the three were seated in the meeting room, Foxmire said, "If you would ask me what our main problem is, it is that the circumstantial evidence is there and we have no 'hook' for the defense."

Lipscomb thought back to the words of his first attorney, Kenneth Merrow, who suggested they come up with a gem to put into the jury's head that maybe Barrelo did this after all. Now all that planning had disintegrated.

Lipscomb listened, despite thinking Foxmire's grin looked forced, like he was trying to make everything sound comfortable. He listened to both lawyers, and as Lipscomb remembered later, "after a lot of talking and a lot of tears," they finally convinced him to agree to the plea bargain—known in the military as a pre-trial agreement.

Two weeks later, Ambrose and Woodward met to hammer out a Stipulation of Fact they could both live with. They used the tapes of Barrelo along with the testimony given by Sergeant Shannon Gilbert. Information from Lipscomb's military records was included, but only to record his length of duty. None of his glowing evaluations were added. The attorneys searched the files of the Bexar County Sheriff, the Guidry Group, the OSI, and the information from Kathleen's counseling sessions. And to all this, the lawyers added every lie Lipscomb had used to cover his actions.

Once the attorneys agreed on the Stipulation, the rules they discussed with Lipscomb began to change. Captain Woodward had to go back to the brig and break the news to Lipscomb.

"The best we could get was 'No Capital Offense' and 60 years. Also the prosecution insisted on a $10,000 fine because they knew you had received Kathleen's insurance," Woodward told him.

Hearing that, Lipscomb realized that his prior decision had gone from bad to worse. "Sixty years?" he said hotly. "I can't do it. I won't do it. I'll not agree to anything that could put me away for that kind of time." His entire body shook as he stared at his attorney. Perspiration caused his clothes to cling to him. "And that fine on top of everything. No, it's too much. I've spent over $100,000 on my defense. There just isn't enough left. And since I've been locked up, I haven't received any salary or benefits. Francine and the kids are getting a grand a month from my folks. Any small nest egg I have is for their emergencies."

Woodward was finding it increasingly difficult to remain sympathetic with his client.

"Bill. This is the best they'll do. What on earth would you suggest?"

Lipscomb said nothing.

"In light of all the evidence against you, think about it. What options do you have? On the plus side, Judge Callinan makes the final decision, and he can't give you a stiffer sentence than the agreement calls for."

Lipscomb's somber mood permeated the cell. Guards walked

by and glanced at him through the bars. He clenched his mouth. "What do I have to do?" he asked.

"I think it's possible for you to get out of the fine. We can probably convince the judge that it wouldn't be you being penalized, it would be your family. Tell you what you'll need to do." He took a tablet out of his briefcase. "Write an admission of guilt. Say how sorry you are and ask that the court not impose a financial penalty. That sort of thing."

Shortly after Woodward left, Lipscomb sat down at his desk/chair combination that reminded him of the desks he had sat in at school, and began writing in his own, poetic style:

"I've never had to memorialize my actions before, but I do so now without rationalizing my faults and accepting fully the punishment society will impose.

"My deepest regret is for the life I've taken from this world. Left behind is a trail of memories; a trail cut short due to my actions. The lives affected by my actions cannot be numbered, but the few I mention deserve some explanation which I can never reasonably justify; no killing can be reasonably justified. To Kathleen's mother and her family, who have suffered beyond comprehension, to my mother and father and family, whose confidence and trust I've abused and must reestablish. To my wife, Francine, who's love I've taken and deceived so unfairly. To Joel and Peggy, whose love was given so freely; and especially to Mary Ann and Billie, who will suffer the greatest loss—I am sorry.

"I accept the shame and humility, and expect my actions not to go unpunished nor accepted. The loss in this tragedy has been great to all; the suffering long enough. The agony I've caused by not accepting my responsibility and by building lie upon lie, will hopefully diffuse in time, and let a healing process begin. The greatest pain will be felt by the children who have been scarred by this tragedy twice. The loss of both parents whose love for them led to the destruction of both, will be long felt.

"I face the humiliation of being the one who killed their mother, and will always live with that label. I had hoped my children would have remembered their childhood without the traumatic and deceitful memories I've caused. I pray God will lessen the hurt in their eyes as I face them and help them grow to mature and responsible adults. Their memory of me will be that of the person who lied to them and killed their mother. I'll forever live with that shame. The humility will be lifelong and their confidence and trust lifelong rebuilding. I pray my debt to society will be eventually paid and their confidence restored. My soul rests in God's hand and I will forever seek His grace and forgiveness for my actions.

"My selfishness destroyed a life; Kathleen wasn't given a second chance. I may not deserve one, but I will strive to attain one through acceptance of my crime and the banishment from my family and society until I've proven my integrity.

"In closing, I apologize to the United States Air Force for the discredit and dishonor I've brought upon this honorable organization. I ask for consideration of my life over the past 34 years in granting what leniency it can in returning me to society and my children's lives, so that I can share their lives and correct whatever can be corrected, while providing for their future well-being.

"I fully realize the extent of punishment that the court can impose and ask only that the court not impose a financial penalty that will jeopardize the future of my wife and our children."

The next week, Foxmire came to Lipscomb's cell with a briefcase full of papers, and the two men exchanged documents.

Lipscomb read the Stipulation of Fact while his attorney read his statement of guilt.

Foxmire nodded his approval of Lipscomb's words, while he sat dumbstruck with the Stipulation.

Lipscomb dropped down to the wooden chair in his cell. His face had turned to chalk. "I, I can't sign this," he stammered. "Things are so ambiguous."

"Bill, it's in lieu of a trial. Either you agree to what's written on that paper, or it's no pre-trial agreement and back to a possible death sentence. I'm afraid the deck's stacked against us. But on the bright side, I talked with Fisher, and he said he's sure he can argue more credit time for you since you spent fourteen months in solitary confinement. That would mean you've served two of your years already."

Lipscomb shook his head and the tears started again.

"Let's go through it one more time, Bill. You failed the lie detector test abominably. Not one person has substantiated your story, and the physical evidence points to you at every turn. Also, it didn't help that you offered Barrelo money not to testify."

With shoulders slumped, Lipscomb signed the Stipulation.

On August 20, 1990, the original date of the court martial, Bill Lipscomb rubbed his clammy hands together as he waited for the formal pleading of guilt to begin. As he saw it, it was less a legal proceeding and more like grandstanding for Kathleen's family to show all her relatives that he had finally admitted his guilt.

He stood with a guard in the hall outside the courtroom, waiting for his turn to march inside. *Probably everyone else has been seated,* he surmised. *I've almost memorized everything about the courtroom. Kathleen's family will probably sit on the left in the visitor's section. I can manage to avoid looking at them when I go down that long aisle. Then I'll walk through those two short swinging doors and turn to the right. I'll be only a few steps from my attorneys then.* He looked down at his manila folder full of papers, and checked for his admission of guilt that the judge would have him read. Then he eyed his Stipulation of Fact. He shook his head. *Damn, I've got to keep that out of sight. No way do I want those words repeated in court.* He tucked the papers back into the folder, and raised his chin.

The bailiff opened the door for him and Lipscomb stood straight and tall, his head erect. His uniform, complete with the master sergeant stripes, had been delivered fresh from the base cleaners, and he had polished his shoes to a patent leather shine. His new haircut was a little short, but earlier he had checked in the men's room mirror, and decided it was acceptable.

Quickly he went in, knowing all eyes were on him. As he walked down the aisle, he could see the two short doors up ahead and knew he had only a few more steps before he'd reach the safety of his attorneys.

Just before he reached his destination, he absently glanced to his left at the elevated jury box, and there they were— Nadine, Darlene, an uncle and aunt, a couple friends, as well as Barney Stegall and Rich Fife. Startled, Lipscomb dropped his manila folder as he reached for the doors and papers flew everywhere. His stoic bearing melted away and his hands shook. The papers rattled as he stopped to gather them back into his folder.

Foxmire temporarily bolstered his client with a motion for additional credit for Lipscomb's 14 months of pre-trial confinement. One of Lipscomb's assistant legal counsels, Fisher, argued that since Lipscomb had been kept in near-solitary confinement conditions, he deserved to be given more credit than the days he actually served. Fisher gave evidence from past trials, and quoted that ''the confinement should not be any more rigorous than necessary to insure the presence of the confinee at trial.''

Judge Callinan agreed, and bestowed on Lipscomb a gift of 236 additional days that he hadn't served. This had the effect of moving his confinement date back to December 2, 1988, over seven months before his arrest.

The judge asked Lipscomb to stand and discuss his plea, and Lipscomb spoke in a faltering voice.

The judge, Lt. Col. Callinan, told him, ''I can't accept a plea of guilty unless the facts support that plea, therefore you have to answer questions about the offense and surrender your right to remain silent. Do you understand that?''

''Yes, sir, I do.''

Callinan continued his thorough, methodical approach and asked Lipscomb how he pled, giving him many opportunities to back away from his decision of guilt. ''Do you have any questions? Are you sure you're doing this of your own free will? Have your lawyers explained about the new penalty of confinement for life?''

Every question was met with, ''Yes, sir.''

Finally, the judge had one last cautionary reminder. ''A plea of guilty is the strongest form of proof known to law.''

Despite all the chances to change his mind, Lipscomb still insisted that he was, ''Guilty, Your Honor.''

''Okay,'' Callinan said, ''I'm the cautious sort. As far as you're concerned, again, is there *anything* in the Stipulation that you disagree with?''

''No, sir,'' Lipscomb assured him.

''Or anything that you think is untrue?''

''No, sir.'' Lipscomb's responses were brief as he struggled to appear unflappable.

The Stipulation was the most damning document of all. In those 13 pages, Lipscomb described every minute detail about the murder. Exactly as it happened.

Chapter Twenty-Four

Now came the final argument by the lead prosecution attorney, Bruce Ambrose. The handsome, Joe College-looking man was smartly attired in his captain's dress blues. He had taken a last-minute glance at his notes, then stacked them on the corner of his table. He wouldn't be needing them.

Capt. Ambrose had confided to the family before his important summation, "I just want you to be prepared for some pretty graphic language, but it's the only way I can get the truth across in court. I helped write the Stipulation, so I know what really happened. I hate the guy."

Ambrose glared at the defendant when he stood to address the court. "I think the most important thing that should be remembered about this case is that strangulation is a *very* painful way to die. The evidence provides merely a dry narrative of the murder of Kathleen Lipscomb. But even a cursory examination of the facts establishes that the maximum punishment now allowed by law is justified. The obstruction of justice alone warrants a dishonorable discharge and total reduction in rank.

By the accused's plea to premeditated murder, he shall receive life in prison as the mandatory minimum, and the evidence fully justifies it. Master Sergeant William T. Lipscomb,'' he said and stared at the defendant who sat staring back, ''committed the ultimate crime in this society, premeditated murder, for which he should now pay the harshest penalty allowed by law. The evidence establishes that this was not a crime of impulse, but instead it was a crime committed after long deliberation and careful planning. There is not one shred of evidence before this court that calls for mercy for this creature.''

Upon saying ''creature,'' he paused and looked at Lipscomb for such a long time that everyone else in the courtroom turned to look at him. Lipscomb deflected their glances by looking at his parents, his only family members in attendance since his five brothers and sisters had opted to stay home. He locked eyes with his mother, but she too stared, and it was the same stare he remembered seeing from the front seat of the family car when he was an 11-year-old boy and had run away from home.

''Instead,'' Ambrose continued, ''the evidence cries out for justice. And in order to hear that cry, we need to examine the evidence and what it means. We can now say that no one reason motivated Sergeant Lipscomb. No one obsession drove him to murder Kathleen. We can say that he had a black heart charred by being the cuckold to Dr. Pearle. We can say that he had an obsession to possess the children. He had a rage to punish Kathleen. But no less important, he was motivated by self-preservation. For this man, the murder of Kathleen crystallized into a very simple solution for his variety of problems. First was the problem of Mary Ann and Billie. By whatever combination of his upbringing, family influence, domineering personality and injured ego, Kathleen could not keep the children. She had to die in order to prevent that.

''Second, and somewhat related, she had to be punished for her affair with the doctor. Now, Your Honor, the rage of love lost to a competitor has sparked countless murders through time. That in and of itself is nothing new. In fact, we also see where Sergeant Lipscomb obtained some measure of sexual revenge through his affair with Sergeant Shannon Gilbert. An affair that Kathleen knew about. But that wasn't enough for him. That level of sexual revenge was not enough. He had to continue the punishment. He had to kill. He had to punish Kathleen for enjoying sex with another man. He had to abuse her body for denying sexual pleasure to him. We also know that sexual revenge was part of the master plan of her murder.

"Remember that during April and May, when Sergeant Lipscomb and Sergeant Barrelo planned her murder, they discussed ways to kill Kathleen in order to divert suspicion from themselves. The sexual assault was part of that master plan. The sexual assault, the murder, taking her nude body to a roadside outside of San Antonio was part of the master plan."

To present what actually happened on June 8, 1986, Ambrose had borrowed from Lipscomb's Stipulation of Fact that he had signed as true and correct. Weighing as his most damaging testimony, it read: "Kathleen arrived at the accused's apartment. The accused and Kathleen talked for a few minutes. At some point, the accused attacked Kathleen and stripped off her blue jeans. He then forcibly had vaginal intercourse with her, and forcibly sodomized her with his penis in her anus . . .

"However, keep in mind, Your Honor," Ambrose continued, "that the accused didn't use a blunt object to simulate a sexual assault on Kathleen's body. He didn't get a brush handle or a broom or some other inanimate object. What did he use? He used his own erect penis. What does that tell us? It tells us he was aroused. It tells us he *enjoyed* it. It tells us that he obtained sexual pleasure through the attack on Kathleen. He found the ultimate sexual excitement in murdering his wife."

Lipscomb showed no emotion as he listened to Ambrose's closing argument, but Kathleen's family would remember him sitting calmly, and coldly stonefaced.

"Third, we have over $314,000 tax-free dollars as a motive. During the divorce hearing, Kathleen proposed with her attorney that the insurance proceeds be placed into a trust if either one of the parties died. The accused knew about the $314,000 life insurance on Kathleen. There was only $50,000 on him. That request from Kathleen sealed her fate, Your Honor. Remember what the accused told Tony Barrelo on Friday, the sixth of June, the very week that he signed that order—that time was getting short; the divorce was about to become final. From the evidence, we learned that his own lawyer counseled him against that provision, and yet he agreed. Why? It's very simple, Your Honor, because he knew he was going to kill Kathleen. He knew that she would be dead before it ever became law.

"What a delicious delight for this man. What a delicious delight. He achieves solutions to all of his problems. He gets the children. He gets his revenge, and Kathleen pays for it with her own insurance premiums. And what a despicable, depraved creature he is."

Again the term "creature," and again the pause. At one time Lipscomb unintentionally glanced toward the jury box, and met Darlene's eyes. She squinted back hatred.

"Strangulation is indeed a painful way to die. We learned that her head filled with blood because the veins were partially occluded, but the arteries were not, so that the blood could not escape, and it built up pressure inside her skull. And that pressure backed up through the veins, the arteries, into the capillaries until those capillaries burst in her eyeballs. Her lungs surely emptied of all the air that was in them, using every molecule that was available to feed her muscles, to give her muscles oxygen for strength. Sometimes children hold their breath just as an experiment to see how long they can do it. What makes them stop? Pain. The body's self-defense takes over. The muscles convulse, forcing the body to breathe. Except in Kathleen's case, she had that cord wrapped around her neck. We know, though, that the cord broke and the accused had to grab it again.

"When that cord broke, Kathleen got a second chance. She got another breath of air. So she continued to fight. She continued to struggle. She was bruised at the jawline caused by a blunt object force, like a fist. She was bruised on the right chest, also caused by a severe blow from a blunt object. She was bruised on the thigh, also caused by a blunt object. Those are signs of a struggle, a fight for life. And as she fought for her life, she was aware. She was aware that she had been lured into a trap. She was aware that William T. Lipscomb was killing her. She was aware that she was about to lose her children, and that they were about to lose her. She was aware that she was being murdered. And so she struggled, she turned, she twisted. Remember the evidence about the bruising on both sides of the neck, caused perhaps by William Lipscomb's own hands, also perhaps caused by her hands. Surely her hands were at her neck, Your Honor, clawing, grasping for that cord, trying to pull it away. Trying to pull his hands away to give her another breath of air. Your Honor, the evidence is overwhelming. Kathleen Lipscomb did not go gently into death's arms."

The hushed courtroom listened, enraptured by Ambrose's powerful delivery.

"She had too much to live for. She had too much love in her life. And yet this man had too much to gain by her murder and too much to lose to let her live. At some point, mercifully Kathleen lost consciousness. But he had to make sure that she was dead, and so he continued to pull, he continued to twist on that cord until her heart stopped and her brain was dead.

"The horrible desecration of her body does not stop there. We know that she was placed in that chest there," he said, pointing to the box that stood in evidence. "Where was that chest? It was in the bedroom closet. Where was the bedroom closet in a one-bedroom apartment? Right next door to the bathroom. Where did the children go when they came back to the apartment? Into the bathroom. One wall separated them from their dead mother. Her body was placed in a duffel bag and then taken to the roadside outside of San Antonio. Does what happen to Kathleen after her death matter? Yes, it matters, it tells us what kind of a sick mind, what kind of a depraved creature it was that killed her and carried out his plan.''

He asked softly, ''Did he kill to obstruct justice?'' Then answered loudly, ''Yes, he certainly did. We know that Kathleen knew of the WAPS cheating. We know that she threatened to expose him. She used that as a weapon to keep custody of the children. Your Honor, there are too many people involved, too much at stake for him to let that risk stay out there, that risk of exposure. She had to be eliminated.

''Did Kathleen suffer prolonged, substantial mental or physical pain and suffering? Yes, her death was not quick. She did not quickly lose consciousness. She fought and she struggled. Her struggle prolonged her death. The sexual assault on her body prolonged her death. When the cord broke, her death was prolonged. Was her pain substantial? The force that caused those bruises caused pain. The cord wrapped around her neck caused pain. Her body was battered and beaten, painfully so. The sexual assault was painful. The loss of oxygen through her muscles was painful. But even more, Your Honor, the greatest pain of all had to be the mental pain, the awareness, the knowledge, the realization of her death.

''Was the murder committed while the accused was engaged in the act of sodomy? Yes, we know that the sodomy occurred before she was dead. Those are the aggravating factors, and the evidence establishes every one. Add to that the cover-up, taking the children to their mother's apartment and leaving the notes on the door to hide his crime, then lying to the Bexar County deputies who interrogated him that night. And the next morning, calling her work place and pretending to be looking for her.

''No amount of remorse from William T. Lipscomb will

wipe away the stain of his murder. And when it is said that Kathleen's murder is tragic, and that nothing can bring her back, that certainly is true. Remember, Your Honor, that every night that he has had to sleep is one night more than Kathleen. Remember that every television program he got to watch in the brig is one more than Kathleen. Remember that every warm touch from Mary Ann and Billie is one more than she got. In this society of laws, there is no redemption for the brutal murder of Kathleen. We, those of us who are left to live, can find justice through the sentence of this court. We can find justice in knowing that his fate is life in prison.''

The captain had finished speaking. His verbal pushing and poking was over, but he stood for another moment, keeping his eyes firmly fixed on Bill Lipscomb, then he walked back to the prosecution table and sat down.

Over the past four years, Kathleen's murder had been discussed, dissected, and absorbed, but never has it been presented more eloquently than by Capt. Bruce Ambrose.

Foxmire rose for his closing argument, but his statement was brief and he waived off arguing the points Ambrose raised because, as he said, ''Sergeant Lipscomb had come in and pled guilty,'' indicating that the point was moot. As for Kathleen's suffering, he tried to present that early on she had lost consciousness and more or less slept through her murder. Finally concluding that ''[Bill] doesn't make apologies for what he did . . . But he is a human being, and people are neither as bad as they sometimes appear nor as good as sometimes they want us to believe.''

Those comments concluded the two-day session.

It would be the last day for the quickly promoted master sergeant to wear his many award ribbons, as well as his master sergeant's stripes. The glowing phrases that had described him for 15 years preceded his last review by Lt. Col. Michael

Saunders: "During this reporting period, it was discovered that Master Sergeant Lipscomb engaged in off-duty criminal misconduct. His judgment, professionalism, and leadership qualities are suspect, and therefore he should not be placed in a position of trust or confidence."

A 10-minute recess followed. After that, everyone would be called back to hear the sentencing. During the break, Rich Fife turned to Nadine. He had been her contact and confidant, the same role Tom Bevans had filled for Darlene. Taking Nadine's hand, Fife said, "It's little comfort when you lose a daughter, but you and Darlene have to be proud of the role you played. We wouldn't be at this point today if you two hadn't taken hold of this case and forced people to see what a great injustice had been done. You should feel pleased with your efforts. I know Kathleen would have been proud of you."

Tears glistened in Nadine's eyes, remembering how many people had told her and Darlene that their efforts were sheer folly. That Lipscomb would never have murdered the mother of his children. Nadine squeezed Fife's hand. "We had a lot of good help," she said, managing a smile.

When the court reassembled, Judge Callinan asked Lipscomb to stand. Lipscomb stood tall and rigid, as if someone were going to pin another medal on him.

The judge looked over his glasses at Lipscomb, and read from a printed page that had been drawn up before his showcase minicourt martial. "Sergeant Lipscomb, as part of your pre-trial agreement, you are sentenced to life at the Disciplinary Barracks at the Leavenworth Federal Penitentiary at Fort Leavenworth, Kansas. You will be dishonorably discharged and reduced to Airman Basic. You will forfeit all pay and benefits. However," Callinan said, clearing his throat, "you will be assessed no punitive fine."

Judge Callinan agreed with Lipscomb's pre-trial agreement and let the term of 60 years in prison stand. But with time off for good behavior, Lipscomb would only serve 10 years before being eligible for parole, making his first parole date December 2, 1998.

September 10 is the anniversary of Lipscomb's arrival at Fort Leavenworth, and each year on that date, he is given a clemency hearing. For his committee appearance, he has memorized the prison's prescribed vernacular of professing his remorse and requesting rehabilitation—two of the criteria that will bring about his release. When he goes before the clemency committee, he also uses his considerable charm and articulate persuasive ability to beg for compassion, to beg for charity, and to beg for mercy—all the things he denied Kathleen.

Epilogue

After Bill Lipscomb went to the Fort Leavenworth Penitentiary, Nadine Adams and Darlene Sanford continued their efforts to keep him there. They have talked to church congregations, civic groups, and businesses, inducing them to sign petitions asking that Lipscomb, because of the brutality of the crime, serve more than the bare minimum of his sentence. They have now sent 5,277 petitions to Fort Leavenworth—more than for any other prisoner in the 150-year history of the institution.

Lipscomb is described as "very mellow" by his prison counselor, and he has been successful in reducing his confinement status to minimum security. His next phase would be the lightest of all—that of trustee.

Tony Barrelo escaped prosecution because the Bexar County Sheriff's Department declined to press charges. Lipscomb has admitted that his neighbor, a Bexar County deputy, passed on all investigative information from the sheriff's office, allowing him to know exactly where the case stood at all times. Sergeant

Dalton Baker received a commendation for his work on the case.

Sergeant Ricky Rios, the only friend of Lipscomb's to cooperate with the OSI, refused immunity and received a reduction in rank. No one else was penalized for the WAPS scam.

Tom Bevans formed Paladin International, a security company, with his FBI-retired father, Tom Sr., in Houston, and Mike Guidry continues in the investigative business in The Woodlands, Texas.

Francine Lipscomb sued her husband for divorce, which became final in January 1995, and relinquished her custody of Mary Ann and Billie. Legally, she still remains their mother.

Rich Fife, Barney Stegall, and Bruce Ambrose have all left the Air Force to pursue careers in civilian life. Dr. Charles P. McDowell is now Chief of the Homicide Branch, Major Crimes Division, in OSI's Investigative Operations Center.

Lipscomb's parents have custody of Mary Ann and Billie Lipscomb, and each year the children visit their Texas family and the cousins are close friends.

Some of the anxiety has left the lives of Nadine and Darlene, but certainly not all. Nadine is active in "Parents of Murdered Children," a support group for the families of victims; however, she still keeps the torch lit for Kathleen.

READ EXCITING ACCOUNTS OF
TRUE CRIME FROM PINNACLE

THE MYSTERIES OF MARY ROBERTS RINEHART

THE AFTER HOUSE   (0-8217-4246-6, $3.99/$4.99)

THE CIRCULAR STAIRCASE   (0-8217-3528-4, $3.95/$4.95)

THE DOOR   (0-8217-3526-8, $3.95/$4.95)

THE FRIGHTENED WIFE   (0-8217-3494-6, $3.95/$4.95)

A LIGHT IN THE WINDOW   (0-8217-4021-0, $3.99/$4.99)

THE STATE VS.   (0-8217-2412-6, $3.50/$4.50)
ELINOR NORTON

THE SWIMMING POOL   (0-8217-3679-5, $3.95/$4.95)

THE WALL   (0-8217-4017-2, $3.99/$4.99)

THE WINDOW AT THE WHITE CAT
                                (0-8217-4246-9, $3.99/$4.99)

THREE COMPLETE NOVELS: THE BAT, THE HAUNTED
LADY, THE YELLOW ROOM
                                (0-8217-114-4, $13.00/$16.00)

*Available wherever paperbacks are sold, or order direct from the
Publisher. Send cover price plus 50¢ per copy for mailing and
handling to Penguin USA, P.O. Box 999, c/o Dept. 17109,
Bergenfield, NJ 07621. Residents of New York and Tennessee
must include sales tax. DO NOT SEND CASH.*